*Governing Academia*

# GOVERNING ACADEMIA

### EDITED BY

## RONALD G. EHRENBERG

CORNELL UNIVERSITY PRESS

*Ithaca and London*

First published 2004 by Cornell University Press

First printing, Cornell Paperbacks, 2005

Printed in the United States of America

Library of Congress Cataloging-in-Publication Data

Governing academia / edited by Ronald G. Ehrenberg.
    p. cm.
Includes bibliographical references (p.   ) and index.
   ISBN-13: 978-0-8014-7282-4 (paper : alk. paper)
   1. Universities and colleges—United States—Administration.   2. Education, Higher—United States—Administration.   3. Educational leadership—United States.   I. Ehrenberg, Ronald G.
   LB2341.G643  2004
   378.1'01—dc21

2003014805

Cornell University Press strives to use environmentally responsible suppliers and materials to the fullest extent possible in the publishing of its books. Such materials include vegetable-based, low-VOC inks and acid-free papers that are recycled, totally chlorine-free, or partly composed of nonwood fibers. For further information, visit our website at www.cornellpress.cornell.edu.

Paperback printing    10 9 8 7 6 5 4 3

*To*

Ｊᴀᴍᴇꜱ Ｏ. Ｆʀᴇᴇᴅᴍᴀɴ

*academic and academic administrator extraordinaire*

# Contents

# III    Governance in Practice

# IV    Challenges from Nonprofits and Nonlegal Legal Influences

# *Preface*

My term as a vice president of Cornell University in the mid-1990s whetted my appetite to study the governance of higher education institutions and ultimately led to this book. As a researcher of the economics of higher education, I am also an avid reader of books by former academic administrators. The one that had the most profound impact on me, in both my administrative and faculty roles, is James O. Freedman's *Idealism and Liberal Education* (1996). For in it Jim said, and I paraphrase him here as I did in my book *Tuition Rising* (2000a), that the best part of being a university administrator was that he was able to raise very fundamental issues with his colleagues on the faculty, the administration, and the board of trustees. Although they did not always respond in the way that he would have preferred, he had the satisfaction of knowing that they were seriously thinking about the issues. His words shaped my career as an academic administrator, and I continue to strive to raise fundamental issues in my research and teaching.

Although I had never met him, as I began to commission the papers that eventually led to *Governing Academia*, it was natural for me to try to see if I could convince Jim Freedman to write a chapter. One of the themes of the volume was to be the relationship between university presidents and trustees and how it varied between public and private universities. Jim had been the president at a major public university, the University of Iowa, and then at a major private university, Dartmouth College, for fifteen years. He also had the advantage of serving on the board of trustees of Brandeis University and could write from the perspective of someone who had served on both sides of the relationship. He very graciously agreed. Because his writings have so heavily influenced the way I behave and my admiration for all that he has accomplished in his career as a scholar, higher education administrator, and public intellect, I also asked Jim if I could dedicate *Governing Academia* to him. Much to my joy he agreed.

The other contributors are also prominent scholars and academic administrators. They come from a wide variety of academic disciplines, including economics, education, law, and political science. All of them have written in a nontechnical fashion to make the volume accessible to a broad audience. Preliminary versions of many of the essays were presented at a conference organized by the Cornell Higher Education Research Institute, which I direct, in June 2002, and the authors all benefited from comments by assigned discussants and during the general discussion.

Since 1995, the Andrew W. Mellon Foundation and the Atlantic Philanthropies (USA) Inc. have provided generous financial support for the Cornell Higher Education Research Institute. This support has allowed me the freedom to pursue my intellectual interests and has provided me with the resources I need to involve many graduate and undergraduate students in research (including three Cornell undergraduates who coauthored a chapter in this volume with me) and to organize conferences, such as the one that led to *Governing Academia*. My debt to these two foundations is enormous, and I am most appreciative of their support.

*Governing Academia*

# Introduction

## Ronald G. Ehrenberg

During recent decades tuition for undergraduate students has risen at rates substantially higher than the rate of inflation at both public and private colleges and universities in the United States.[1] These high rates of tuition increases led Congress to establish the National Commission on the Costs of Higher Education in 1997 to conduct a comprehensive review of college costs and prices and to make recommendations on how to hold tuition increases down. Parents of college students, taxpayers, and government officials all wanted to know why academic institutions can't behave more like businesses—cut their costs, increase their efficiency, and thus keep their tuition rates under control.

Part of the answer to this question, and the subject of *Governing Academia*, is how higher education institutions are governed in the United States. In some states, coordinating boards oversee both public and private higher educational institutions and help to rationalize course and degree offerings across institutions. In other states, their focus is solely on how public higher education is organized and administered.

Public higher education is often organized into a system, or several systems, of academic institutions, with governing boards elected or appointed for each system or for individual institutions. For example, in New York State, there are two public systems, the State University of New York (SUNY) and the City University of New York (CUNY). Each of these multicampus systems has a single board of trustees that, among other things, appoints the president of each campus, approves program offerings at each campus, and sets tuition for the entire system. In contrast, in Florida the governor and legislature recently approved a change in how their system of public academic institutions is governed, eliminating the single statewide board of trustees for the whole public university system and establishing boards for the individual cam-puses.[2] Private higher educational institutions always have boards of trustees.

The size and composition of boards, along with whether the trustees are appointed or elected, differ across institutions in both the public and the private sector. For example, the governor of Florida appoints all of the board members for that state's public universities, but all of the board members for the University of Michigan are elected in bien-nial statewide elections. At Princeton University, a leading private aca-demic institution, alumni elect some of the board members, the board itself elects some members, and the governor of New Jersey appoints a member.

Boards of trustees have fiduciary responsibility for all that goes on at an academic institution. However, typically they delegate most of their authority to the institution's president and become involved only in major policy decisions. The president in turn appoints a team that includes central administrators, as well as deans of individual colleges within multicollege institutions. These administrators then oversee the institution in conjunction with a system of faculty governance that specifies the sharing of decision-making power between faculty members and administrators. Increasingly, other staff and students are also involved in decision making.

Faculty members play a key role in the governance of academic institutions. They are the creators of new knowledge and, along with students, the key participants in the educational process. Hence, on educational matters the faculty often reigns supreme. Such matters include admission standards, curriculum, graduation requirements, faculty hiring and promotion processes, and the like. While trustees for-mally retain the final authority on academic matters, in practice they rarely overturn administrative recommendations. Administrative rec-ommendations, in turn, are heavily influenced by faculty decisions.

This system of shared governance between trustees, administrators, and faculty members has often led to the perception that no one is really in charge of academic institutions. An often-repeated phrase is that an administrator trying to lead the faculty faces the same problem as a person trying to "herd cats." Other observers have described academic institutions as "organized anarchies" (Cohen and March 1986). As a result, it should not be a surprise that changes in academia come only slowly and that it is difficult to get institutions to focus on economic efficiency and holding down costs.

The governance of academic institutions also relates to how they are organized and how revenues flow and costs are allocated across the institutions. Some universities, for example, place the sciences, social sciences, and humanities within a single college of liberal arts and sciences. Others have separate colleges for each of the three disciplinary groups. The different forms of organization may well influence the decisions that are made within a university. So too may the systems used to allocate revenues and costs. Some institutions treat the whole institution as a single budgetary unit, while others treat each unit as a "tub on its own bottom" and hold each unit responsible for balancing its own budget.

Because of the Supreme Court decision in the *Yeshiva* case, very few private colleges and universities have faculty unions.[3] However, many faculty members at many public institutions are covered by collective bargaining agreements, as are many other employees in both public and private universities. The last few years have also seen a dramatic growth in the number of campuses at which graduate teaching assistants have won the right to bargain collectively over their working conditions.

Higher education is subject to a set of governmental regulations and the requirements of what might be called "nonlegal legal influences" on academic governance and the decisions at universities. Government regulations include environmental, nondiscrimination, and immigration rules—the most recent of the latter to hit academia is the USA PATRIOT Act, which was enacted as an outgrowth of 9/11 and will increase the costs and decrease the ability of American academic institutions to enroll foreign students. Nonlegal legal influences include intellectual property issues, the role of donors in determining policy, insurance carriers' requirements, accreditation bodies, higher education academic consortia and athletic conferences, and sole-source service providers. Each can have a substantial effect on the cost structure of an academic institution and on the efficiency of its operations.

Finally, higher education in the United States has traditionally consisted of a nonprofit private sector and a public sector. However, the last decade has seen the growth of accredited for-profit higher education institutions—one notable example is the University of Phoenix, which is now the largest (in terms of enrolled students) private higher education institution in the United States. The growing competition from the for-profit institutions, whose governance structure is often more corporate in nature, is putting pressure on the nonprofit and public higher education institutions to meet the competition, and this in turn may affect how they are governed.

*

The chapters in this volume cover all the aspects of higher education governance just discussed. The focus of each is on what social scientists know about that aspect of governance and on the types of future research that might be undertaken to help us better understand how to improve the performance of these institutions.

The chapters in part 1 deal with state governance of higher education and boards of trustees. The section begins with an essay, "Presidents and Trustees," by James O. Freedman, a former president of major academic institutions, both public and private, who now serves on the boards of several other institutions and whose experiences uniquely qualify him to write on this topic. His essay addresses the differences in roles that the boards of public and private institutions play and the interactions of an academic institution's president with the board in each of these types of institutions. His experiences lead him to suggest how boards can improve their functioning and how a president and his or her board can maximize their joint effectiveness in guiding their institution.

Benjamin Hermalin has a long-standing interest in the functioning of boards of directors of corporations and nonprofit institutions and how boards influence the performance of these organizations. In "Higher Education Boards of Trustees," Hermalin points out how an understanding of for-profit corporate boards may provide insights into how academic boards of trustees operate, and indicates crucial differences between corporations and academic institutions that make it unlikely that all of the findings with respect to corporate boards will carry over to academic boards.

Donald Heller's chapter, "State Oversight of Academia," first discusses the history of state governance of higher education and what the social outcomes of our higher education system are likely to be. He then asks whether how states choose to administer higher education has any impact on the end results.

Part 2 focuses on how the organization of a university and the allocation of revenue and costs across units can affect outcomes at the institution.

In "Darwinian Medicine for the University," Susanne Lohmann treats the university as an institution whose organization has evolved over a long history to help solve problems of information and commitment. She stresses that aspects of the university that may appear to outside observers to be defects, such as the tenure system and impermeable departmental boundaries, are actually subtle design solutions that have evolved to help facilitate the university's goals. Thus any proposal to reform university governance needs to be crafted very carefully, with a full understanding of the institution's local history and environment. While institutional governance rules tend to get etched in stone, it is important to judge carefully whether they are *defects* of the system that need to be changed or *defenses* of the system that help it to achieve its goals.

Thomas Hammond's "Herding Cats in University Hierarchies" presents a "bottom-up" perspective of how the formal structure of universities can affect the outcomes from their decision processes. Using simple illustrations that deal with the way an institution might group four different departments into two colleges, he shows how the method of grouping will bring different types of information, different packages of advice, and different sets of conflict to the attention of top-level administrators. Thus the optimal way to structure a university depends on the types of information, advice, and conflicts that the administrator considers most important.

John D. Wilson's "Tiebout Competition versus Political Competition on a University Campus" compares centralized budgeting models with decentralized budgeting models that treat each unit as a "tub on its own bottom." Under a broad set of circumstances, he shows that the decentralized budgeting models, which often are more formally referred to as "responsibility center management," or RCM models, yield less efficient outcomes than the more centralized ones. In particular, he argues that the centralized budgeting models provide better incentives to increase educational quality. Given the movement of many universities toward RCM models, his essay is an important one.

Part 3 concerns shared governance and collective bargaining in academia. Over thirty years ago, the American Association of University Professors conducted the last major survey of academic institutions that ascertained the extent to which faculty and administrators shared governance in a variety of decision-making areas. In "How Academic Ships Actually Navigate," Gabriel Kaplan reports the results from a new survey of governance at academic institutions that he undertook at the turn of the twenty-first century. Despite concern by faculty nationwide that their role in governance has diminished over time, Kaplan finds that faculty play a significant role in governance at many institutions and that their authority is greatest in their areas of expertise—curriculum, degree requirements, and hiring and promotion. In contrast, administrators and boards have more authority in budget making, long-run strategy, and facility issues.

"Collective Bargaining in American Higher Education" is a product of the work of three Cornell undergraduate students, Daniel Klaff,

Adam Kezsbom, and Matthew Nagowski, and myself. After reviewing what social scientists know about the effects of faculty unions, we present the results of the first study of the impact of collective bargaining on staff salaries in higher education and discuss the emerging phenomenon of graduate student unions. Using data for a set of public research universities provided to us by a data exchange consortium, we investigate the effects of graduate student unions on graduate assistants' salaries, hours of work, and other economic outcomes. The competition to attract first-class graduate students to major research universities appears to have more effect on these outcomes than does collective bargaining per se.

The chapters in part 4 deal with the external forces that affect governance and how academic institutions behave. In "Nonprofit and For-Profit Governance in Higher Education," Brian Pusser and Sarah Turner address the growing importance of the for-profit sector in higher education, the differences in governance between the for-profit and nonprofit sectors, and how the growing importance of the for-profit sector will likely influence governance in the nonprofit sectors. They caution that one impact of the growth of the for-profit sector is that nonprofit and public higher education institutions may be forced to behave more like the for-profits, which in turn will reduce the rationale for public subsidies, either directly in the form of state appropriations or indirectly in the form of tax exemptions.

Michael Olivas, in "The Rise of Nonlegal Legal Influences on Higher Education," provides four case studies of nonlegal factors that influence higher education governance in the sense that they dictate policy responses and constitute the complex features of statutory, litigative, or regulatory requirements. The four cases Olivas addresses are the roles of insurance carriers, accreditation, consortia, and sole-source providers. He shows how pervasive the influences of these nonlegal legal influences are on academic institutions' behavior.

In the conclusion, I summarize the major themes in this volume and look to the future. I discuss the trends in the environment—including growth in enrollments at a time when many state governments are limiting their financial support for public higher education institutions; the increasing use by many academic institutions of part-time faculty, non-tenure-track full-time faculty, and adjunct faculty; and the growth of collective bargaining for graduate assistants and adjunct faculty on higher education campuses—that will likely influence higher education governance in the years ahead.

I

# PRESIDENTS, TRUSTEES, AND EXTERNAL GOVERNANCE

# CHAPTER ONE

# Presidents and Trustees

## JAMES O. FREEDMAN

Boards of trustees, comprised principally of lay representatives, are a distinctly American institution, quite different from the ministries of education and faculty guilds that have often controlled higher education in Europe. For a university president, few relationships are more crucial than that with the board of trustees. A mutually respectful relationship can be a source of support and strength. An uneasy or wary relationship represents a lost opportunity. (I use "board of trustees" throughout, even though the official name for public universities in Iowa and some other states is "board of regents.")

Having worked with two boards, one public and one private, I venture to testify to some of the similarities and differences I found between them.

I begin with a truism. Just as presidents differ from institution to institution—in intellect, personality, preparation for the position, professional working style, educational vision, and personal ambition—so do boards. Given the immense variation in the range of possible relationships—there are, after all, more than three thousand colleges and universities in the United States—it is a tribute to the flexibility and tolerance of the protagonists that so many presidents and boards, functioning in such diverse contexts, work together as well as they do.

University governance has existed, historically, in an ebb and flow of accommodation (and acrimony) between presidents and boards of trustees. In *Making Harvard Modern* (2001), their extended examination of Harvard in the twentieth century, Morton and Phyllis Keller note that the Harvard Corporation, which they characterize as "a combine of clerics" in the early nineteenth century, had evolved by the late nineteenth century into "representatives of Boston's socioeconomic elite, out to make Harvard the special preserve of their caste" (18). With the passing decades even more changes came.

By the first half of the twentieth century, the balance of power had shifted from the seven-member corporation to a series of strong presidents (Charles W. Eliot, A. Lawrence Lowell, and James Bryant Conant) who drew their authority to govern from the vigorous exercise of their office. Thereafter, as the Kellers demonstrate, governing Harvard "in practice depended as much on its president's personality and purpose as on its venerable institutional structure (18)."

Another student of Harvard history, Henry Rosovsky, the former dean of the faculty of arts and sciences, has written in *The University: An Owner's Manual* (1990, 261), "Governance concerns power"; it is about "who is in charge; who makes decisions; who has a voice; and how loud is that voice." Presidents and trustees abut at the epicenter of that power. In my experience, there is always an uneasy tension between the commitment of board members to support the president on academic issues and their desire to exercise their statutory authority independent of the president on matters they deem to be of governance. There is a converse tension in the president to act only with the advice and consent of the board on as many matters as possible even as he seeks to protect from encroachment by the board what he deems to be the essential prerogatives of his academic authority. In seeking to exercise their respective reservoirs of power, presidents and trustees can find few hard-and-fast rules as to how to strike the proper balance.

## Members of the Board

When I first met the nine members of the University of Iowa board of regents, I was greatly impressed by the diversity of their stations in life and by their midwestern modesty. They were six men and three women: a small-town lawyer; a former lieutenant governor; an African American physician who also served as a county medical examiner; a union official who was a meat-packer by trade; a rural farmer; a professional farm manager; an owner of a family agribusiness; and two housewives, one of whom had chaired a local school board. None had a national reputation.

Appointed by the governor to staggered six-year terms, they were the salt of the earth—not a captain of industry among them. This was a board of commonsense men and women, honest and reliable, devoted and hardworking, in awe of their public service responsibilities; each brought to the task the earnest hope that he or she was up to the job.

By contrast, the Dartmouth board of trustees, only slightly larger at a size of thirteen men and one woman, was more homogeneous. Its members were wealthy; most had achieved high and professional standing, and some were socially prominent: Wall Street CEOs, investment bankers, venture capitalists, and corporate lawyers. One was a university president. All were Dartmouth graduates. They were self-assured, competitive, and socially poised, accustomed to commanding and to being listened to. A number had national reputations. Some felt entitled to be regarded as authoritative voices on particular areas of governance. Most bore their trusteeship as a social credential and a confirmation of their station. Dartmouth was an important part of their personal history, and they cared that the college be true to its traditions. In the manner of many with a lifelong attachment to an institution, they were at pains to ensure that the college was loved by its alumni, even more perhaps than that it was respected by the wider world.

The board members at Iowa, drawn from a wider social spectrum and a more diverse set of occupations, tended to have a more realistic appreciation of the limits on the president's power to dominate his constituencies. The board members at Dartmouth, most of whom had substantial management experience, albeit in more authoritarian and hierarchical institutions, tended to assume that a chief executive officer could readily impose his will upon faculty and students alike if only he wanted to.

One of the strengths of the Dartmouth board was the fact that the governor of New Hampshire, by prescription of the 1769 charter from King George III, was an ex officio member. Even a governor who rarely attends board meetings—and most attended no more than one a year—can be helpful in many ways, for example, in fending off ill-considered legislative incursions, attracting national figures to the campus, and intervening with federal officials.

Ironically, the governor of Iowa was not an ex officio member of the board. Indeed, the two governors with whom I served adopted, at least publicly, an apolitical stance on most issues before the board. Only after I was appointed as president did the board chairman arrange for me to meet the governor.

There are advantages, of course, to a board composed entirely (or almost entirely) of alumni. As Robert M. Rosenzweig (1998, 124), the former president of the Association of American Universities, has noted, alumni typically "have demonstrated their attachment to the institution by long service to it in various volunteer capacities and frequently by their financial contributions."

But alumni can also be indifferent to an institution's shortcomings and unduly resistant to proposals that threaten to alter its familiar character. By contrast, trustees who are not alumni are more likely to see the institution with less complacency and through clearer lenses, although some observers are dubious that non-alumni trustees can summon the institutional devotion that the task requires.

Should the president be a member of the board? At the University of Iowa I was not; at Dartmouth I was. I cannot say that it made much difference, although I did feel at Dartmouth that I was more than simply a professional executive hired to do a job. I was a colleague of the other board members with a shared responsibility in every aspect of their work.

Peter T. Flawn (1990, 20), the former president of the University of Texas at Austin, has added a different set of considerations: "In general, it enhances the position of the president if he or she is also a member of the board. . . . However, in the case where the board is divided, either on political or philosophical grounds, and the president as a member of the board must break the tie in a number of significant votes, board membership can create the extra pressure that leads to early departure from the presidency." These two boards, then, presented different social and professional profiles, but they were similar in the conscientious performance of their responsibilities.

Board Size and Membership

Boards of the size of those at the University of Iowa (nine) and Dartmouth (fourteen) are unusually small. Many boards, both public and private, are as large as forty to sixty trustees. Princeton's board, for example, has forty members; the University of Pennsylvania's, fifty-six. There seems to be no rule as to the relationship of the size of a board and its institution's status as public or private.

It is possible that boards of, say, less than fifteen members do not allow for sufficient representation of important substantive areas that ought to be represented in the making of informed decisions. Moreover, such boards usually do not have sufficient seats to include many major donors whose continuing generosity may be ensured or encouraged by such recognition.

Every few years, the Dartmouth board studied whether to increase its size, and each time it concluded to make no change, preferring to preserve the sense of collegiality and heightened responsibility that accompanied its small size to risking the dilution of these qualities in becoming larger. Often in boards of forty to sixty members, the executive committee exercises effective authority, seeking formal approval from the entire board for decisions already essentially made. These considerations lead me to believe that boards of no more than about twenty-five are an optimal size.

## Selection of Trustees

At a public university, the president rarely participates in the selection of board members. The choices, of course, are those of the governor, made with the advice and consent of the state senate. (In a few states, including Michigan, prospective board members stand for election as candidates of political parties.) I believe that the governor of Iowa would have welcomed suggestions from board members, channeled through the chairman, and he may well have received some, but a president is well advised to be cautious in associating with any candidate in what is still a political process.

At Dartmouth, the board partially perpetuated itself by selecting half (seven) of its members. The alumni chose the other half (seven) in contested three-candidate elections. In comparing these two selection processes, Henry Rosovsky (1990, 280) has written that "elections are more likely to reflect populist consensus" while "self-perpetuation will, with a considerable degree of certainty, produce a conservative bias."

Some of Dartmouth's elected trustees were, indeed, well known among alumni, sometimes because of their athletic achievements as students. One had been a Rhodes Scholar and an All-American basketball player who went on to play for the Boston Celtics. Another had been the quarterback of an undefeated football team, pre–Ivy League, that had won the Lambert Trophy and finished the season ranked fourteenth in the country. Both were popular candidates, although one would probably not call them "populist".

The board of trustees must have a sufficient breadth of expertise or interests that its members can effectively meet a number of important responsibilities. In a public institution, the attainment of this versatility depends on the care that the governor takes in making appointments.

It is easier for a private institution, in which the board at least partially perpetuates itself, to respond to the importance of having board members with specific areas of expertise, for example, finance, investments, real estate, communications, higher education, development, science, medicine, technology, and engineering. At some private institutions, the desire for expertise in higher education has led to the appointment of former university presidents from other institutions; for example, Gerhard Casper, the former president of Stanford University, serves as a member of the Yale Corporation, and I serve on the boards of Brandeis University and Hebrew Union College.

Discussions at Dartmouth about selecting new board members were interminable. No subject provoked more vehement opinions or more excited debates. Selecting successor trustees seemed a little bit like what I imagine the process of selecting saints to be: few candidates seemed worthy of annointment.

Should faculty members or students be members of the board? During the 1960s, public pressure grew to appoint faculty members and students as board members (or at least as nonvoting representatives to the board). Advocates of these proposals saw them as an enlightened effort to democratize the governance of academe. Many colleges and universities adopted such proposals, with uneven consequences that persist until today.

Neither the University of Iowa nor Dartmouth had faculty or student members on its board, although a governor of Iowa did use one of his nine official appointments to name an undergraduate student leader—a junior at Iowa State University—to the board.

In my judgment, it is a mistake to provide for faculty or student members on a board. Both face expectations that they act in a representative, rather than a fiduciary, capacity. Responsibility to a constituency is inconsistent with sound management. Moreover, student representatives are rarely qualified by experience or training for the important decisions required of trustees. Finally, the presence of faculty members or students in the boardroom will inevitably inhibit discussion of some issues, for example, evaluation of a dean or an administrative officer. Assessing faculty and student opinion is an important function of a board, but there are better ways for a president or a board to acquire information about campus opinion than allocating places on the board to faculty members or students.

At both public and private institutions, trustees typically serve for approximately a decade, although members of the Harvard Corporation serve for life. There is no statutory limitation on the length of time that University of Iowa trustees may serve, but the practice of successive governors has been to limit them to twelve years (two six-year terms). Ten years is the prescribed limit at Dartmouth (two five-year terms) with minor exceptions.

Because the president is a member of the Dartmouth board, I had an opportunity, although never a decisive one, to influence the selection of the new members whom the board itself appointed. Perhaps it is true, as Robert M. Rosenzweig (1998, 124) has written, that "private institutions are especially vulnerable to a situation in which the president comes to dominate the selection of new trustees, ending up with a board that is beholden to the president and not disposed to challenge presidential judgment." I never enjoyed such a satisfying experience.

In my experience, nominating committees want the president to be comfortable with new board members and therefore seek to accommodate her wishes, particularly if they are strongly felt. But presidents need to be aware that discussions of prospective board members can be fierce—especially when substantive issues such as affirmative action for minorities or women are concerned—and can leave permanent scars.

Trustees at private institutions are more likely to have emerged from a wide-ranging merit-based search conducted by the board, sometimes with the assistance of a professional search firm, than those nominated by a governor at public institutions. Indeed, given that the appointment is, short of a judgeship, the most prestigious that a governor could confer, I was surprised at how few names Iowa governors could sometimes gather from which to select new board members.

Responsibilities of Trustees

What is it that trustees are supposed to do?

In the conventional statement of board responsibilities, variations on five chief duties are usually listed: (1) to select and support the president; (2) to formulate and pursue the institution's mission and purposes; (3) to oversee the educational program; (4) to nurture the institution's tangible assets; and (5) to care for the institution's intangible assets, especially academic freedom, the commitment to excellence and impartiality, and its ethical standards. No wonder that Clark Kerr and Marian Gade (1989) refer to trustees as "the guardians."

It is easy to append to this list the unexceptional bromide that in meeting these responsibilities trustees ought to engage in governance, which is precisely their domain, and avoid engaging in management, which is the president's domain.

Frank H. T. Rhodes, the former president of Cornell University, has written, in *The Creation of the Future* (2001, 220):

> The role of the board is governance, and there is a world of difference between governance and management. Governance involves the responsibility for approving the mission and goals of the institution; for approving its policies and procedures; for the appointment, review, and support of its president; and for informed oversight of its programs, activities, and resources. Management, in contrast, involves the responsibility for the effective operation of the institution and the achievement of its goals, within the policies and procedures approved by the board; the effective use of its resources; the creative support of the highest standards for teaching, research, and service. The responsibility of the board is to govern, not to manage.

But the line between the two is often difficult to discern in practice, as each side sometimes seeks to press its advantage against the other. When each side acts in good faith, the line is best established case by case in a dialogue of shifting accommodation and mutual respect. In the end, of course, the board of trustees has the legal authority to establish the line by a raw assertion of power. But a board that intrudes on the president's administrative prerogatives risks serious trouble.

Perhaps everyone would agree that a decision to establish a new professional school speaks of governance, just as a decision to set the next year's academic calendar speaks of management. But what of a more complicated decision, for example, to construct a new building, and the subsidiary decisions of where to locate it on the campus and how to determine what its architectural style should be? Such decisions implicate both governance and management. One of my predecessors as president of Dartmouth, Ernest Martin Hopkins (1916–1945), once wrote to a friend:

> I have never seen a group of directors of a business concern, or the trustees of a college, no matter how unanimous in the large, that would not break into sharp differences of opinion over a program of building. . . . Our board of trustees is no exception at this point. At the last meeting we presented the formal plan of development of the College plant for the long future . . . and immediately, as always happens, the Trustees in their individual capacities wanted this, that, and

the other building located differently, disliked the tentative sketches of suggestion for the elevations, and gradually advocated about as many different provisions as there were members of the Board.

In light of the generality of the constraints dividing governance from management, one might expect that institutions would provide new trustees with an extensive orientation program. Orientation programs are especially important because many trustees, on beginning their university service, seek to act like directors of for-profit corporations. Yet the missions of universities, whether public or private, are quite different from those of corporations.

In fact, few institutions, public or private, provide even an adequate orientation program for new trustees; at both the University of Iowa and Dartmouth, the orientations consisted mostly of issuing large notebooks of rules and regulations, long-range planning reports, and official bulletins—a process hardly likely to educate new trustees about the culture of the institution they are about to govern and the nature of their responsibilities. Both institutions seemed to believe that trusteeship, like marriage, is a learn-as-you-go enterprise.

Although both trustees of universities and directors of for-profits have fiduciary duties of care and loyalty, the primary goal of for-profit organizations is to enhance shareholders' investment, often by modifying their missions through mergers, acquisitions, and divestment. As William G. Bowen (1994, 21), the former president of Princeton University, has commented, "A key responsibility of for-profit boards is to identify businesses that should be sold off as well as to probe the desirability of striking out in quite new directions."

Universities, by contrast, serve no shareholders. They do not seek to make profits. But they do have a firm commitment to their institutions' historic traditions. In fulfilling that commitment, they may sometimes have an obligation to maintain an academic activity that is central to the institution's educational mission, for example, the department of classics, even though it is disproportionately costly.

Although both for-profit corporations and universities must be concerned with their standing among many external constituencies, the identity of these constituencies is quite different. For universities, these constituencies will include alumni, donors, public officials, fund-raising consultants—relationships that usually require trustee involvement; for for-profits, it will be government regulators, investors, suppliers, customers, accountants, auditors, Wall Street analysts, lawyers, and bankers—relationships normally handled by management.

The tendency to conflate the "bottom-line" fiduciary responsibility of a for-profit corporate director with the mission-oriented responsibility of a university trustee can be awkward. It ought to be one of the responsibilities of the president and the board chair to orient new trustees to their task.

### Supporting the President

Some business school professors teach that chief executive officers can expect to have little impact on a strong organizational culture. To the extent that this observation is true, it doubtless applies to educational institutions no less than corporations. But it is not invariably true. There are notable instances in the history of higher education of presidents who have defied that teaching and strengthened the academic status of their institutions, for example, Robert Maynard Hutchins at the University of Chicago and Derek Bok at Harvard. It is important, therefore, to search out the sources of their leadership success.

In my judgment, perhaps the principal source has been the long-range support of the board of trustees. For this reason, I regularly emphasized to the trustees with whom I served that the most significant function of the board is to establish clearly the principles that will guide the institution's educational aspirations. What a president needs most from members of the board is a confident, informed commitment to the vision that they have mutually set, so that she can focus her sights on the long term.

In the end, it is the board that has the best opportunity to see the future of the college as a whole, unlike other groups, such as alumni and students, that see it only from afar and sporadically or from too near and constantly. Of her many constituencies, trustees are the one on which a president absolutely must be able to depend. In *A Woman's Education* (2001, 45), a memoir of her decade as president of Smith College, Jill Ker Conway testifies to the way an effective board supports a president: "In this highly charged setting, the Board of Trustees was the only counterweight a newly arrived president could deploy. I came to admire and like my board colleagues a lot, because having cast their vote for change, they stood firm."

The president must be assured that the board will not become so distressed by the turbulence that occasionally disturbs every academic community that it may prematurely consider modifying the fundamental aspirations of the institution. He needs trustees who are critical but loyal, and who will draw on their external credibility and visibility to defend the institution in the public arena.

I did everything I could to make certain that both boards I served understood that trustees are stewards of the many diverse interests that comprise the university—most useful when they are active rather than activist, detached and independent, divorced from any of their personal political antecedents, and immune to the pressures of specific constituencies, the appeal of popular prejudices, or the familiar tyranny of the urgent. Boards of public universities have a special obligation to protect their institutions from political pressure and interference.

In addition, if board members are to provide effective support to the president, they must be prepared to commit a substantial amount of time to the task. When a board meets either nine times a year, as the University of Iowa board did, or five times a year, as the Dartmouth board did, with many additional meetings of committees (e.g., academic affairs, student affairs, budget, personnel, investment, real estate, development), board membership must be regarded as an active working commitment, not an honorific or decorative sinecure.[1]

It is essential, too, that board members act in such a manner as to respect the president's autonomy. The president must be perceived as the leader of the institution. Moreover, the faculty must regard the president as their representative, independent of the board. If the board, by clumsy or heavy-handed actions, makes it appear that a president is too often carrying out the board's specific wishes (in the manner of "a hatchet man"), perhaps against the suspected views of the president himself, the president's capacity to lead will suffer.

At the time that my appointment at Dartmouth was announced, the board made clear that my principal charge was to strengthen the college's intellectual quality and raise its academic profile—"to lift Dartmouth out of the sandbox," in the often-quoted words of an anonymous trustee. The faculty could not have been more pleased with this charge, but many alumni and students found it threatening.

What did I—the first president since 1822 who was neither an alumnus nor a faculty member—know of Dartmouth's traditions? Would I appreciate the "work-hard, play-hard" culture of which so many alumni and students were proud? Did I intend to emulate my alma mater by "Harvardizing" the institution? Was I about to create a student body of geeks—of students, as I declared in my 1987 inaugural address, "whose greatest pleasures may come not from the camaraderie of classmates, but from the lonely acts of writing poetry or mastering the cello or solving mathematical riddles or translating Catullus"—rather than the traditional one of well-rounded students? Without the vocal and public support of the board, I doubt that I could have weathered the storm, especially among alumni, that these speculations incited.

In supporting the president, trustees must be careful not to form opinions about her on the basis of casual comments made on social occasions. The members of a public board are likely to be more accessible to faculty members, students, and alumni than are private boards; they are, after all, public officials. This can be a positive circumstance; a board of trustees that listens to many voices, from many constituencies, is likely to be better informed than one that does not. But board members must calibrate their accessibility so that it does not encourage the belief that there is an alternative channel to the board that bypasses or diminishes the perceived authority of the president, and, by extension, other senior administrative officers.

*Evaluating the President*

One of the board's most important responsibilities is to systematically evaluate the president's performance, ideally on an annual basis. In my experience, the conduct of such a review, even when it is informal and even when the board is pleased with the president's performance, makes all of the participants uneasy. Moreover, the risks of miscommunication are always present. Yet communication of this kind is an essential form of the president's accountability to the board.

From a president's point of view, an annual evaluation is a great protection. She needs to know whether the board is satisfied with her performance—academic administration and planning, budgetary and fiscal management, faculty, student, and alumni relations, fund-raising, and external relations—and she especially needs to know whether individual members of the board are critical of any of her specific actions. She needs warnings if her performance is deemed deficient, as well as suggestions as to how to remedy her deficiencies. As one commentator has written, "The board should hold the president's feet to the fire, but make it a friendly fire!"

For a public institution the difficulties of a presidential evaluation may be greater than for a private institution. Because a public president holds a position of public trust and may even be a controversial figure in the state, it is essential that the board, in evaluating the president, resist the perception that it is vulnerable to political pressure, especially from the governor or outspoken legislators. The board must also be able to assure the press, as a matter of public accountability, that such reviews have regularly been held, even as it must decline to provide the press with a written document encapsulating the review.

Under the Dartmouth practice, the chair of the board, along with two trustees of my choosing, would meet with me approximately once a year (specifically not at salary time) to discuss my performance as well as my working relationship with the board. The goal was not to assign a "grade" but to help me be more effective. The chair made clear that these performance reviews were not intended to be an annual referendum on my tenure. In addition, the chair always sought my feedback on how the board could make its own performance more effective. As Clark Kerr and Marian Gade (1989, 94) have written, "Boards should realize that when they evaluate a president's performance they are also evaluating their own performance in selecting, advising, and supporting the president."

In my experience, these meetings were invariably helpful. Nothing critical that the board ever told me came as a surprise. I was already aware of those areas of my performance that needed strengthening and realized that any concerned observer would readily note them as well.

### Fund-Raising

Is fund-raising a trustee responsibility? Providing assistance in an institution's fund-raising efforts is certainly a common expectation of trustees of private institutions. It is a rare private board that has not appointed a number of trustees precisely because they are significant donors and therefore in an unembarrassed position to ask for significant gifts from others.

For presidents of private institutions, the most important fund-raising efforts involve calling on prospective donors in the company of a trustee. Often the trustee has made significant contributions to one or more of the prospective donor's favorite charitable causes, and now the time has come for reciprocity.

At public institutions, the role of trustees in fund-raising is invariably more limited. Some trustees feel disabled from participating in fund-raising because they hold a public office and do not want to risk even the remote possibility of impropriety that sometimes attaches to financial dealings in a political environment. Others are sometimes inhibited

by the fact that their board governs several public institutions, thereby creating dilemmas of favoritism.

I discussed fund-raising prospects with the board chair at Dartmouth or another trustee on at least a weekly basis; I cannot recollect ever discussing them with the board chair or a trustee at the University of Iowa.

## The Chair of the Board

A good board chair is a president's godsend. Because the trustees are the president's most reliable constituency, and because the chair is the first among equals around whom authority inevitably coalesces, he is in a position to be an important source of support in the professional life of a president. His role is unavoidably political.

My predecessor at Dartmouth, David T. McLaughlin, perceptively wrote, "The president needs an advocate, a full partner who is an advisor, counselor, and confidant—a person who can help interpret the board to the president and the president to the board and give critically constructive guidance privately and in a non-threatening manner" (private memo). Similarly, the board chair is an essential person in translating to alumni and external audiences the values that the president, with the board's support, is seeking to implement.

It is essential, as President McLaughlin indicates, that the president and the chair of the board be able to talk intimately. One of the important roles of the chair is to serve as a sounding board for the president, helping her to temper and refine her views and suggesting other persons who might be useful in that process.

In my experience with three chairs at the University of Iowa and five at Dartmouth, every one consistently exercised self-restraint in intervening in policy matters; they helped me think my way into and through problems, they tested my premises, but in the end they rarely said anything more directive than "use your best judgment." Because these relationships were built on mutual respect, several of these chairs remain, to this day, close personal friends.

One of a chair's most useful functions is to help the president, especially in her early years, understand the institution's culture and appreciate its power. This is especially valuable when the president is an outsider, as I was at Dartmouth, where a tenacious alumni and student culture had created a unique mythology, illustrated by Daniel Webster's (1819) oft-quoted assertion before the U.S. Supreme Court that "it is, sir, as I have said, a small college, and yet there are those who love it."

However much presidents may value their relationship with the chair of the board, few are thrilled to work with a chair who lives in the community where the college is located. They fear, probably correctly, that the chair will be awash in dinner-party and coffee-shop gossip about the president. (They would have a similar fear about resident board members.)

The fact that the University of Iowa is located in a small town—away from the state's population centers—made it unlikely that the chair would be a local resident. Dartmouth, too, is located in a small town, but one that is a retirement community and year-round vacation spot for thousands of alumni. None of the chairs with whom I served happened to reside or vacation in Hanover, but that possibility may well occur in the future. When it does, the chair would do well to avoid drawing too many conclusions about the president from the inevitable analysis of her performance that sprinkles local conversation. And the president would do well to place some trust in the good sense and discriminating worldliness of the chair.

Perhaps the distinguishing mark of a public institution is its status as an instrumentality of state government. Public universities exist in a political environment. Their relationships with the governor and the state legislature (especially the leadership) are crucial; on them state appropriations depend. The rule at Iowa was that only the chair of the board could negotiate with the governor or the legislative leadership about the university's budgetary requests. The rule was designed to protect the president from being drawn into political conflict. To be sure, the president testified on behalf of the university at committee hearings and was free to meet with legislators socially, but he was not free to lobby.

Among the consequences of this rule was the frequent election of board chairs who had political experience. The three chairs with whom I served at Iowa had been, respectively, a state senator, the state's Republican national committeeman, and the chair of the governor's fund-raising efforts.

Because the board chairship is a leadership position, the permissible length of a chair's tenure is an important matter. A chair's tenure ought to be long enough to permit him to grow into effectiveness and to form an effective partnership with the president (perhaps five years) but not so long that he becomes complacent. The term of the chair at Dartmouth was typically no longer than three years—too short a period to be able to take advantage of one's experience at the head of the table. At Iowa, most chairs served five or more years.

## Avoidance of Surprise

Presidents must always deal openly and honestly with board members; that much is a given. But one precept instilled in me by eight different chairs is of special import: board chairs do not want to be surprised. Every one of the chairs with whom I served, at both Iowa and Dartmouth, insisted that I share with them every intimation I might have about events that had not yet emerged from what Othello called "the womb of time," even if my anticipatory suspicions seemed far-fetched. Thus, I would always take care to inform the chair about deans or prominent faculty members who were considering job offers elsewhere, even when I believed it unlikely that they would accept them, or about student unrest, even when I doubted that it would erupt into confrontation or demonstrations. A chair does not want to be unprepared when confronted by the press or by other board members.

In time, my conduct in this respect became institutionalized at Dartmouth into a regular agenda item known as "KPAN." I was asked to report at every meeting on the problems that *K*eep the *P*resident *A*wake at *N*ight.

On more than one occasion, the chairs to whom I reported had useful problem-solving suggestions that had not occurred to me. The chair, in turn, could exercise his discretion as to whether to alert the members of the board to my incipient apprehensions, weighing that course against the possibility that my apprehensions might never come to pass.

For public trustees, the avoidance of surprise is especially important in financial matters, such as facilities construction, which involves committing large sums of taxpayers' money, often in the tens of millions of dollars. Once the decision is made, litigation challenging the board's procedures, financial estimates, adherence to environmental protections, and compliance with ethical standards usually follows—especially from disappointed bidders complaining, inter alia, about the selection of out-of-state professionals.

Given this setting, public trustees regard themselves as watch dogs for the taxpayers. They understandably want sufficient time to become familiar with the details of each project, well in advance of its adoption, lest they fail to anticipate the vulnerabilities to which the media and lawyers will inevitably point when judicial proceedings are initiated.

Another matter of acute interest to boards is personnel. Few responsibilities of a university president are more important than the selection of administrative officers, especially provosts and academic deans. In appointing academic officers, a president has an opportunity to place her mark on a school and give it a direction she favors. Trustees properly seek advance notice of such appointments.

In my experience, presidents are often reluctant to share their thinking with the board during their course of deliberation, for fear that members of the board may limit their freedom of choice by lobbying for one candidate over others. Yet board members have a point in arguing that selection of the dean of an important school, such as one of business, law, or medicine, especially if the president seeks to redirect the school's programmatic emphasis, is a matter of governance, not merely of internal management. Rarely are boards pleased to learn of a prospective appointment when it is virtually a fait accompli, a few hours before a press release is issued.

Having appointed four provosts and ten deans during sixteen years of service, I can testify to the value of not drawing the lines of competing authority too sharply. I found it valuable to rehearse, with board chairs, the strengths and weaknesses of the final group of candidates. As a result of such discussions, the chair was in a better position to test my evaluation of the candidates, explain my thinking to board members, and alert me to avoidable pitfalls that the appointment of specific individuals might present. Board chairs readily appreciate that, in the end, a president can be held accountable for the manner in which she administers the institution only if she can work with associates of her own choosing.

In the public sector, the chair's advice might be to give the governor advance notice of the appointment of the dean of a particular school (like the medical school, which received significant state funding, or the law school, from which the governor may have graduated). In the private sector this advice might be to place courtesy calls to a number of the school's most prominent alumni and donors.

In my experience, board members are always interested in the appointment of deans, especially of professional schools. This interest was more intense at Dartmouth than at the University of Iowa. Because many Dartmouth trustees held two degrees from Dartmouth—an undergraduate degree and a professional degree—and were the parents of alumni children, they had a proprietary interest in the schools' future. This intimacy fed an appetite for insider information.

Most of all, board members in both sectors were interested in the appointment of the vice president for finance. This was an appointee whose work on budgets and investments was an essential predicate to one of the board's most important responsibilities. In addition, board members felt themselves better qualified to assess the credentials of a prospective financial officer than of an academic dean. In such instances a president is wise to value the opinions of board members; it makes no sense to appoint a vice president for finance about whom the board, itself highly competent in matters of finance, has significant doubts.

## Nature of Meetings

One of the most important differences between boards of public and private institutions has to do with the nature of their meetings. The meetings of public boards typically are governed by state laws providing for "open meetings" or "government in the sunshine." For the University of Iowa, these laws deemed any conversation about public issues among five or more members of the board to be a public meeting that must be held pursuant to formal rules, including notice to the general public and access to the print press and television cameras.

Many decisions were too sensitive to be risked in an open meeting televised statewide. In these circumstances, the board chair was compelled to cajole consensus before the meetings by consulting in at least three groups of four or fewer members. This, of course, gave the eventual meeting something of a rehearsed and stilted air.

Moreover, the president's political desire to make a vigorous, even passionate, presentation on behalf of the interests of one of his constituencies—for example, salary increases for faculty, new recreation facilities for students, enlarged medical coverage for staff—was sometimes diminished by the fact that the decision had been already arranged beforehand.

Did this mean that the closed meetings of the Dartmouth board were more effective? Certainly the discussions were more vigorous, more contentious, and more frank. Sometimes, these discussions among board members, accustomed to advocacy in their own professional circles, seemed undisciplined, full of interruptions and raised voices, but in the end the private setting in which they occurred undoubtedly enhanced the quality of the meetings.

In virtually every state, the strongest proponents of open-meeting laws are the media, which reflexively regard them, in dignity, as next to the First Amendment. But few who have operated under the restrictions that open-meeting laws impose regard them as conducive to the quality of collegiate decision making necessary for good government.


## Conclusion

An examination of the boards of trustees at two institutions alone is hardly a basis for generalization, but it does suggest certain modest comparisons.

That differences would exist between a public and a private institution were to be expected—in this case differences between (1) the method of selection and personal profiles of board members, (2) the extent to which meetings must be open to the public, (3) the institutional and political environment in which the respective boards operate, and (4) the obligation to engage in fund-raising.

The similarities, however, are striking—(1) in the size of the two boards, (2) the conscientiousness of the board members, (3) the commitment to supporting the president on academic matters and evaluating his performance on a regular basis, (4) the leadership role of the board chairs, (5) the intense desire to avoid surprise, and (6) the weakness of orientation programs.

# CHAPTER TWO

# Higher Education Boards of Trustees
## Benjamin E. Hermalin

niversities and colleges in the United States are overseen by
boards of trustees, regents, overseers, or similarly titled entities. With respect to their place in the hierarchical structure,
such boards are similar to boards of directors in corporations. Indeed,
for nonstate institutions of higher education, their legal status is effectively the same. Although similar in structure to corporate boards,
they—and in fact nonprofit boards more generally—have not received
much scrutiny from economists. The purpose of this chapter is to
suggest ways in which economists could go about making amends and
trying to anticipate some of the difficulties they may face. In addition,
this essay attempts to point out how our understanding of for-profit
corporate boards may provide insight into boards of trustees and
suggest questions to investigate.

As Kerr and Gade (1989) observe, within the United States, boards
of trustees and boards of directors come from the same legal tradition.[1]
Indeed, institutions such as Harvard and Yale are among the oldest corporations (in the legal sense) within the English legal tradition. And
almost as long as there have been corporations, there has been criticism
of the boards that oversee them.[2] Yet, in the for-profit arena, corporations are the dominant form of business organization. Similarly, in the
United States the "corporate" model is the dominant model in higher
education. Moreover, there are two separate pieces of evidence to
suggest that it is a pretty good model: First, state colleges and universities have almost invariably copied this model even though there is no
legal requirement for them to do so. That is, for instance, a state

university could easily be overseen by civil-service bureaucrats in some state agency of higher education, similar to the way many states oversee grade K through 12 education. To be sure, the corporate model could simply be some historical accident; but if it were a truly poor form of organization, one might have expected to see some alternatives arise in American higher education (for instance, because of emulation of alternative models observed in Europe or utilized by the service academies, such as West Point).

The second piece of evidence is that there are alternative models employed elsewhere in the world (a point also made by Kerr and Gade [1989]). In particular, there are models in which universities are controlled by ministries of education (e.g., as in France). There are models in which they are controlled by faculty guilds (as were Oxford and Cambridge until nineteenth-century reforms). There are even models in which they are controlled by student guilds (as was Bologna University, the oldest in the Western world).[3] Yet all these models seem to yield universities that are generally perceived as inferior to American universities organized along the corporate model. Although neither of these pieces of evidence is conclusive proof that the corporate model is the best or even a superior model, they at least make clear that it can't be a particularly terrible model, at least vis-à-vis alternatives.

But the historical durability of the corporate model and its apparent success relative to alternative models only begs further questions. What, in fact, do boards of trustees do? How do they affect what happens in colleges and universities? What can we reasonably expect of them? Why if it's a successful model has it generated so much criticism?[4] Moreover, the possible fact that the corporate model is the best available model is merely a relative comparison, and doesn't deal with whether boards satisfy some absolute objective (i.e., achieve some *un*constrained optimum) or are just the least bad of the available evils (i.e., achieve some constrained optimum). In the context of for-profit corporations, these questions and issues have recently received considerable attention, primarily in the form of empirical analyses, but also in terms of some theoretical treatments.

The next section of this chapter explores what lessons from empirical work on boards of directors might apply to boards of trustees. It also considers to what extent this empirical work can serve as a road map for future work focused directly on boards of trustees. The section following it turns to theoretical issues concerning directors and governance.

What We Know about Corporate Boards and How It Might
Apply to Trustees

In a recent survey of the literature on corporate boards, Michael Weisbach and I (Hermalin and Weisbach 2003) made the following observations. First, formal theory on boards of directors has been quite limited. Most of the work has instead been empirical, seeking to answer one or more of the following three questions:

1. How do board characteristics such as composition or size affect the achievement of firm objectives?

2. How do board characteristics affect the observable actions of the board?

3. What factors affect the makeup of boards and how they evolve over time?

Research thus far has established a number of empirical regularities. First, board composition, as measured by the ratio of inside directors (e.g., executives of the firm) to outside directors (e.g., executives of outside organizations),[5] is not correlated with firm performance.[6] However, the number of directors on a firm's board is negatively related to its financial performance. Second, board actions *do* appear to be related to board characteristics. Firms with higher proportions of outside directors and smaller boards tend to make arguably better—or at least different—decisions concerning acquisitions, poison pills, executive compensation, and CEO replacement, ceteris paribus. Finally, boards appear to evolve over time depending on the bargaining position of the CEO relative to that of the existing directors. Firm performance, CEO turnover, and changes in ownership structure appear to be important factors affecting changes to boards.

To what extent should we expect a similar picture to hold for boards of trustees? Anecdotal evidence (e.g., Bowen 1994) suggests that large boards are no more effective in higher education than in the corporate world, although I am unaware of any formal statistical analyses for boards of trustees demonstrating that size is negatively related to performance.[7] Other results, such as those pertaining to acquisitions, poison pills, and changes in ownership, are clearly less applicable to higher education.

One problem with replicating these studies using data for boards of trustees is deciding how to define—to say nothing of measuring—"firm objectives" in the higher education context. When it comes to boards of trustees, there is no unambiguous dimension along which to measure performance—does one measure research, teaching effectiveness, fundraising success, or what? Moreover, even if we let researchers decide to concentrate on one dimension,[8] there is no unambiguous yardstick to employ for most dimensions—is research, for instance, measured by articles in scholarly journals, citations, grants received, faculty memberships in prestigious scholarly societies, or what?

The definition-of-objectives problem is not the only problem facing a would-be researcher addressing question 1 as it relates to boards of trustees (i.e., how do board characteristics affect objective attainment?). Other problems face the researcher as well. First, many of the board characteristics that have been hypothesized to matter in the corporate context are either not meaningful or difficult to define in the higher education context. For instance, given that typically the only director from management is the university or college president, one might conclude that there is not much scope for an empirical analysis of the impact of insiders versus outsiders. On the other hand, one might object that even the definition of "insider" is unclear: There are boards of trustees, for instance, that include student representatives or faculty representatives. Are they insiders, outsiders, or something that has no real analog in the corporate world?

Of course, even if there weren't issues measuring performance or the factors that we hypothesize could determine performance, there is no reason to suspect that an attempt to answer question 1 would reveal anything.[9] As reviewed in Hermalin and Weisbach 2003, almost all such attempts in the corporate context are inconclusive; that is, researchers typically find no evidence that corporate board characteristics affect firm performance.[10] The one exception, in fact, has been the relation between board size and corporate performance (Yermack 1996; Eisenberg, Sundgren, and Wells 1998), where it has been found that larger board size is associated with worse performance. However, as I discuss later, there are reasons to wonder whether those results indicate a causal relation; that is, this association need not mean that larger boards *cause* worse performance.

In retrospect, there are two reasons why we should perhaps not be surprised by the lack of clear results when looking empirically at whether board characteristics affect firm performance. First, firm performance is relatively volatile and buffeted by many forces. Moreover, it is not clear whether board characteristics have an immediate or more delayed effect on performance. Given the difficulties in measuring performance clearly and not knowing whether the effects of board characteristics show up in the short term or the long term, it is not surprising that detecting a relationship between characteristics and performance would be difficult, at least as a statistical matter. Although some measures of university or college performance are no doubt less volatile over time than financial performance measures, they are likely harder to assess accurately, so the "noise" problem—the difficulty of differentiating a true relation from random variation—would likely be equally severe were one to attempt to explain university or college performance on the basis of trustee characteristics.

The second reason not to be surprised is that presumably organizations want to perform well. If there is some way in which board characteristics affect performance, organizations should ensure that their boards exhibit those characteristics that yield optimal performance. That is, if there is an optimal set of characteristics, we should expect, all else equal, for organizations to adopt these characteristics. In steady state (equilibrium), then, there should be no meaningful differences in board characteristics with respect to performance, which means— unless there are a number of firms in the sample still in the process of adjusting toward these optimal characteristics—there isn't the variation in the explanatory variables necessary to detect the relation between board characteristics and performance. Put another way, recall that to detect that a characteristic affects performance, we need to see that institutions that set the characteristic one way systematically perform differently from institutions that set it another way; but if it is optimal for all institutions to set the characteristic a single way, and they do, then it is impossible to see how *variation* in that characteristic, given that it doesn't exist, is systematically related to variations in performance.

This notion of optimality in steady state or equilibrium also raises questions of how one would interpret any apparently conclusive results from addressing question 1 empirically (see Hermalin and Weisbach 2003 for a complete discussion). In particular, one can imagine that the set of board characteristics that would be optimal in terms of performance under a given set of circumstances differs from the set that would be optimal under a different set of circumstances. If, in fact, all organizations adopt the board structure that is optimal for them given their circumstances, then any relation found between board structure and performance would necessarily be meaningless—the correlation is simply the consequence of both structure and performance being correlated with the underlying circumstances. For instance, suppose that the more complex an organization is, the more difficult it is to manage well. Because of the difficulty in managing such a complex organization, it might be optimal to have a large board. A large board would, perhaps, allow for a range of expertise on the many problems confronting a complex organization. At the same time, because it is difficult to manage, a complex organization's performance would be worse ceteris paribus than a simpler organization's. Given my premises, one would readily find institutions with smaller boards outperforming those with larger boards, but this relationship would *not* indicate that small boards *cause* better performance. In particular, it would be an erroneous policy prescription to encourage an organization with a large board to shrink it—the organization would end up with a board that was *less* well suited to its specific purposes, and its performance would be even worse than before.

This "equilibrium" caveat could, however, be less pronounced for boards of trustees than boards of directors. For-profit firms are subject to the forces of economic Darwinism—in the long run, competition from more efficient firms either induces improvement in inefficient firms or drives them out of business. It is, thus, difficult for a for-profit firm to maintain a board structure that grossly departs from optimality for an extended period of time. Universities and colleges, while not wholly immune to Darwinian forces, are not, as a rule, hit with them as strongly (a point also made by Bowen [1994, 9–13]). This is especially true of well-endowed and state institutions. Moreover universities and colleges are much more affected by other, noneconomic forces, such as political pressures and a greater need to respect tradition, which could yield and perpetuate boards that are nonoptimal in structure (this would seem especially true of state institutions, where there is little reason to imagine that the political process will yield an optimal board).[11] Consequently, we can expect much greater variation in the characteristics and structures of boards of trustees than boards of directors, which, in turn, means there could be hope of having sufficient variation in the independent variables to detect their impact on performance.

Table 2.1 "confirms" the hypothesis of great variation. It summarizes some of the characteristics of the trustees of four universities. Although the table reflects the considerable heterogeneity in boards of trustees, it also raises doubts about finding any relation between institutional performance and the structure of the board and its characteristics. While admittedly four is a rather small sample, it is worth noting that all four of these universities are widely considered to be among the very top universities in the United States. Looking at the variation in Table

Table 2.1. Four Universities and Their Trustee Characteristics

| University | Method of Selection (composition) | Number of Trustees | Frequency of Regular Meeting |
|---|---|---|---|
| University of California[a] | 18 regents appointed by governor for 12-year terms<br>1 regent (a student) appointed by the regents for a 1-year term<br>4 state officials: governor, lieutenant governor, speaker of the assembly, and superintendent of public instruction<br>2 alumni officials: president and vice president of the alumni associations<br>President of the university | 26 | 6 times annually |
| University of Michigan[b] | 8 regents elected in biennial statewide elections<br>President of the university | 9 | 12 times annually |
| Harvard University | Two boards:<br>Corporation (7 members) self-perpetuating with consent of board of overseers (includes president of the university); members appointed for life<br>Board of overseers elected by alumni at large | NA | Corporation meets 15 times annually[c] |
| Princeton University | 13 alumni trustees (elected by alumni for 4-year terms), one of whom, at least, must be an alumnus/a of the graduate school<br>4–8 term trustees, elected by the board for 4-year terms<br>Governor of New Jersey<br>President of the university<br>Unspecified number of charter trustees, elected by the board for 10-year terms | 23–40 (currently 39) | 5 times annually |

*Sources*: Except where noted, sources are the respective Web sites of the universities.
[a] Nine-campus system.
[b] One main campus and two secondary campuses.
[c] Kerr and Gade 1989, 60.

2.1 and the uniform excellence of these schools, the hypothesis that the structure of its board of trustees has no effect on a university or college's performance would seem the more logical hypothesis than that it does have an effect. Hence, while higher education offers greater variability in boards than does the corporate world, there still seems no reason to expect to find that these boards matter for institutional performance, at least in an empirically detectable way.

A potentially more profitable issue to tackle is question 2—how do board characteristics affect the observable actions of the board? In the corporate board arena, this question has been a more fruitful line of research than question 1. Specifically, evidence indicates that both board composition and size are systematically related with the board's decisions regarding CEO replacement, acquisitions, poison pills, and executive compensation. Because the first and last of these have greater relevance in the higher education context, I will limit my review to these two sets of findings.

The most commonly discussed responsibility of the board of directors is to choose and to monitor the firm's CEO (see, e.g., Mace 1986). Indeed, rather than make day-to-day decisions, boards appear to play a crucial role in picking the firm's CEO and to view their primary responsibility as monitoring and potentially replacing him. One way, therefore, to evaluate the board's effectiveness is by looking at the quality of these decisions.

A large number of articles have documented that there is a positive relation between CEO turnover and poor performance in large corporations, as well as in other types of organizations.[12] The standard interpretation of this relation is that it measures the board's monitoring; when performance is worse, the board is more likely to find the current CEO unacceptable and to make a change.

Simply documenting a relation between poor performance and an increased probability of CEO turnover, although suggestive of board monitoring, is nonetheless far from conclusive. After all, a sense of failure or pressure from shareholders could explain this relationship. To better identify the role played by the board, Weisbach (1988) tested whether the effect of firm performance on CEO turnover varies systematically with board composition. His results indicate that when boards are dominated by outside directors, CEO turnover is more sensitive to firm performance than it is in firms with insider-dominated boards. This result is consistent with the view that outsider-dominated boards—those a priori likely to be independent of management—are responding to corporate performance when they make CEO-retention decisions. In contrast, turnover in insider-dominated boards is not performance-driven, suggesting that insider-dominated boards make turnover decisions for reasons unrelated to corporate performance. This is not surprising: Inside directors' careers tend to be tied to the CEO's, which gives them incentives to advance the CEO's career regardless of the stock price. Consistent with this tied-career explanation is evidence from Borokhovich, Parrino, and Trapani (1996) and

Huson, Parrino, and Starks (2000), who find outsider-dominated boards are more likely than insider-dominated boards to replace a CEO with someone from *outside* the firm.

Yermack (1996) and Wu (2000) performed a similar analysis of CEO turnover, measuring the impact of board size on the relation between CEO turnover and firm performance. These researchers estimated similar equations to those of Weisbach 1988, except that they considered how board size changes the relation between firm performance and CEO turnover. Yermack and Wu found that firms with smaller boards have a stronger relation between firm performance and CEO turnover than do firms with larger boards. This finding is consistent with the view that smaller boards are more effective overseers of the CEO than are larger boards. In particular, in response to poor performance, they may not be paralyzed by free-riding or otherwise plagued with inertia the way larger boards are.

To interpret these studies, the key issue is whether the relations they uncover are causal. In other words, do the particular attributes of the board, such as composition or size, directly affect the board's monitoring? Alternatively, it could be that boards are independent for some other reason (as suggested, e.g., by the bargaining-game model of Hermalin and Weisbach [1998], which I discuss later). Although observationally difficult to distinguish, it is hard to imagine that it is the board characteristics per se that matter; rather what is at issue is whether the board is dominated by a CEO. A dominated board will not monitor regardless of its visible characteristics; however, visible characteristics tend, on average, to be correlated with independence from the CEO. Conversely, a board made up of directors who wish to be independent of management will arrange themselves, in term of size and composition, in a way that best facilitates oversight of management.

Another role of the board is to set and to oversee the firm's compensation policies. A view, prevalent since at least the time of Berle and Means (1932), is that CEOs can exert control over their boards and use this control to extract "excessive" levels of compensation. For example, Michael Eisner, the longtime CEO of Disney, was able to have his personal attorney appointed to the Disney board, and even got him a seat on the compensation committee (see *Wall Street Journal*, 2 February 1997). Not surprisingly, Eisner has been one of the most highly compensated CEOs in recent years.

Core, Holthausen, and Larcker (1999) studied the relations among board composition, ownership structure, and CEO pay. Their results suggest that firms with weaker governance structures tend to pay their

CEOs more. In particular, they found that a CEO's pay rises with the number of outside directors appointed during his tenure, the number of directors over age sixty-nine, board size, and the number of busy directors, where "busy" is defined in terms of the number of additional directorships held by a director.[13] In addition, both Core, Holthausen, and Larcker (1999) and Hallock (1997) found that CEO pay increases when a board contains interlocking directors (e.g., when the CEO of firm A sits on firm B's board and the CEO of firm B sits on firm A's board). Finally, Yermack (1996) found that the pay-performance relation for CEOs decreases with board size, suggesting that small boards give CEOs larger incentives and force them to bear risk more so than do large boards. This evidence suggests that CEOs' influence over their boards does result in higher pay for them.

It seems plausible that similar studies investigating how trustees make decisions about replacing college and university presidents and setting their compensation could be undertaken, although to the best of my knowledge such studies have not yet been conducted.[14] Of course, to some extent, any such studies would face many of the same empirical problems raised earlier (e.g., defining trustee types, measuring performance, etc.). In addition, the data collection could be more daunting than it is in the corporate setting: Although the *Chronicle of Higher Education* does, for instance, collect and report salary information for university and college presidents (see Ehrenberg, Cheslock, and Epifantseva 2001), collecting data on trustee characteristics and certain measures of performance (e.g., research output) could be more difficult.

Replicating studies of how different types of boards of trustees respond to performance in their decisions to retain or remove their institutions' presidents would be fascinating. One potential pitfall would be the noise that exists because not every change in president is due to the removal of the incumbent. Although presumably exogenous causes of change, such as death, can be dealt with, it is still the case that some separations are voluntary (e.g., the president retires) while others are involuntary (e.g., the president announces she is retiring, but would have preferred to stay on if the trustees had permitted her to do so). Weisbach (1988) discusses some of the ways in which voluntary separations might be distinguished from involuntary, but, as he notes, the consequences of failing to identify correctly the two types of separation need not be fatal: Leaving voluntary separations in the sample adds noise to the regression analysis but should not bias the results; the only consequence, therefore, would be that statistical tests would not be as strong as ideal.

In addition to replicating the analyses conducted for corporate boards, research on boards of trustees could consider the effect of boards on decisions that are unique to higher education. One example of this type of work is Lowry 2001b, which examines how differences in trustee selection across different public universities affect the setting of tuition and other fees. Lowry found that tuition and other fees are lower, ceteris paribus, the greater the representation on the board of trustees of "external" trustees, defined as state officials serving ex officio or trustees selected by the governor, state legislature, or popular election.

The third type of empirical analysis has been to answer the questions, What factors affect the makeup of boards and How do they evolve over time? These studies typically measure the impact of *changes* in a firm's characteristics on subsequent *changes* in board composition. Looking at changes minimizes the potential joint endogeneity problem that would arise if one considered levels (i.e., distinguishing the effect of firm characteristics on board characteristics from the effect of board characteristics on firm characteristics).

Hermalin and Weisbach (1988) took this approach and estimated the factors that lead to changes in corporate boards. They found three sets of factors that predict changes in the board. First, poor firm performance increases the likelihood that inside directors leave and that outside directors join the board. Second, the CEO succession process appears to be intertwined with the board selection process. When a CEO nears retirement, firms tend to add inside directors, who are potential candidates to be the next CEO. Just after a CEO change, inside directors tend to leave the board, consistent with the hypothesis that these directors are losing candidates to be CEO. Finally, after a firm leaves a product market, inside directors tend to depart and outside directors tend to join the board. Denis and Sarin (1999) confirmed these findings on a much larger sample of firms from a nonoverlapping time period. They found that large changes in board composition tend to occur after abnormally poor performance and around the time of a CEO change.

Replication of studies of this third type using trustee data could be difficult for a number of reasons. First, whereas corporate directors serve relatively short terms,[15] many trustees serve far longer terms (e.g., the ten- to twelve-year terms of trustees or regents of Princeton and the University of California—see Table 2.1). This suggests fewer turnovers in trustees,[16] which makes detecting sensitivity of changes in board composition to institutional performance more difficult. A second difficulty could be the now familiar difficulty of measuring performance, or more precisely focusing on the relevant measures of performance. A third difficulty is defining different types of trustees, an issue raised earlier.

One strategy would be simply to avoid the third difficulty by just looking at what increases turnover rates, regardless of type of trustee. In particular, a reasonable prediction is that events that increase "headaches" for trustees, such as scandals or financial problems, also increase turnover. Another possible line of research would be the "flip side" of the question Lowry (2001b) asked: He hypothesizes that political pressures cause "external" trustees to hold down fee increases. Is there evidence for such pressures? Do, for instance, fee increases lessen reelection rates for elected trustees? Do they influence state elections more generally?[17]

In this section, I have reviewed the empirical literature on corporate boards to see the extent to which it can serve as a road map for similar work on boards of trustees in higher education. At an abstract level, much of the work on corporate boards could be replicated for boards of trustees, but, as I've indicated, there are reasons to suspect that in a number of instances such work is unlikely to yield interesting results. This is particularly true of attempts to determine how the characteristics of the board of trustees affect the achievement of institutional objectives (i.e., question 1). Measuring both the variables to be explained and the explanatory variables could prove messy. Moreover, there are fundamental theoretical reasons to question whether any significant relationship should exist and what, if one were found, it would mean. The one line of inquiry on this dimension of which I would be less negative would be to determine whether a *statistical* relation between board size and performance, which has been established in the corporate setting (Yermack 1996; Eisenberg, Sundgren, and Wells 1998) and hypothesized by Bowen (1994) for higher education, indeed exists for higher education. But should such a relation be uncovered, I would caution against necessarily accepting the "obvious" causal interpretation.

As noted earlier, more fruitful lines of research would be to address questions 2 and 3 in the board of trustees context. With respect to question 2—how do characteristics of the board affect its observable actions?—there are a number of interesting analyses to be conducted. For instance, one could extend the analysis of Ehrenberg, Cheslock, and Epifantseva (2001) to see whether board characteristics affect how the various determinants they studied influence presidential pay or even

whether board characteristics *directly* affect presidential pay. In particular, based on the work of Main, O'Reilly, and their coauthors (O'Reilly,
Main, and Crystal 1988; Main, O'Reilly, and Wade 1995), one would
hypothesize that the socioeconomic status of trustees will have a significant effect on presidential compensation. One could also seek to do
a similar study to that by Ehrenberg and colleagues, but seek to explain
the change in the president rather than her compensation, and then add
in board features as Weisbach (1988) did in the corporate board context.
Finally, more work like Lowry's (2001b), which looked at the role of
board of trustee characteristics on important higher education decisions
(e.g., fee setting), would be most welcome.[18]

For question 3, a sensible focus would be on the determinants of
trustee turnover. Basic facts need to be uncovered, such as the underlying rate of turnover. Beyond that it would be good to know what
the determinants of turnover are. Of particular importance would be to
see what actions affected the tenure of elected regents of state schools
and, more generally, the extent to which political issues affect trustee
tenure.

## Governance Theory and Its Application to Boards of Trustees

The prototypical view of hierarchy is that those who hold higher positions in the hierarchy control those beneath them. Under this view, the
board of trustees should have all the power with regard to the running
of universities and colleges.[19] Reality, of course, is clearly different, and
there are a number of reasons why.

One reason that boards cannot possess all the power is that they don't
possess the necessary knowledge, incentive, and time. Most boards of
trustees consist primarily of *lay* trustees, that is, trustees who are not
academics and whose primary employment is not in higher education.
They, thus, haven't the time to make all the decisions and must rationally delegate much of the decision making to the officers of the college
or university.[20] Such delegation necessarily implies the ceding of power.
In the same line, the lack of necessary knowledge and experience makes
the trustees reliant on the officers for background and briefings, which
again shifts power to the officers. Finally, as with any group effort, there
is the usual "teams problem," whereby each individual trustee under-
provides effort because he feels that he can leave the work to his fellow
trustees (i.e., an individual trustee will "free-ride" on the efforts of the
other trustees).[21] This means less attention overall to the institution

and, in particular, less oversight of the administration and a power vacuum that administrators (and others) will seek to fill.

Organization scholars sometimes refer to such shifts of power as the board retaining the right to *govern* (oversee) while management is granted the right to *manage* (take action).[22] But even the board's right to govern is not absolute. A second reason, then, that the board cannot possess all the power is that it must also make concessions on the right to govern, at least in a de facto sense. These concessions are part of the bargaining—implicit or explicit—between the president and the board over the latter's ability to govern. This bargaining model, set forth in Hermalin and Weisbach 1998, runs as follows: At any point in time, the board can fire the current president and draw a new one from the relevant population of new presidents. Such a decision is rational only if the board concludes the current president is less able than a president randomly drawn from this population is likely to be.[23] Conversely, if the board doesn't wish to replace the current president, then that means the trustees see her as better, in expectation, than any available replacement. But this makes her a "rare commodity," which in turn bestows on her bargaining power vis-à-vis the board. She can, of course, use this bargaining power to extract more compensation and perks from the board. But, as Michael Weisbach and I showed, she will also use it to gain looser governance and less oversight.

Although written in the context of corporate boards, the Hermalin and Weisbach model carries over straightforwardly to higher education.[24] Indeed, it may be even more powerful in that latter context than the former. Observation suggests that changing a university or college president is a more costly undertaking, particularly for board members, than is changing a corporate CEO. It's rare to have an internal successor, who's been groomed for the job, just sitting there at a college or university, whereas succession planning is an ongoing process at most corporations (see, e.g., Vancil 1987 for a study). Moreover, even when a corporation goes outside for a new CEO, the process can be done more quickly and less publicly than it can in most college or university settings. Raising the cost of replacing the president increases her bargaining power and, thus, results in less oversight in equilibrium.

The president may also gain bargaining power to the extent that faculty and students are effectively her allies. A large proportion of a college or university's assets are in human capital—moreover, in human capital that is exceedingly mobile (at least in comparison to most corporate alternatives). Particularly on academic issues of importance to the faculty, the president can utilize that mobility to strengthen her bargaining power vis-à-vis the board of trustees. Similarly, to the extent that conflict between board and president adversely affects applications or yield, the president can capture bargaining power. Ironically, though, this bargaining-power story also means that a president who loses the support of faculty or students may lose a tremendous amount of bargaining power vis-à-vis the board, even if she has otherwise proved to be a strong administrator. Ultimately, then, there is a greater devolution of power from the board and top management to the employees (faculty) and customers (students) in higher education than there is in the typical corporation.

In the Hermalin and Weisbach model (1998), the manner in which the president secures less oversight is by having trustees appointed who are less "independent" of the president. Operationally, less independence means the trustee finds oversight more costly personally, enjoys reduced personal benefit from oversight, or both, ceteris paribus. Comparing the higher education and corporate contexts, it seems reasonable to imagine that the personal benefits of oversight are lower in the former than in the latter: Trustees do not have the financial incentives (stock, stock options, fear of being sued) that corporate directors have. In addition, to the extent trustees see their positions as honorific, they may enter the board expecting not to work hard, which could lead them to act as if they have a high disutility of effort.[25] In contrast, corporate directors presumably understand that they are making a serious commitment. So, all else equal, we could expect boards of trustees to be less effective monitors of management than corporate boards. Moreover, in the Hermalin and Weisbach model, the bargaining between boards and presidents never results in the boards becoming *more* effective monitors—either effectiveness is unchanged, if the president has insufficient bargaining power, or it is reduced.[26] Hence, one can see the Hermalin and Weisbach model as predicting that boards of trustees should be less powerful overseers of presidents than corporate boards are over CEOs, a prediction that is consistent with anecdotal comparisons, such as Bowen's (1994).

Another model that could be applied, a variant of the ideas in Hermalin and Weisbach 1998, would be to imagine that the board of trustees needs to be sensitive to many objectives. In this sense, the board is analogous to a consumer who may wish to buy many different goods. One of these is oversight of the president and other administrators. If, however, the president appears able and capable, then the benefit of monitoring relative to other objectives is lower. A lower relative benefit is analogous to a higher cost; hence, the situation is similar to a consumer who sees the price of one good rise—he consumes less of that good and more of the other goods. Similarly, the board will "purchase" more of its other objectives. For instance, it may add "honorific" trustees to reward large donors (or potential donors); it may expand to allow for greater diversity on the board to mollify critics; or it may expand to have a greater range of expertise. But whatever the motive, the board may rationally respond to capable management by pursuing courses of action that lessen its effectiveness as a monitor. Moreover, although rational, many of these actions are in some ways irreversible—large donors cannot readily be dropped; it is hard to shrink a board, particularly at the expense of diversity. Although it is admittedly a sample of one, it is nonetheless consistent with this view that Princeton's board is currently just one trustee shy of its permitted maximum (see Table 2.1).

A diverse board, while desirable for many reasons, can also result in a weaker board with regard to oversight. Unlike a corporation, which ostensibly has a single objective—to make money—a university or college has multiple objectives. If these different objectives acquire different champions on the board, or even if there is simply considerable disagreement about their relative importance, then the board can become dysfunctional.[27] A power vacuum at the top means more power devolves to the president and others in the institution.

To summarize, there are a number of reasons to expect the governance and management exercised by a board of trustees to be relatively weak:

1. Lack of expertise on the part of lay trustees, which increases reliance on the president and other administrators for information and guidance.

2. Lack of time to devote to the job, which increases the amount of delegation to the president and other administrators. This also means less effort expended on monitoring.

3. Free-riding (teams problem), which reduces the amount of oversight.

4. Bargaining power of a successful president, which leads to less monitoring.

5. Bargaining power of faculty and students, which reduces board power in general, but can also bolster the president's bargaining power vis-à-vis the board to the extent she can mobilize the bargaining power of these other stakeholders.

6. The temptation to use the board for nonoversight purposes, such as to reward large donors or increase diversity.

7. Divisiveness among the directors, which results in a power vacuum at the top.

Although there are all these reasons to imagine that boards of trustees will be "weak," it is worth remembering that not *all* institutions are, necessarily, governed by weak trustees. For instance, political or other pressures could make trustees attentive and focused. Restrictions imposed by charters and by-laws on board size or selection could limit the amount of power a board can bargain away. Finally, in some instances, the board will consist of "strong" trustees, who, by dint of their personality, political clout (e.g., a state governor), or financial clout (e.g., a large donor), are able to "recapture" some amount of power from administrators.[28] On net, however, given that the majority of complaints about boards, corporate or collegiate, is that they are insufficiently vigilant (see, e.g., Berle and Means 1932; Chait and Taylor 1989; Lipton and Lorsch 1992; Jensen 1993; Bowen 1994), the seven reasons for weakness just given would, in whole or in part, seem to apply to most boards.[29]

In contrast to their critics, at least two members of the board, its chair and the president, typically view the board as functioning well according to survey results presented in Kerr and Gade 1989. Chairs give their boards passing marks on all issues except the issue of raising and securing adequate funding (see Kerr and Gade 1989, Table 3, 89). Of particular interest, is that 80 percent or more of the chairs describe their boards' review of the president, its delegation of authority to the president, and its level of commitment and involvement as "good" or "excellent" (Kerr and Gade 1989, Table 3). Presidents are somewhat tougher graders, but nonetheless tend to assign good marks as well. Interestingly, the presidents' views vary from the chairs' on the questions of authority, where they give lower marks.[30]

How can one reconcile the good marks assigned by presidents and board chairs with the criticism leveled by observers (including faculty—Kerr and Gade [1989] report considerable faculty dissatisfaction with their institutions' boards, see their Table B-11)? Part of the answer is simply that people typically assign themselves higher marks than outside observers do—a fact made abundantly clear to me first as a professor and, more recently, as an academic administrator. Another part, though, and one consistent with the Hermalin and Weisbach bargaining model, is that chairs and presidents are reasonably satisfied with the, perhaps implicit, agreement they've reached concerning the degree of oversight and involvement of the board. Outside parties, who may not understand this bargaining or who wish or believe that one side or the other could have been more effective bargainers, are more inclined to express dissatisfaction with the outcome. (An analogy would be the not uncommon occurrence of the rank and file expressing dissatisfaction with the contracts that union leaders achieve with management.)

Personally, my sympathies lie more with the chairs and the presidents than with the outside critics. Within the reality that trustees face—the trade-offs, the true incentives, the allocation of bargaining power, and so on—they achieve the best solution possible in terms of oversight and control. To be sure, we can conceive of better oversight and better control. But we can also conceive of two-hour flights from New York to Tokyo—something that, in the world we currently live in, is not going to happen. To be sure, there are board failures: Occasionally, trustees shirk duties that can be reasonably expected of them; sometimes they could reasonably be tougher bargainers; sometimes they accept actions that we would rightly expect them to reject; and so forth. But one must be careful not to make idiosyncratic mistakes the basis of a condemnation of a system. To do so would be analogous to asking that the rules of football be rewritten because occasionally receivers drop passes and quarterbacks throw interceptions.

Although much of the existing theory of governance, derived in the context of considering for-profit firms, can be exported to nonprofits, such as colleges and universities, there are certainly differences between for-profit and nonprofit firms that could call for the development of new models. In particular, the fact that some nonprofits, like institutions of higher education, have multiple objectives pushed by multiple stakeholders means that there are governance issues that are absent or less pressing in the for-profit realm, where presumably making money is essentially the only objective. For instance, an argument could be made that while the purpose of governance in a for-profit is to ensure effective achievement of the one objective, to make money, the purpose of governance in a college or university is to keep the various stakeholders content to continue with the school and to engage with each other.

To give a concrete example, students want a greater variety of courses. With a finite faculty, more variety means more teaching by the faculty. The faculty, in contrast, want less teaching because they have other uses for that time, such as conducting research. The administration's task is, therefore, to achieve a compromise that keeps each group sufficiently satisfied. The role of governance is, thus, to ensure that the administration properly affects a compromise solution, a role made difficult by the lack of clear performance metrics and uncertainty over objectives on the part of the governors. Although the basic toolkit of the modern economic theorist, including agency theory, game theory, and information economics, can be employed, the model that will be constructed from this toolkit could easily be far different from any model built in the for-profit context.

As these new models are built, they will start to shape how we perceive the role of the board of trustees and will give further guidance toward models and theories of its functioning. This is not to say that the seven points made previously will be shown not to apply or that insights from corporate boards will be shown to be nonapplicable to higher education. Rather, these new models and theories will add additional points to those made previously and will help us think about the relative importance of all these points in understanding the functioning of boards of trustees. Because, however, mapping out a research agenda for looking at higher education governance more generally is beyond the scope of this chapter, it is not feasible to say more on this point at this time.

Conclusion

This chapter has considered boards of trustees of institutions of higher education. The aim has been to consider how the insights that have been gained over the years concerning corporate boards of directors, whether empirical or theoretical, could be applied to boards of trustees. To a large extent, the focus has been on the degree to which this earlier research on corporate boards can serve to guide future research on boards of trustees.

For the most part, the theory of boards should apply to both directors and trustees. The principal differences are in degree. The basic insights concerning lack of expertise, lack of time, free-riding among board members, and the Hermalin-Weisbach bargaining model (1998) apply to both directors and trustees, although, as discussed, they could loom larger in the trustee context. The dependence on highly mobile human capital creates problems for higher education governance that are less pronounced in most corporate settings. Higher education also suffers from two other issues not generally present in the corporate world: first, a temptation to use the board for purposes other than governance; and second, a susceptibility to divisiveness on the board that comes from less focused objectives as compared to the essentially single objective of corporations. Although there is every reason to believe that theoretical insights about boards derived from the for-profit corporate context apply to boards of trustees of colleges and universities, with some modification, it is also true that colleges and universities face governance issues unlike those typically seen in the for-profit context. As some of these issues enjoy greater study, a consequence will be that our perception of the role and functioning of the board of trustees will be adjusted. That is, the corporate model provides a good picture of boards of trustees, but a more complete picture awaits advances in the theory of collegiate and university governance.

With respect to empirical analyses of boards of trustees, analyses of corporate boards are generally good guides concerning what to study and what can be found. In particular, it is unlikely that any analysis will find a relation between characteristics of boards of trustees and the overall performances of the institutions in question.[31] More promising lines of inquiry are with respect to whether trustee characteristics help explain specific board actions (e.g., presidential compensation and replacement, setting of fees, specific types of expansion, etc.) and with respect to what causes turnover in trustees.

When I began to formulate this chapter, I started with two beliefs: first, that boards of trustees are very much like corporate boards of directors; and second, that boards are a reasonably good solution to a set of governance problems affecting any complex organization, whether for-profit or nonprofit. Basically, I still hold to both beliefs. As discussed, there are differences between the two types of boards, and these differences will have an impact on both empirical and theoretical analyses. Nonetheless, these differences are primarily ones of degree and not of substance. Both directors and trustees are, for instance, imperfect agents with respect to oversight of management, but institutional aspects of colleges and universities suggest that trustees could be the more imperfect agents, at least in some dimensions. Moreover, despite the criticisms that both types of boards engender, I still maintain that they are a reasonably good solution within the constraints within which they operate. Corporate boards, for instance, do in the end replace incompetent management, and there is every reason to believe that so too do boards of trustees. The real evidence is that despite numerous critics, alternative organizational forms have generally not functioned better. This is true in the for-profit context, where the corporate form with directors is the dominant form of organizing a large company. And it is true in the college and university context, where American universities, with their boards of trustees, dominate higher education and have outperformed, along any reasonable metric, non-American universities organized along different lines.[32]

# CHAPTER THREE

# State Oversight of Academia
## DONALD E. HELLER

Much attention has been focused in recent years on the topic of state governance of higher education. Numerous journal articles, books, and reports have examined how states organize the governance structures of public higher education, how these structures are changing, and the impact of these structures and changes on higher education institutions, students, and the public at large.[1] The topic has not escaped attention from the popular press; newspapers and magazines regularly cover public higher education in general and focus particularly on proposals for changing the governance of a state's higher education institutions.

While attention has been focused on *how* states organize the governance of their public higher education institutions and systems, there has been much less research on the *impact* of these decisions on outcomes. This chapter reviews the literature on this topic by addressing the question, What impact does state governance have on the outcomes of higher education?

The chapter opens with a brief history of state support for and governance of higher education. It then presents an overview of the expected outcomes of public higher education. This includes both social outcomes and private returns to individuals. Social outcomes include higher education's contribution to general economic development; preparation of individuals for entry into specific careers and professions in the state; continuation of the education of the citizenry begun in the K through 12 sector; prestige maximization; and avoidance of negative social outcomes (such as unemployment or criminal behavior). Discussions of private outcomes for individuals have traditionally focused on preparation for entry into labor markets.

One of the issues dealt with by many researchers is the discordance between institutional interests and broader state goals. States generally try to establish governance and funding mechanisms that will promote statewide goals, however they are defined. Institutions, however, generally try to work within these constraints to maximize their own goals, which may diverge from the broader state goals.

After examining the outcomes of higher education, the chapter turns to the research on state governance structure and outcomes. The chapter concludes with some thoughts regarding future research on the topic.

## State Support for and Governance of Higher Education

Higher education has existed in the United States longer than the nation itself.[2] Harvard College, founded in 1636, was the first higher education institution in the colonies. While the earliest colleges were private, state support of higher education began with public allocations to these largely church-chartered institutions.[3] This support was often in the form of the granting of public lands, and authorization for the running of lotteries to benefit the institution. Many state governments in the late eighteenth and early nineteenth centuries began to provide direct financial assistance from general tax revenues to support a number of private colleges and universities.

The first truly "public" institutions of higher education were chartered in the late eighteenth century, primarily in the South and Midwest. These institutions received direct state subsidies, though their control can best be described as "quasi-public" because of the degree of autonomy generally granted to their trustees. In some institutions, the trustees were self-perpetuating, thus putting the overall control of the institution beyond public reach. Brubacher and Rudy (1976) note that it was well into the nineteenth century before many state legislatures began asserting governance control over these public universities by reserving the right to appoint trustees. They designate the University of Virginia, founded by Thomas Jefferson in 1819, as the "first real state university" (p. 147) for the following reasons:

• The university had a board of visitors appointed by the governor of the state.

• The state provided initial capital and ongoing funds for the operation of the university.

• The university was founded to be free of "domination by any and all religious sects" (p. 149).

• Provisions were made for free tuition to selected poor students from throughout the state.

This mixing of state support for both public and private institutions of higher education continued into the early nineteenth century. A turning point, however, was the famous *Dartmouth College* case of 1819, in which the state of New Hampshire tried to assert control over Dartmouth College because of its chartering and support of the institution. The New Hampshire Superior Court found in favor of the state, ruling that Dartmouth was a public institution. On appeal to the U.S. Supreme Court, the defense of the college and its independence from the state was passionately argued by Daniel Webster, in an oft-quoted speech before the court:

> This sir, is my case. It is the case, not merely of that humble institution, it is the case of every college in the land . . . for the question is simply this: Shall our state legislature be allowed to take that which is not their own, to turn it from its original use, and apply it to such ends or purposes as they, in their discretion shall see fit? Sir, you may destroy this little institution . . . but if you do . . . you must extinguish, one after another, all those great lights of science, which, for more than a century, have thrown their radiance over the land! (quoted in Rudolph 1990, 209–210)

The Supreme Court ruled in favor of Dartmouth, thus effectively closing the door on any further attempts by the states to gain control of private institutions. The *Dartmouth* case clarified the distinction between public and private colleges and universities in the United States. Following *Dartmouth*, states began to focus their financial assistance for higher education on the publicly controlled and supported institutions, and phased out most of the direct appropriations to private institutions.

Simultaneous with the focusing of financial aid on those institutions deemed purely public, states—which had expanded public higher education largely through the support provided by the Morrill Land Grant Act of 1862—turned their attention to the issue of how these institutions should be governed and controlled.[4] During the nineteenth century some states, including Michigan, California, and Minnesota, granted constitutional autonomy to the flagship institution in the state in order to "remove the management of public universities from the reach of 'meddlesome politicians'" (McLendon, 2003). Most states, even those not providing constitutional protections for institutional autonomy, meddled little in the affairs of the public higher education institutions within their borders. Zumeta (2001, 161) notes that "political leaders tended to be somewhat in awe of highly educated men . . . they *trusted* academic leaders to lead the schools in the broad directions both parties wanted to go. . . . Moreover, most state governments had little capacity for more than occasional, fairly limited involvement in academic affairs."

Through the late nineteenth and early twentieth centuries, however, states began to assert more authority over many of their public higher education institutions through the development of statewide or systemwide governing boards, through the development of laws and regulations applying specifically to higher education, and in some cases, through the removal of the constitutional autonomy of the institutions.

The trend of assertion of state authority over higher education institutions grew through most of the twentieth century until the last two decades, when "the 1980s and 1990s witnessed a variegated array of state-level reform (sometimes referred as 'restructuring') initiatives representing several different patterns of activity, rather than one dominant movement" (McLendon, 2003). These "different patterns of activity" included both a continuation of the trend toward more state authority over public institutions in some states than in others, and a movement toward the granting of more independence and autonomy to colleges and universities or individual public systems. McLendon describes this latter movement as one of "deregulation/decentralization . . . whereas, in the 1980s, this form of state activity primarily involved dispensation from state procedural controls, recently it has broadened to include substantive areas of campus functioning (greater campus authority over academic programs, for example) and, occasionally, has involved the restructuring of entire governing or coordinating systems." As McLendon notes, no matter what the nature of the structural change imposed by each state, "rare is the governance initiative that does not claim to improve efficiency, promote competition or coordination, or reduce costs."

In a recent report, the Education Commission of the States (2002) reviewed the status of postsecondary governance structures across the fifty states and the District of Columbia. The Appendix provides the details of these structures for each state. Three states had no statewide postsecondary governance structure; twenty-five had coordinating boards, eight had planning boards, and fifteen had governing boards. The vast majority of board members were appointed by the governors of each state, many with legislative approval. The size of these boards ranged from seven to thirty-two members, with the average size being thirteen members. The governance of the individual institutions in each state ranged from states such as Alaska, Georgia, and Maine that had just one system governing all the public institutions, to states, like Texas, with separate governing boards for each individual institution.

Thus, the beginning of the twenty-first century finds public higher education in a state of flux, with some states opting for improved quality and efficiency in higher education through assertion of more statewide authority, and others attempting to achieve the same goals through a devolution of power to individual campuses or system boards. The next section describes in more detail the outcomes expected of public higher education institutions and systems.

## Outcomes of Higher Education

Going back to the early development and expansion of public institutions of higher education in the nation, there were often conflicting views of what the mission of these institutions should be and how that mission should be carried out. The focus on the Morrill Land Grant Act of 1862 was in the development of public universities "where the leading object shall be, without excluding other scientific or classical studies, to teach such branches of learning as are related to agriculture and the mechanic arts" (Rudolph 1990, 252). While the legislation appeared to establish a clear mission for these institutions, there was not uniformity in the interpretation of how it should be accomplished. Brubacher and Rudy (1976, 63) note that "the National Grange and the Farmers' Alliance made constant complaint that the new colleges were too theoretical and classical in their curricular offerings and had little to offer the average farmer. Indeed, many of these new foundations did seem to go to great lengths to imitate eastern liberal-arts colleges in order, among other things, to attain what was then considered academic respectability." This example is emblematic of the tension that has existed since between how public colleges and universities interpret their role in serving the state, and how policymakers (and often, the public at large) see that role.

Over one hundred years later, some researchers have concluded that the mission of higher education is still poorly defined and articulated.

Cohen and March (1986, 3), in their study of the college presidency, argue that "the American college or university is a prototypic organized anarchy. It does not know what it is doing. Its goals are either vague or in dispute." They further describe an "organized anarchy" as an organization with "problematic goals. It is difficult to impute a set of goals to the organization that satisfies the standard consistency requirements of theories of choice. The organization appears to operate on a variety of inconsistent and ill-defined preferences. It can be described better as a loose collection of changing ideas than as a coherent structure. It discovers preferences through action more often than it acts on the basis of preferences."

Others, however, argue that the role of higher education in serving society can be more clearly defined and described. Bowen (1977, 55–59) divided the goals of higher education into two categories: those for individual students and those for society as a whole. He further described these goals as follows:

Goals for Individual Students
   1. Cognitive learning
   2. Emotional and moral development
   3. Practical competence
   4. Direct satisfactions and enjoyments from college education
   5. Avoidance of negative outcomes for individual students
Goals for Society
   6. Advancement of knowledge
   7. Discovery and encouragement of talent
   8. Advancement of social welfare
   9. Avoidance of negative outcomes for society

He further describes thirty-three different outcomes within these nine broad categories. Bowen (p. 54) warns, however, that "not all of the goals are achieved in practice, and some of them may not even be achievable. . . . Many are shared goals pursued jointly with the family, the school, the church, the media, governmental agencies, and the workplace."

The Institute for Higher Education Policy (1998, 20) created a similar taxonomy of the benefits of higher education, dividing these outcomes into two types, economic and social, and accruing to two realms, the individual or the public. Included in the public economic benefits were such outcomes as "increased tax revenues, greater productivity, and increased workforce flexibility." Private economic outcomes included "higher salaries and benefits, higher savings levels, and improved working conditions." Public social outcomes included "reduced crime rates, increased charitable giving/community service, and increased quality of civic life." Private social outcomes included "improved health/life expectancy, better consumer decision making, and increased personal status."

Two notions—Cohen and March's of the ambiguity of preferences of institutions, and Bowen's of the difficulty of achieving particular goals— are crucial to understanding the role of higher education institutions in American society. For if Cohen and March are correct that higher education institutions themselves cannot articulate a clear set of goals and objectives (and other researchers have agreed with their conclusion), then it is difficult to expect an external entity, namely, a state bureaucratic agency, to be able to clarify and identify a set of goals for the institutions. And if Bowen is correct that although a set of goals can be identified for colleges and universities, it is difficult to achieve many of them and impossible for higher education to achieve some of them by itself, then it is even harder for external entities to hold the institutions accountable for the accomplishment of those goals and production of the outcomes.

States have struggled with implementing mechanisms for assessing how well higher education institutions are producing these outcomes, generally choosing to use a "carrot" rather than a "stick" approach. Many states have opted to implement "performance funding" or "performance budgeting" programs, where some portion of base or incremental appropriations is awarded to institutions based on how well they performed on specific criteria established by the states.

The Rockefeller Institute of the State University of New York at Albany has conducted a survey of state practices in the areas of performance funding and budgeting (Burke and Modarresi 1999). The Rockefeller Institute defines the two practices as follows: "Performance Funding: state funding tied directly to the *achievements* of public colleges and universities on specific performance indicators (money awarded after performance achieved). Performance Budgeting: state governments use indirectly reports of system or institutional achievements on performance indicators as a context in shaping the total budget for public higher education and/or its institutions (indirect influence on budget levels)" (p. 16). Under these definitions, performance funding mechanisms more tightly couple the awarding of funds with institutional performance, while performance budgeting more loosely couples the two by using performance indicators as one criterion in what otherwise may be largely a political, incremental, or formulaic budgeting process.

The Rockefeller Institute survey found that by 1999, sixteen states had implemented some form of performance funding for public institutions (up from ten states in the survey conducted two years earlier), and twenty-three states had implemented performance budgeting (up from sixteen in the earlier survey). The study found that the earliest implementation of performance funding was in 1979 (Tennessee), while performance budgeting was first implemented in 1975 (Hawaii). Another interesting aspect of the study was an examination of the source of the performance funding or budgeting processes. The researchers identified the following parties as having initiated the programs in one or more states: higher education coordinating board, governor, legislature, and system office.

Zumeta (2001, 157–158) reviewed a number of state efforts at increasing the accountability of higher education institutions and concluded that the impetus for these efforts included

- private-sector management ideas permeat[ing] the public sector
- extreme financial pressures on states during the economic slowdown of the early 1990s . . . followed closely by the mid-decade tax revolt and Republican electoral ascendancy
- the discretionary nature of spending on higher education, in contrast to program areas driven by federal or judicial mandates
- the large increases in public-sector tuition prices and resulting public concern over the affordability of college

Perhaps the most ambitious foray into performance funding was made by the state of South Carolina. In 1996, the General Assembly passed legislation mandating the use of thirty-seven performance indicators for allocating appropriations to the thirty-three public higher education institutions in the state (Schmidt 1997). The legislation's chief sponsor, State Senator Nikki G. Setzler, justified the change by stating, "To make higher education more accountable, we must first define what we expect from the system. [The plan] will bring us a system of excellence rather than a system that supports mediocrity" (Schmidt 1996, A26). By 1999, 100 percent of the state's appropriations were to be based on such measures as quality of faculty, instructional quality, administrative efficiency, and the user-friendliness of the institution. The all-or-nothing nature of the program was in contrast to that of most other states, where generally less than 5 percent of appropriations were tied to performance indicators.

The ambitions of the South Carolina legislature were never realized, however. A legislatively mandated review of the state's performance funding system was conducted in 2001 by the South Carolina Legislative Audit Council. The Audit Council's report (South Carolina Legislative Audit Council, 2001, v) indicated that "in FY 99–00 and FY 00–01, the years in which funding was to be based *entirely* on performance, the [appropriation] amount affected by performance scores was 3 percent each year." The study found that while the state's Commission on Higher Education complied with the 1996 mandate by developing the specific indicators and collecting the data on institutional performance, the indicators

> do not provide a comprehensive assessment of institutional quality. Reasons that the performance measurement system should not be used as the sole determinant of institutional funding include: changes and volatility of the system, problems in measurement, the narrow focus of the indicators, and the use of some indicators that may be inappropriate for some institutions. . . . Performance funding has had little effect on the elimination of waste and duplication in higher education. (p. vi)

In its response to the audit report, the commission noted that it was "substantially in agreement with the Council's recommendations" (p. 33). The commission also agreed to revise the indicators and how they were collected. Even with the Audit Council's conclusions, the state has continued the performance funding program, though all parties appear comfortable with the fact that the state has not fulfilled the initial legislation's obligation to put 100 percent of the appropriation for each institution at risk.

Research on Governance Structures and Higher Education Outcomes

McLendon (2003), in his analysis of some of the recent trends in state governance and coordination, points to "the new *accountability* demands of the states. . . . A 'new thinking' about accountability emerged in which concerns about performance 'outputs' replaced the older emphasis upon resource 'inputs.'" South Carolina's performance funding program is an example of one state's interest in using state authority to promote institutional accountability. As McLendon notes, this focus on the outputs to the higher education production process has replaced the measures traditionally used to evaluate higher education—how money has been spent, how many students have been enrolled, how many faculty were employed, and so on. But these *outputs* are distinct from the type of *outcomes* described by Bowen (1997) or the Institute for Higher Education Policy (1998). In addition, a focus on outcomes has to embody an agreement on and understanding of what those outcomes should be and, equally importantly, how they should be measured and evaluated.

Bowen's nine goals for higher education, while relatively easy to conceptualize and understand, are very difficult to measure consistently given the wide range of higher education institutions in the country, the varying types of students served by those institutions, and the differing needs of individual states. For example, it is reasonable to expect that all institutions that have at least in part a mission to teach students (which includes almost all of the more than thirty-six hundred colleges and universities in the nation) would be expected to promote some forms of Bowen's goal of cognitive learning, in which he includes such outcomes as "verbal skills," "quantitative skills," "intellectual tolerance," "wisdom," and "esthetic sensibility" (pp. 55–56). But what about the goal of promoting emotional and moral development in students, under which Bowen includes "personal self-discovery," "values and morals," and "refinement of taste" (pp. 56–57)? The focus on these types of outcomes is likely to be very different for institutions whose missions are to serve primarily traditional-aged, full-time residential students, than for a community college that serves largely a part-time, adult-learner student body.

Bowen's goals for society include such outcomes as "direct satisfactions and enjoyments received by the population from living in a world of advancing knowledge, technology, ideas, and arts," "enhancement of national prestige and power," and "'improvement' in the motives, values, aspirations, attitudes, and behavior of members of the general population" (pp. 58–59)—all outcomes that may be expected of some higher education institutions but not others, but all extremely difficult to measure and assess.

Thus, any attempts at assessing the relationship between higher education outcomes and aspects of state governance and control are hindered by the inherent ambiguity, imprecision, and vagaries of defining what institutions are supposed to be doing. The somewhat sparse literature relating these two reflects this difficulty. My review of the literature for this chapter from the key disciplines—higher education, political science, policy studies, and economics—discovered no studies

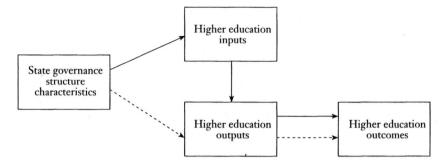

Figure 3.1. Model of research on higher education governance structures and outcomes.

that directly addressed this relationship between statewide governance structure and higher education outcomes. The few related studies can best be described by a single, common feature: the use of proxies for higher education outcomes, rather than the direct measurement of the outcomes themselves (as described by Bowen [1997] or the Institute for Higher Education Policy [1998], for example), or as one researcher described the problem, "Education is a good in which the inputs are often used as measures of output, because of the difficulty in doing the latter" (Toma 1990, n. 3).[5]

These proxies tend to be the inputs to and/or outputs from the higher education production function as shown in Figure 3.1. Some studies focus on the relationship shown by the solid arrows, attempting to trace the effect of governance structure through the production process to outcomes. Others bypass the input portion of the process, relating governance structure directly to outputs, denoted by the dashed arrows.

Volkwein and Malik (1997) examined predictors of the degree of flexibility enjoyed by the higher education institutions in a state. Flexibility was measured in two dimensions: financial/personnel flexibility and academic flexibility. The predictors included state economic, social and demographic, and political attributes (including higher education governance structure), along with characteristics of the higher education institutions themselves. As the authors (p. 18) noted, "Most organizational behaviorists believe that an increase in monitoring activities increases operating costs, both for those doing the monitoring and for those being monitored."

In this cross-sectional study using 1995 data, the authors found no relationship between governing board structure and either academic flexibility or financial/personnel flexibility. In fact, none of the state-level characteristics were predictive of the degree of academic flexibility enjoyed by the campuses, and only one—the state's population—was found to be modestly related to financial/personnel flexibility (with campuses in larger states enjoying less flexibility).

In a second analysis in the same study, Volkwein and Malik used many of the same variables to predict the quality of the public higher education institutions in the state in two realms: faculty quality (as measured by data from the National Research Council [1995] survey of doctoral programs and a study conducted by researchers Hugh Graham and Nancy Diamond [1997]), and undergraduate student quality (as measured by student selectivity data from college guidebooks and rankings). The researchers found that the state's higher education governance structure (in 1995) was not related to the measures of either faculty or undergraduate quality, controlling for the other statewide and institutional characteristics. Another interesting finding in the study was that neither academic nor financial/personnel flexibility was related to faculty or student quality, thus belying the conventional wisdom that "the less regulation the better."

In a later study, Volkwein, Malik, and Napierski-Pranci (1998) took this analysis one step further to examine if many of the same predictors from their earlier study were related to the level of satisfaction enjoyed by administrators in public colleges and universities, because "regulatory activity may reduce managerial job satisfaction, which in turn increases turnover and lowers organizational productivity and adaptation" (p. 45).[6] Using data from a survey of twelve managers in each of 144 public institutions across the country, they measured satisfaction in five realms: "overall satisfaction," "intrinsic satisfaction," "extrinsic satisfaction," "work conditions," and "relationships with others" (p. 52). While they did not explicitly include a measure of the state governing board structure, they did include as predictors the same academic and financial/personnel flexibility measures from the earlier study. The two flexibility measures were not found to be related to any of the five types of satisfaction, leading the researchers to conclude that there was "little direct relationship between administrator satisfaction and most state and campus characteristics, including the regulatory climate" (p. 59).

Volkwein and colleagues' measures of institutional administrative and academic flexibility were used in another study as predictors of the supply of public higher education in the states (Berger and Kostal 2002). The authors of this study divided each flexibility measure into three categories, low, medium, and high, and used these measures along with other covariates to predict the supply of public higher education in each state from 1990 to 1995. They found that states where public institutions enjoy greater levels of both administrative and academic flexibility tend to have lower public enrollment rates, confirming their hypothesis that "a college or university with relatively loose regulations can devote more resources to activities for which there is weak demand but which, nonetheless, are important to its staff (e.g., nonfunded research or providing spaces for relatively high-cost graduate and professional students)" (p. 107).

Lowry (2001a) used cross-sectional data to examine the effects of a number of predictors on institutional revenues and expenditures. His four outcomes include institutional revenues from the state (appropriations, grants, and contracts), revenue from tuition and fees (net of institutional financial aid), expenditures on research, and expenditures on public service (all four variables are measured per one-hundred-thousand voting-age residents in the state). His predictors include state economic data (tax revenue and per capita income), demographic data (educational attainment and age distribution), the number of higher education governing boards in the state, and campus attributes (enrollment, quality rating, revenues and expenditures in other categories). He describes his rationale for including the number of governing boards as a predictor as follows: "Public universities in states that have fewer governing boards should be able to lobby more effectively, and thus obtain more state government funding" (p. 108). Of the four outcomes in his study, Lowry found the number of governing boards to be related only to the level of state funds received by the institution. He noted that the "coefficient for the number of governing boards is negative . . . consistent with my expectation that a large number of boards makes it more difficult for public universities to engage in effective lobbying [of the state]" (p. 113).

In a related study, Lowry (2001b) broadened his measures of state governance structure to include (1) whether the state had a statewide coordinating board; (2) the number of campuses governed by the board; (3) the percentage of trustees who are state government officials or who are selected by the governor, legislature, or voters (what he labels "external trustees"); and (4) his earlier measure of the number of governing boards in the state. His outcomes in this study included net tuition and fee revenue (again after deducting institutional aid), along with the level of expenditures in five categories: instruction, student services, academic support, institutional support, and plant operations and maintenance. Lowry's analysis showed that the presence of a statewide coordinating board was negatively related to spending on instruction, student services, and academic support, while spending on instruction increased in relation to the number of governing boards in the state. He also found that a larger number of external trustees is related to lower levels of expenditure on instruction, student services, and institutional support. Lowry (2001b, 859) is somewhat circumspect in his interpretation of these results:

> It cannot be said from these results that there is one best model for public university governance for two reasons. First, it is not clear that public universities subject to more or less political control are unambiguously better or worse.... Since I do not analyze educational outcomes I cannot say what students in high-tuition states get for their money, but increased spending on activities such as instruction, student services, and academic support may lead to benefits for many students.

Zumeta (1996, 367–368) examined statewide higher education governance structures in the late 1980s to determine whether states fell into one of three "policy postures toward private higher education": "laissez-faire," "central planning," or "market-competitive." He simplified and reduced state higher education governance structures into two types: (1) regulatory coordinating boards and (2) consolidated governing boards, the latter being a stronger form of statewide control over the public higher education system. He then used the structure measure along with a number of other state-level variables—including per capita income, tax effort, population growth, and college participation rates—as predictors to determine which of the three policy postures the states took toward private higher education. The key finding with respect to governance structure was that the existence of a consolidated governing board, a "stronger" form of governance, was a predictor of states adopting the laissez-faire approach.

A key issue regarding Zumeta's research, however, is the direction of the effects he found. While he included the type of governance structure as a predictor of the type of policies, or posture, toward private higher education in the state, it is entirely plausible to question whether the relationship works equally in the opposite direction. In other words, rather than the existence of a consolidated governing board being the cause of this set of laissez-faire policies, it may be this general attitude toward the private sector of higher education which causes states to adopt a stronger, more active approach toward the management of the public higher education sector. In most states, many of these laissez-faire policies would be considered outside the purview of a statewide governance board and would instead be the responsibility of a state legislature—the body generally responsible for the assignment of authority to any statewide governing or coordinating board for higher education.

Another interesting approach to the issue of analyzing the relationship between governance structure and public higher education outcomes is that taken by Toma (1990). She posits that a beneficial outcome of public higher education would be an input-output mix mimicking that of private colleges and universities, because "private universities must be relatively responsive to consumer demands in order to survive, and . . . are more successful at producing students with earned degrees" (pp. 3–4). She uses data on public governing board structure along with state demographic and financial data in 1982 to predict three outcomes across all public institutions in the state: (1) the ratio of tuition revenue to state appropriations (a higher ratio would be a more "private" financing model), (2) the pupil-teacher ratio (a lower ratio is more akin to private institutions), and (3) the percentage of faculty that are tenured (a lower proportion being more indicative of private institutions).[7] Her measure of governance structure is the ratio of the number of public universities in the state to the number of governing boards, a larger number indicating a more centralized approach to governance.

Toma notes an important methodological concern with her models: that the measure of board structure may not be exogenous. In an earlier study (1986), she tested this premise and concluded that board structure is in fact not exogenous, for "educators (or other high-demand groups) would be expected to lobby for centralized board structures as a means of securing an input-output mix closer to that which they desire" (Toma 1990, 4). To overcome this problem, she ran two sets of models, one with each state's actual measure of board centralization and one with a centralization measure predicted on the basis of a series of statewide demographic and financial variables.[8]

Her results in both sets of models were consistent, that a *more* centralized board structure was related to outcomes *less* indicative of a private model of higher education: less reliance on tuition revenues, higher pupil-teacher ratios, and a higher proportion of tenured faculty. In the models using the actual board structure, the coefficients were smaller for all three outcomes than in the models using the predicted board structure, confirming her hypothesis that "educators in states that rely heavily on tuition as a source of revenue or that have small percentages of tenured faculty, will lobby for the centralization of the governing boards" (p. 6).

Hearn and Griswold (1994, 171) examined the factors that predicted whether states were likely to enact postsecondary education policy innovations. These innovations included whether states

> required assessment of undergraduate students
> required tests for teaching assistants
> offered a tax-exempt college savings bond
> offered a prepaid college tuition plan
> restricted or taxed college businesses
> made vandalism of animal-research facilities a crime
> allowed nontraditional paths for certification of K–12 teachers
> required that high school teachers not be education majors

The authors hypothesized that states with more centralized governance structures would be more likely to enact one or more of these innovations. They included as covariates measures of state population, educational attainment, and the region of the country in which the state was located.

The results from this study were mixed. The authors' hypothesis concerning the effects of structure was confirmed for innovations in academic policy (the first, second, and sixth items above)—states with more centralized structures were more likely to have enacted one or more of these innovations. Also confirmed was that states with more centralized structures were more likely to restrict or tax college businesses. However, the authors found that these same states were *less* likely to enact alternative certification programs for K–12 teachers. They concluded that centralized governance structures were most influential on what they labeled the "core *educational* activities" (p. 183) of public colleges and universities.

While the Hearn and Griswold study used a single-year cross section of state data to examine the determinants of policy innovation, McLendon, Heller, and Young (2001) used a pooled time-series analysis of state-level data from 1981 to 1998 to examine the relationship between governance structure, state political and demographic measures, and the probability that states would enact higher education policy innovations. They also added to the list of predictors a measure of "policy innovation diffusion" (p. 27), to determine whether adoption of policy innovations in one state influenced the adoption of innovations in neighboring states. The authors grouped states into two governance structure categories: (1) a planning agency or weak coordinating board and (2) a regulatory or consolidated board. The study examined six higher education policy innovations also grouped into two categories:

(1) regulatory innovations (performance budgeting, performance funding, and mandated assessment of undergraduates) and (2) financing innovations (merit scholarships, prepaid tuition plans, and college savings plans).

The results of this study partially confirmed Hearn and Griswold's earlier findings (1994). While McLendon and coauthors (2001) found few determinants of whether states would enact regulatory innovations, they did find that governance structure was moderately related to whether states would enact financing innovations: "states with planning agencies or weak coordinating boards were 6.8 percent less likely to innovate in the area of postsecondary financing than were states with more centralized boards" (p. 30).[9] The study found, however, that policy diffusion was a much stronger predictor of innovation in the higher education financing realm than were other variables.

Conclusion

This review has covered a broad range of studies. The researchers used similar measures of the public higher education governance structure in states, generally revolving around some assessment of the degree of control that the statewide bureaucracy enjoyed over the colleges and universities in the state. However, the dependent variables modeled in these studies were quite diverse and were only indirectly related to the type of higher education outcomes articulated by Bowen (1977) and the Institute for Higher Education Policy (1998). To assess whether governance structure can influence these outcomes requires the reader to accept certain assumptions about the relationships among the four realms shown in Figure 3.1.

Even accepting the use of inputs, and in some cases outputs, to the higher education production process as a proxy for outcomes, the evidence regarding the effect of higher education governance structures is mixed. Lowry (2001a), in his study of the relationship between governance structure and institutional revenues and expenditures, found that more centralized structures were related to higher levels of state funding for public institutions, but found no relationship to levels of spending. If one accepts the model shown in Figure 3.1 indicating that the outputs of the higher education production process (i.e., spending levels, credit hours, bachelor's degrees) are more closely related to outcomes, then a discovered relationship between governance structure and inputs is less informative than one between structure and outputs.

Lowry's other study (2001b) did find more of a relationship between governance structure and spending in certain categories, but he notes the limitations of relating increased spending to improved outcomes (see the quotation from Lowry 2001b, 859, in the previous section).

The two studies conducted by Volkwein and colleagues (1997, 1998) found no relationship between statewide governance structure and the academic and administrative flexibility enjoyed by the state's higher education institutions, an attribute best described as an input to the higher education production process. Toma's 1990 research related governance structure directly to outputs and found what is perhaps the strongest and most consistent results among the studies reviewed here, that more centralized governance structures were less indicative of an output mix akin to that of private institutions (and therefore judged to lead to better outcomes).

Perhaps the largest area of agreement in all these studies is the inherent limitation of this type of research. A recounting of some of the caveats expressed by these authors includes the following:

• "Education is a good in which the inputs are often used as measures of output, because of the difficulty in doing the latter" (Toma 1990, n. 3).

• "Because our focus was on innovation alone and because even there we made no attempt to judge 'good' versus 'bad' innovations, we cannot definitely address the larger questions involved in the choice of one or the other of the more centralized governing arrangements" (Hearn and Griswold 1994, 183).

• "Since I do not analyze educational outcomes I cannot say what students in high-tuition states get for their money, but increased spending on activities such as instruction, student services, and academic support may lead to benefits for many students" (Lowry 2001b, 859).

The implications for further research on the topic of governance structure are quite clear. There is little disagreement in the literature regarding the acceptance of the outcomes offered by authors such as Bowen and the Institute for Higher Education Policy. Different parties may place varying weights on the values of each of these outcomes for individuals or society, but there is broad consensus on the examples offered by these authors.

Researchers need to examine ways to effectively measure these higher education outcomes, and to do so in a manner that is methodologically sound. The task is not a simple one, however. It is complicated by the inherent difficulty of conducting experimental or even quasi-experimental research in the social sciences. For example, measuring the increase in wages enjoyed by college graduates compared to those not attending college—a key outcome in today's policy debates regarding who should pay for the cost of higher education—is confounded by the fact that college graduates generally possess many other attributes (academic ability, work ethic, and other skills) that are valued in labor markets. Similarly, some studies have attempted to analyze how public colleges and universities have contributed to a state's economic growth and development through their tripartite missions of teaching, research, and service. But measuring this contribution in the absence of knowing how the public investment in these institutions would otherwise be directed (if they did not exist) is inherently flawed.

While this task is not impossible, it does pose challenges for researchers. Until methods are found for overcoming these limitations, it will be hard for policymakers to judge how, or even if, the higher education governance structure in their states should be changed.

# INTERNAL
# GOVERNANCE
# AND
# ORGANIZATION

CHAPTER FOUR

# Darwinian Medicine for the University
## Susanne Lohmann

### The University: Its Defects and Defenses

Darwinian medicine explores the evolutionary origins of sickness, with the goal of treating the sick more effectively (Nesse and Williams 1994). By spelling out what evolution had in mind, so to speak, when it endowed the human body with the propensity to get sick, Darwinian medicine helps us to assess the benefits and costs of alternative medical interventions.

The distinction between *defects* and *defenses* is central to Darwinian medicine. A broken leg is a defect—one would not want to leave it alone just in case some good came of it. A fever, on the other hand, is a defense: it brings discomfort, it creates tissue damage, it depletes nutrients, and in extreme circumstances the patient might die from it. But fever also serves useful functions: it keeps bacterial pathogens in check, it serves as a signal to the patient to take it easy, and under ordinary circumstances it helps the patient survive. Darwinian medicine takes the position that fever is an evolved response, with the implication that we must trade off the costs and benefits of suppressing a fever when treating it.

This chapter applies Darwinian medicine to the university. Much that looks like a defect of the university is in fact a defense. Defects are bad; they need to be eliminated. Defenses look bad, but they are subtle

The ideas in this chapter are drawn from my book in progress, *How Universities Think*. I thank the Ford Foundation and the John Simon Guggenheim Memorial Foundation for their generous support.

design solutions that evolved in interaction with a demanding environment; they need to be preserved, or at the very least it needs to be recognized that eliminating them comes at a cost. The vexed institution of tenure is an example of a defense, as are the impossibly rigid boundaries separating the disciplines.

Effective university reform must distinguish between defects and defenses so it can eliminate the defects and go lightly on the defenses. Making such distinctions requires an understanding of what the university is *for*—what problems the university was designed, or evolved, to solve.

I contend that the function of the university is to enable deep specialization. The structures of the university emerged to solve several problems: how to nurse deeply specialized scholars, how to protect them from each other and the outside world, and how to pool the results of their distributed inquiries.

The problems to which the university is a response are hard problems, and there is no free lunch. Institutional solutions are generally second best in the sense that they constitute the best solution feasible in light of environmental constraints (in which case they are a defense), or they are less than second best (in which case they are defective).

As a necessary by-product of fulfilling their productive functions, the structures of the university have a tendency to ossify. It is precisely because the powerful incentives and protections afforded by these structures are intertwined with their potential for ossification that it is hard to disentangle where the defects of the university end and its defenses begin.

The university's built-in tendency to ossify and the commingling of defects and defenses explain why the structures of the university are so resistant to change and improvement—why they are hard to change in the first place, and hard to change for the better.

To complicate matters, ossification implies that a solution that worked well initially (it started out as a defense) can become dysfunctional over time (it ends up becoming a defect). For this reason, any practical project of reforming the way the university is governed needs to respect its thick history and local detail. Armchair theorizing cannot say definitively, "This is a defect—off with its head" and "That's a defense—better not mess with it."

The remainder of this chapter is structured as follows. I begin with a short history of the university. Drawing on history, I argue that the structures of the university that enable deep specialization are naturally and inherently resistant to change. What makes the university strong is precisely what makes it weak. I spell out how institutions of higher education can be designed to remain intellectually vibrant and structurally pliable even though their constituent elements—deeply specialized scholars and discipline-based departments—are doomed to ossify.

## A Short History of the University

In the history of the human race, the medieval university stands out as one of the great political institutions of all time. It drew Western Europe out of the Dark Ages and into the light. It invented cosmopolitan structures and norms that are still with us today.

Two archetypes emerged in twelfth- and thirteenth-century France and Italy. Paris offered a free space for the theological debates that prepared the way for the Reformation. In Bologna, students trained in the legal statutes and reasoning that would come to support increasingly complex political and economic institutions all over Europe.

In both cases, a complex institution crystallized, the result of a decentralized process of annealing. The institutional structures in Paris and Bologna were shaped by conflict with their environment, and in similar ways, but they ended up at opposite ends of the governance spectrum, Paris controlled by its faculty, Bologna by its students.

Paris attracted students from all over Europe. They came to hear the charismatic Peter Abelard apply the scholastic method to questions of speculative theology, such as whether the bread and wine consumed during mass truly turn into the body and blood of Christ, or only in spirit. In an age permeated by religion, in which any position outside of that defined by the church was considered heresy and heretics were burned at the stake, the *sic et non* (pro and con) exploration of a theological issue was nothing short of daring, and Abelard's students picked up on the fact that he was onto something big.

The University of Paris thus started out as an amorphous group of faculty and students collecting in and around the Cathedral School of Notre Dame, with few norms and no internal oganizational structure in place. Over the years, the faculty fought with the church over rights and entitlements, including in particular the right to appoint new faculty. The pope and the emperor were drawn into these fights, and the faculty played them off against each other.

Migration, boycott, and violence pushed forward the cause of the faculty. It helped that the medieval university had no physical plant—the faculty could threaten to leave for another city and take the university (themselves and their students) with them. On occasion, this threat was realized, in which case it led to new university foundings in surrounding cities; mass migration turned out to be the mechanism by which the idea of the university, and its emerging structures, spread.

As each bitter conflict was resolved, some protective piece of structure fell into place—some right was awarded here, another entitlement there. Pieces of structure were negotiated to prevent future conflict, or to encourage nonviolent conflict resolution, or for damage-control purposes. In this way, over the course of a century, an extraordinarily complex institution emerged brick by protective brick. In a decentralized process planned by nobody, structures evolved that protected the inhabitants of the university from the outside world. Thus, in the midst of the Middle Ages, an era not known for its intellectual tolerance, the university carved out a safe space for scholarly inquiry.

Because it was the faculty who led the fight against the church, Paris ended up with a governance structure dominated by the faculty: it was the faculty who voted on the issues of the day, staffed the administration, set the curriculum, and appointed new faculty.

As the university became increasingly differentiated into schools and departments, and factions within schools and departments, and factions within factions, it became internally conflicted. The members of a faction tend to reserve the most intense feelings of hatred for their intellectual neighbors rather than for the inhabitants of faraway worlds. This makes it very hard for faculty in the same, or closely related, fields to agree on appointments and curriculum design.

Protective structures followed faculty infighting: strong walls sprang up to separate the departments and schools, and federalist structures emerged. The voting procedures that aggregated the preferences within and across departments and schools became ever more complex. The university thus developed an intricate internal organization to protect the faculty from each other.

Meanwhile, students flocked from over the mountains (the northern and western parts of Western Europe) to study law in Bologna, and it was they who led the fight that created a great university. Foreign students did not have the same rights and entitlements as the citizens of Bologna. They were vulnerable to exploitation by the local townspeople, especially landlords and tradesmen, with no legal recourse. If a drunken student got into a fight and killed a local, he would be judged by a jury consisting of local citizens, and the outcome would not generally be favorable—hence the students' demand to be judged by their student peers.

The foreign students banded together for reasons of protection. They formed nations, that is, groupings of students with shared geographic origins. Collectively, they fought the Commune of Bologna for rights and entitlements. Here, too, the weapons of choice were migration, boycott, and violence. Once again, in the course of a century a complex institution emerged, loaded with rights and entitlements protecting its inhabitants from the outside world—but now, because it was the students who carried the water, the university ended up with a governance structure dominated by students: it was the students who voted on the issues of the day, staffed the administration, set the curriculum, and appointed the faculty.

The institutional structures that emerged in Paris and Bologna include bottom-up governance, representative assemblies, decentralized federalist structures, complex voting procedures, and institutionalized forms of conflict resolution (the latter snuffed out the violence that used to be an inevitable by-product of conflict).

The idea of the university emerged, manifesting itself in rights and norms such as *ius ubique docendi* (the right to teach at any institution after graduating from one of them), open access, open information, and free inquiry. These norms, powerful as they are, are ultimately derivative to the institutional structures of the university: a norm of free inquiry is not worth much without a structure in place that protects the inquirer from being imprisoned, killed, or (worst of all) ex-communicated.

The Middle Ages saw the emergence of complex voting procedures in the Italian city-state and of bottom-up governance processes in the medieval guild; but the politics of the city-states remained violence prone, and the guilds did not exactly embrace ideas of open access and open information. The university was unique in the astonishing combination of structures and norms it developed, allowing its inhabitants to engage in peaceful intellectual inquiry and protecting them from the outside world and from each other.

In its early fighting years, the medieval university was as intellectually vibrant as its structures were pliable. Once its structures, and the associated protections, got locked in, the university ossified intellectually. The scholastic method, wild and wonderful in its early years, matured and joined the establishment, finding its apotheosis in Thomas Aquinas's *Summa theologica* (the title itself has an end-of-history quality, quite unlike Abelard's title, *Sic et non*, which has an open-ended air about it). The scholastic method degenerated into an ever more refined system of logic-chopping exercises applied in a mindless and mechanical way to questions of great irrelevance, as in, how many angels are there on a pinhead? As the society surrounding the university became more interested in history and language, and more empirically oriented, the scholastic method was doomed.

The medieval university missed the boat come the Renaissance. In Italy, many universities continued to apply the scholastic method for one hundred years after the society around them had reinvented itself in full. The intellectual underpinnings of the Renaissance were developed in private academies outside the university. Humanist ideas got picked up by newly founded universities, including universities in northern Europe far away from the geographic center of Renaissance action.

During the religious wars of the sixteenth and seventeenth centuries, institutions of higher learning were established by local rulers seeking prestige and control (the principle of *cuius regio, eius religio* applied not only to countries, but also to universities). The university in Europe was in decline in the seventeenth century and became utterly moribund in the eighteenth century. It was missing in action during the Enlightenment and the Scientific Revolution, which largely took place outside the university, in private academies, societies, and salons. Many of the leading scholars and scientists were independently wealthy, and it was their wealth, not the protective structures of the university, that afforded them "a room of their own."

After a steady decline lasting several centuries (and contradicting the idea of history being an "ever upward-lifting" process), nineteenth-century Germany entered the world stage with a couple of innovations that, together with the inventions of the medieval university, came to define the modern university.

Progressive reformers developed the norms of *Lehrfreiheit* (freedom to teach) and *Lernfreiheit* (freedom to learn). Wilhelm von Humboldt, in particular, promoted the idea that science is not a fixed body of knowledge that students can mechanically learn by heart. Our understanding of the world is necessarily incomplete, and the quest for knowledge is an ongoing enterprise of which students must be an integral part so they can partake in the emerging understanding, which is as much about process as it is about results. Even while Humboldt established the primacy of research over teaching, his humanist approach emphasized the unity of inquiry and learning. It was thus that Germany developed the idea and institution of the deeply specialized research professor who combines research and teaching on a single discipline-based subject.

Deep specialization and the disciplines emerged in tandem, and for a reason. Because the world is complex and the individual brain is limited in its cognitive grasp, the task of figuring out how the world works needs to be split up into manageable pieces, but then the results of all the distributed inquiries need to be pulled together to form a synoptic picture—the ultimate goal, after all, is to help the human race gain control over harsh and capricious Nature (including human nature). To this end, the university slices the world into a hierarchically ordered set of disciplines and fields within disciplines and subfields within fields. A deeply specialized scholar will spend his life tending to some obscure question, which in isolation is pointless. His research gains meaning and impact only if it is pooled with the research of other scholars who are working on the same or closely related questions, and the research of a group of scholars gains meaning and impact only if it connects and cumulates within the larger discipline.

In Germany, discipline-based deep specialization had a powerful impact. Germany started out economically backward and as an intellectual backwater. It emerged as a leader in the industrial revolution in large part because of its universities. German science and industry flourished as a result of its pathbreaking research and teaching in physics, chemistry, agriculture, forestry, and other disciplines of central importance to industrialization.

In the case of Germany, university reform was shaped by an element of design—Humboldt's brilliant ideas as they manifested themselves in the newly founded University of Berlin. The vibrant German model was copied all over the world, including the United States (Johns Hopkins, Cornell, Chicago). In Germany, it ossified. Deep specialization, and its attendant narrow-mindedness, battled the humanist desire for holistic understanding—and won. Lack of competition and inflexible bureaucracy contributed to the decline. Today, the German university is largely moribund.

The idea of the university, and its institutional manifestation, was refined over the course of eight centuries. The university is a hybrid mix of bottom-up elements, which were shaped by evolution, and top-down elements, which are the result of deliberate design. The structures and norms of the university allow people to conduct systematic and cumulative research and thereby gain a better understanding of the way the world works. The medieval university with its emphasis on speculative theology and law helped Western Europe shake off the suffocating yoke of the church and develop complex political and economic institutions. The German university with its cutting-edge applied research and humanistic teaching ideals contributed to the industrialization of the German economy and the consolidation of the German nation.

## What Makes the University Strong Makes It Weak

The history of the university gives us an idea of what the university is *for*. The university is home to structures that nurse and protect and connect deeply specialized scholars.

There is a dark side to the history of the university. It is largely a history of ossification punctuated by bursts of intellectual vibrancy and structural innovation. In the large sweep of history, change occurs not because existing scholars, departments, and institutions move with the times, but through replacement. New ideas and methods are developed by new generations of scholars working in newly founded disciplines. New structures that support new forms of inquiry and learning emerge in newly founded universities.

Existing institutions do change—some of them, some of the time. When institutional change occurs, it is typically in response to the political or economic threat posed by competitors. Departments have a harder time reinventing themselves, and when they do, it is because of generational turnover, for individual scholars tend not to change at all.

The tendency of the university to ossify is an integral aspect of its positive function to enable deep specialization. As knowledge cumulates, it necessarily moves on. Inevitably, areas of inquiry that are vibrant today will be overrun by the masses tomorrow and be dead meat the day after. But the constituent elements of the university—deeply specialized scholars and discipline-based departments—cannot easily change their stripes simply because their stripes are the way they are for a reason.

Tenure is supposed to give individual scholars the freedom to think unthinkable thoughts, embark on high-risk-high-return research programs, stand up to "the powers that be," and so on. It doesn't always work that way, or even most of the time. In the university, it is the tenured faculty, above all, who are the fundamental source of ossification.

The problem is in part emotional, in other part cognitive, and it lies in the scholarly brain. First, the identity of a scholar, his connections and loyalties, are defined by his socialization in graduate school.

Second, as a result of his graduate training, his brain is locked into seeing the world in a particular way, and he is blind to new ideas and methods that slice the world in a different way.

To understand the nature of the problem, we need to take a look at graduate school. It takes about seven years for an uncommitted amateur to become an engaged scholar. Graduate school shapes the student emotionally and cognitively as it draws him into a scholarly community. It is the peer group that adopted him in graduate school that will later write referee reports when he submits articles to journals, and outside letters when he comes up for tenure.

A scholar who changes horses in midcareer loses the support of his peer group and is forced to reinvent himself from scratch. This requires personal courage and the willingness to take a risk, and these are not traits the tenure system selects for. Past behavior is the best predictor of future behavior, and it is a rare occurrence for a scholar who was conformist enough to attain a tenure-track position and achieve tenure to suddenly buck the trend and cook up wild and wonderful ideas in midcareer, let alone in old age.

Graduate school brainwashes the student—literally, in the sense that it rewires his brain connections—into becoming a *Fachidiot*, that is, an expert who has a very particular way of seeing the world. The expert is equipped to make extremely fine distinctions on one dimension even while he is blind to the existence of other dimensions.

Laypeople are as easily impressed by experts as they are contemptuous of them, and for good reason: they are awed by the subtlety of expert analysis, especially if it gives them purchase on some part of the world, and they deplore the experts' inability to apply common sense and take a holistic view of a problem. The universally felt ambivalence toward experts tells us something important about the existence of a "budget constraint" in the human brain. A layperson who turns into an expert does not stay the same on all dimensions of his thinking except for the one dimension on which he gained expertise: the expert's ability to see in great depth on one dimension reduces his appreciation of other dimensions. And indeed, the expression *Fachidiot* translates as "he who knows a lot in his area of expertise but is a total idiot when it comes to other areas."

The multiyear process of enculturation by which a student becomes a scholar generates an emotional and cognitive lock-in. The problem is that (undesirable) lock-in is a necessary by-product of (desirable) deep specialization. If the purpose of the university is to reap the gains from deep specialization, there must be a process in place that turns uncommitted amateurs into engaged experts, and such a process necessarily produces *Fachidioten* with rigid identities and warped cognitions.

The *Fachidiot* is nothing by himself—he is necessarily part of a group consisting of like-minded individuals competing with other groups. Part of the explanation of ossification lies in the individual expert's brain, but the other part can be found in the expert's social embeddedness, or in the interaction of expert brains.

The workings of scientific groups can be understood only with reference to the evolution of those parts of the human brain that are in charge of regulating social interaction.

Social cognition and social emotions developed in the human brain approximately thirty thousand to three hundred thousand years ago. In this ancestral environment, humans clustered together in tribes of 150 members, or thereabouts, and they were continually at war with other tribes. The emotional and cognitive makeup of the human race is designed to support cooperation within tribes and competition between tribes. Humans work well in groups of 150—this is the number of people who can interact regularly, communicate face to face, and learn to trust each other.

The clusters that form the backbone of scientific networks typically count about 150 members. Groupings of scientists have a small-town feel to them—think of the pervasiveness of gossip, which serves both a social policing function and an epistemological function, as in "you can't trust his regressions, he always fudges the data."

Scientific clusters play an enormously important motivational role—important because deeply specialized inquiry can quickly become dreary and alienating, and there needs to be something in place to keep scholars chipping away at some minuscule problem that in isolation is utterly meaningless. Within clusters, scholars give each other the emotionally comforting sense of belonging to a community and the spiritually uplifting sense of contributing to a larger purpose, and they dole out professional recognition and status.

Scholars are energized not only by within-group approval but also by between-group competition. A scholarly peer group typically stands in an enemy relationship with a competing group that largely shares its way of viewing the world but comes up with a competing answer to some critical question. The identity of a scholar is defined in large part by the opposition to the competing group whose members are seen as stupid, or wicked, or both.

Consider, for example, two groups that are obsessed with questions concerning the size and stability of the money multiplier. One group "proves conclusively" that the money multiplier is large and stable, whereas the other group "demonstrates beyond any doubt" that the money multiplier is small and unstable. The two sets of results yield opposite conclusions about the proper conduct of monetary policy, and each group considers the policy prescriptions of the other group to be utterly irresponsible.

At times, the two groups converge on some theoretical or empirical point, but then they immediately part ways on some new dimension of the problem, as a result of which their disagreement about the proper conduct of monetary policy keeps right on ticking. To the uninitiated, it looks like new arguments and evidence keep on chasing the same old conclusions. But scientific progress manifests itself in the gradual creep of conclusions made possible by the partial convergence of the competing factions. Then again, it is possible that the gradual creep is moving around in a circle—scientific progress doesn't follow automatically from factional conflict.

Factionalism at its best ensures that the two sides of one dimension of an issue get explored thoroughly before the conclusion moves on—at which time a new dimension opens up, and its two sides in turn get explored thoroughly. Scholars end up doing a thorough job not because they are obeying an ethical mandate to explore all sides of the issue thoroughly, or because they care about the truth, but because the two sides of a given dimension "belong" to two competing groups and because there is a process in place that moves the system on to a new dimension when the exploration of a given dimension is exhausted. Scholars are intensely driven by the prospect of beating "the others"—of bombing them out of the water by demonstrating definitively that the money multiplier really truly is large and stable over time—not! As a motivating force, the social utility of their research pales in comparison, which is just as well because the ultimate purpose of their research can be quite obscure at times.

Factionalism does not figure prominently, or even at all, in formal philosophies of science. The idea that factional conflict drives scientific progress sits uncomfortably with the normative ideal of the lone scholar in single-minded pursuit of the truth dispassionately engaging in classical hypothesis testing. The scientific process is loaded with social cognition and social emotions. If science is successful, it is because its motivational structures are consistent with the cognitive and emotional makeup of the human brain, and in particular with the human desire to cooperate in small groups and compete with other small groups. Factionalism is the motor of scientific progress, and historically it is factionalism that has moved the university out of its ossification trap.

Disciplines ossify in a very peculiar way. Factional conflict keeps them moving, and so the inhabitants of a discipline tend to believe they are making progress over time, and indeed, sometimes they are. But one important function of the disciplines is to protect the established lines of inquiry, and when those lines become obsolete, they keep right on protecting.

Disciplinary job market and reward structures shape which kinds of inquiry are advantaged and which kinds are not. They tend to discourage interdisciplinary research, and since the cutting edge often lies in the interstices of the disciplines, this is a problem.

Disciplines are controlled by journal editors and leading scholars who collectively decide what gets published in the top journals, who is awarded tenure, and which activities are to be supported by grants and showered with honors. There are selection biases in place that create a tendency for self-perpetuation. Perhaps most importantly, there is a natural bias toward gerontocracy that benefits scholars who are in mid-career or even "over the hill." This is the group from which journal editors and leading scholars are drawn, and they will tend to favor traditional work and support clones of themselves.

Scholars are part of a scientific network that cuts across universities, and this network typically covers a specialized subfield within a discipline. In their home institution, scholars are members of a discipline-based department that includes many different specialized subfields. Like disciplines, departments consist of scholars who clone themselves in hiring and promotions because they feel emotionally more comfortable with people who think like them; because they feel threatened by newcomers with different ideas; and simply because the new is the wicked.

The logic of departments, however, differs from the logic of disciplines. Departments have two special problems: a morale problem and a problem of Balkanization. First, a department consists of a mix of cosmopolitan scholars who are part of national networks, scholars with local loyalties who are involved in teaching and administration, and scholars who have given up on life and are deeply frustrated. Second, the department contains a collection of narrowly specialized scholars who don't interact with each other intellectually because they don't speak the same language.

The morale problem is fundamental to the university because of the random nature of scientific progress. Some scholars work out, and most don't, and many of the deeply specialized scholars who don't work out end up as flotsam. The value of the university lies in those who work out—it's just that it's impossible to predict in advance who that will be. Prediction is impossible because the attributes that make an individual scholar excel are only partially located in her brain—they mostly lie in the interaction between her brain, the surrounding brains, and the environment. The successful scholar is in the right place at the right time, and the idiosyncratic attributes of her brain connect with the idiosyncratic attributes of the brains around her in just the right way. With the right combustive mix in place, the resulting insights, which are collectively produced, find novel application to problems posed in the literature or the outside world. When this occurs, the effect is magical, and this is what the university is all about. The problem is, most of the time there is no magic, and the question is, what should we do with the empties?

The university is a cruel institution. It takes the best and the brightest, promises them the world, and then it throws most of them to the dogs. The vast majority of scholars start out as fresh-eyed and bushy-tailed newly minted assistant professors; their careers peak as they become tenured associate professors; and from then on their human capital declines steadily for reasons that are mostly not under their control. As a result, there is a lot of bitterness and resentment floating around in the heads of the tenured faculty. If the resulting morale problem is not properly addressed, it will stand in the way of intellectual renewal because frustrated faculty will clog the collective decision-making processes of the university. A well-designed university picks up its burned-out faculty and moves them into other activities they can take pride in, such as teaching or administration.

(Empathy with burned-out tenured faculty might come across as misplaced, given that the tenured faculty contribute to the overproduction of Ph.D.s, as a result of which many of the best and brightest never reach the level of assistant professor in the first place, which creates a lot of unhappiness. A mind is a terrible thing to waste, and this mass wastage of minds is a disgrace to the university. Politically speaking, however, frustrated tenured faculty are more important than are the rejects of the academy: the latter don't vote.)

To understand the problem of Balkanization—and to see why this is a hard problem—consider the example of an economics department whose stated goal is to hire and promote "excellence." Of course the stated goal of the department will not generally correspond to the actual goals of all faculty in the department: there are always some faculty who get very anxious about hiring and promoting scholars who are better than they are, and for this reason alone mediocrity can beat excellence. For now, let's go with the stated goal. It turns out that excellence is a rather vague goal, and once the highly specialized faculty begin to entertain concrete candidates, they will disagree violently on who is excellent. (Not that there is any actual violence: in this respect, the structures of the university are doing their job.) The economic theorists, the labor economists, the macroeconomists, and the economic historians—they all support different candidates, and since each group constitutes a minority in the department, no candidate would ever gain majority support if each group voted its preferences.

A malfunctioning department is Balkanized, and its members will not agree on anything, including hiring and promotions. Such a department will ossify quickly.

A well-functioning department will follow a decision-making process involving logrolling, that is, reciprocal deference to specialized subgroups. Today, it is the turn of the labor economists to identify their desired candidate, and everybody else holds their nose and votes along. Tomorrow, it is the turn of the macroeconomists, and everybody supports *their* selection sight unseen.

As a result of this universalistic decision-making process, the department will tend to hire and promote ever more of the same: scholars who are excellent as conceived by traditionally defined and narrowly specialized groups. Suppose the cutting edge in economics is a new field that encompasses parts of traditional fields (an example might be political economy, which cuts across monetary economics, international trade, public finance, and much else besides). Or suppose the cutting edge is not represented in the department at all (an example might be behavioral and experimental economics, which includes elements of psychology and uses empirical tools that are not standard fare in other subfields of economics). Then the department will fail to hire candidates on the cutting edge because the labor economists and the macroeconomists will use their turn to hire clones of themselves. And if the department hires one of "them" by accident, the outsider will do less well come promotion time because departmental resources are allocated by subfield and the political support structures are tied to the subfields. Thus, there is a seminar series in labor economics and in macroeconomics, and not in political economy or experimental economics, and so the scholarly misfit will have relatively less opportunity to connect with his peer group. External labor economists and macroeconomists, not political economists or experimental economists, are asked to write tenure letters, and so the scholar who is neither fish nor fowl will end up looking weaker than he really is—on paper, which is what matters in a bureaucratic promotion system.

And of course if the cutting edge involves interdisciplinary inquiry, an economics department that is oriented exclusively toward meeting the standards of the discipline of economics cannot cope at all.

But let us not kill the departments and disciplines all too quickly. They have evolved to protect scholars from each other and from the outside world, and their protection function is all too easily overlooked. Structures that mute conflict tend to be underappreciated when they do an excellent job because little if any conflict is observed in equilibrium—and so people forget about the problem that is being solved by the structures and "see" only the pathological implications of the structures. Based on their partial understanding, they propose structural reform. It is only when the structures are torn down and conflict breaks out that it becomes apparent that the structures were doing some good.

Consider, for a moment, an economist and a historian who are coming up for tenure. They have very different takes on the issue of globalization. The economist thinks "more is better," and he has money and material goods in mind. In his Panglossian world, everybody benefits from free trade, especially the poorest of the poor, and if the countries that are political and economic basketcases would only adopt the superior political and economic institutions of the West, they could work their way out of poverty and achieve the same high standards of living as the West.

In comparison, the historian looks through the glass darkly. She sees globalization as the direct descendant of colonialism and imperialism. If the West is rich (and it is of course merely materially rich; spiritually it is impoverished), it is because the West stole from the poor—it extracted resources from the countries it colonialized and as a byproduct screwed them up politically and economically, which is why many of the former colonies are such a mess.

The economist despises the historian for her nonrigorous method— thick description of local and historical detail, no grand theory, lots of left-wing ideology. The historian is horrified at the way the economist acts as if a reductionist theory can apply universally to all countries and explain all of history: what an impoverished understanding it is that economics promotes!

Now imagine the two (or their friends in their respective departments) could vote on each others' tenure cases. It would be a disaster. Neither of them would survive. And yet it is arguably useful for the university to have both (or even more than two) sides of the globalization debate represented in its walls. And it does—because the tenure process neatly separates faculty who can't possibly get along: economists vote on economists, and historians vote on historians.

Deeply specialized scholars and discipline-based departments are the way they are for good reason. They are the engines behind scientific progress, a dynamic force that has changed the face of the earth, and yet they are deeply conservative.

## Managing Change in the University

Universities are all about deep specialization. This is why they can get stuck in time—and do. The question is how institutions can be designed to remain intellectually vibrant and structurally pliable even if their component parts necessarily ossify.

At the level of the individual scholar, little if anything can be done; ditto at the level of the departments and disciplines. At the level of the institution, there is hope, though history tells us that there is no easy solution to "the problem of the university."

The single most important factor affecting the quality and content of the research and teaching in an institution—the factor that determines whether the institution is on the knowledge production frontier—is the selection of academic personnel. For good *and* for bad, the selection of academic personnel (recruiting and promotions to tenure) is firmly controlled by the departments, which are self-governed and self-perpetuating.

So what's a reform-minded university leader supposed to do? The decision-making processes in her departments are impenetrable. She cannot effectively order the departments to hire and promote scholars on the cutting edge: she does not have the specialized expertise to challenge the faculty if they fail to do her bidding. For the same reason, a university president cannot set up an effective incentive scheme. If she promises a 10 percent pay raise to the faculty in all departments whose hiring and promotion practices are on the cutting edge, one of two things will happen. Either the faculty will claim that they are hiring and promoting on the cutting edge, in which case the president lacks the wherewithall to check the faculty's claims. Or, if the president defines an operational measure of the cutting edge, the faculty will play to the measure, and since the measure is necessarily simplistic relative to the reality of the (deeply specialized) cutting edge, the incentive scheme will end up backfiring awfully. In the last resort, the president could get rid of the departments altogether. But departments are efficient ways of collecting deeply specialized scholars and organizing their teaching. And in the modern era it is highly ranked departments that define a highly ranked university, and the ambitious president cares deeply about improving her rankings.

What the president can do is put into place structures that promote internal competition and thereby exert pressure on the departments to become more flexible and nimble-minded. Internal competition can be achieved by piling cross-cutting structures on top of the departmental structures. For example, an interdisciplinary program might draw on the discipline-based departments to staff its courses. Internal competition can also be put into place by linking units of the university that naturally have something in common even while they pander to different constituencies. For example, there is an overlap in the research and teaching of the economics department and the business school.

The idea is to connect the units of the university in a way that encourages resources to flow in the direction of (relatively) better performance. So, for example, if the interdisciplinary program is vibrant and does a better job at attracting students than do the discipline-based departments, then the dean could allocate faculty positions to the interdisciplinary program. The faculty who get hired into the interdisciplinary program would be housed in one of the feeder departments, which ensures that there is some discipline-based quality control going on. The presence of the interdisciplinary program changes the personnel selection process in a subtle way: the departments retain their veto powers but they lose their agenda-setting powers—they can prevent candidates from getting hired and promoted, but they cannot select candidates. This solution is not perfect: there will be some excellent interdisciplinary candidates who will not pass muster with the departments. But it does allow for change at the margin: there will be some candidates whom the departments would not have chosen to put on the agenda, but once those candidates are on the agenda, especially if they are not seen to be directly competing with candidates the departments have identified as their own, they can attract a majority of the departmental vote. With this solution in place, the home departments will grow over time in the direction of the interdisciplinary "action."

Along the same lines, both the economics department and the business school could offer business economics to undergraduates. If students self-select into the courses taught by the business school because the faculty in the business school take teaching more seriously, and if resources follow the flow of students, there will come a point where the economics department will have to rethink its "take-no-prisoners" approach to undergraduate teaching and overhaul its dated curriculum.

To promote change, decentralized structures must preserve diversity even while they enable competition. Diversity is valuable for two reasons. First, it keeps a multiplicity of perspectives alive. The scientific process is inherently deeply uncertain: we do not know which strains of research and teaching will be valuable tomorrow. Universities need to hedge their bets. When the action moves on, they must have someone on the ground who will pick up the ball. Second, diversity allows experimentation to occur. Diverse departments engage in different activities, and some activities will turn out to be more successful than others. The less successful departments can then adopt the successful experiments.

Diversity and competition complement each other: it is diversity that makes people and projects stand out in the first place, and it is competition that allows for the dissemination of better-performing strategies and successful experiments.

To preserve diversity, decentralized structures must be messy and loose. The competition between the units must be limited in scope. All-engulfing competition has a tendency to homogenize—if everybody is chasing the same rewards under identical environmental constraints, everybody will end up behaving the same way, and if there are selection effects, there will be a homogenization of types.

One way to limit competition is to put multiple cross-cutting and partially contradictory performance criteria into place. Different departments can then choose to meet different combinations of criteria. This way each department is forced to confront competitive pressures, and yet it can maintain a unique profile because it gets evaluated by a unique combination of performance standards.

Designing effective decentralized structures is difficult because we must give up our natural tendency to think in binary extremes. On the one hand, we do not want each academic unit to operate as an independent and isolated island, with no performance measure in sight. This will lead to poor performance in research and teaching for sure. On the other hand, we do not want to put into place simplistic quantitative performance standards that apply uniformly to all units. Such a scheme will surely backfire, first, because it fails to respect local detail and, second, because faculty will max out on the dimension of their performance that is being measured even while they continue to shirk on other dimensions.

While it is important to implement some degree of competition, which necessarily implies the use of performance standards, we must avoid incentivizing everything in sight. The university must retain some free and open spaces for playful exploration and random happenings. There is a need for incentives, but incentive schemes should not be so tightly wound that they prevent faculty from working on projects that will pay off only in the long term, or that are high-risk high-return, or politically controversial.

Leaving slack in the system makes state legislators nervous because they suspect that the slack will be exploited by lazy deadwood faculty, and they don't want the taxpayer to pay good salaries to faculty who are doing nothing but living the good life. But we must keep in mind that it is not the first goal of the university to avoid paying faculty for doing nothing. (Indeed, given the potentially debilitating morale problem of the university, there is something to be said for paying the nonproductive faculty well.) The first goal of the university is to enable deep specialization, and if there is one thing history tells us, it is that deep specialization occurs when scholars are given a room of their own—unsupervised and unincentivized slack, for short.

Last but not least, ossification depends on the university's relationship to the outside world. Departments and disciplines that are not linked to constituencies outside the university can keep right on trucking in self-referential circles. They will move with the times if they are permeable to the outside world. In medicine, faculty who want to get National Institutes of Health (NIH) grants must select research topics and employ methods that find the approval of the NIH, and since the NIH is tied to Congress, and Congress is accountable to the American people, new developments in the external society feed into the medical schools and influence medical research. Thus, we now examine whether doctors treat African American patients differently, and we now include women subjects in medical trials.

In the short space of a decade, biology has completely resliced itself as a discipline in response to the external job and profit opportunities offered by biotechnology. The case of biology is instructive because it shows us how important it is not to go all the way: molecular biology has lost its slack because it has been taken over by the profit motive. Ideally, the university is partially permeable to the outside world, and it is best for it to have multiple cross-cutting connections and multiple contradictory external constituencies.

Managing change in the university is not about putting centralized command-and-control systems in place or defining simplistic profit centers and performance standards or infusing the university with business values—this would be the death of the university. On the other hand, if the university is left in the hands of the faculty, it will surely turn into bone. Managing change is about designing decentralized structures that encourage competition, preserve diversity, and keep the university connected to the outside world.

CHAPTER FIVE

# Herding Cats in University Hierarchies: Formal Structure and Policy Choice in American Research Universities

## Thomas H. Hammond

Research universities in the United States are often described in nonhierarchical terms, and there are good reasons for this perspective. Department chairs and higher-level administrators, for example, find it all but impossible to fire tenured faculty members: as long as these faculty members meet minimal standards of teaching and personal behavior toward students, even the most pugnacious and intemperate critics of the university administration can remain employed until they make their own decisions to retire. Moreover, the initial recommendations on promotion and tenure are largely in the hands of departmental faculty members, and higher-level reviews of these recommendations are almost always conducted by committees dominated by tenured faculty members. Even the search committees that do the initial screening for new hires are dominated by faculty members, as are the final recommendations of whom to hire. Proposals to change departmental curricula are primarily developed by departmental faculty members, and higher-level reviews of these proposals are usually made by committees dominated not by administrators but by other faculty members.

I would like to thank Robert Birnbaum, Marvin Peterson, M. Christopher Brown, Craig Volden, Robert Pahre, Susanne Lohmann, Ken Koford, and two anonymous reviewers for their encouragement and for their helpful comments on early drafts.

Furthermore, the faculty members' disciplinary training, coupled with their own personal concerns and interests, largely governs their choices of research topics; higher-level administrators can affect these choices only at the margin. And those faculty members who are the most productive researchers (in publications and especially in grantsmanship) are often in a position of strength when bargaining with department chairs and higher-level administrators: a threat to decamp for another university usually carries considerable weight in salary negotiations, teaching loads, and research support. In general, it is the imbalance between the faculty members' knowledge of their own fields and the administrators' ignorance of most of these fields that makes it difficult for the administrators to exercise great control over these promotion-and-tenure, hiring, curricular, and faculty-retention decisions.

These general characteristics of research universities have given rise to a well-known simile: managing institutions populated by such independent-minded academics is like "herding cats." In fact, Cohen and March (1974) even advanced a conception of research universities as "organized anarchies": the faculty members' problematic goals, unclear technology, and fluid participation in decision making are taken as suggesting that the universities can be described in decidedly non-hierarchical terms.

The views of Cohen and March have been echoed by other students of these academic institutions as well. For example, in describing research universities as organized anarchies, Birnbaum (1988, 159–160) suggests that

> The traditional organization chart with its boxes representing offices connected by lines representing channels of authority provides one very powerful metaphor for thinking about tight coupling in organizational structure. But a metaphor more appropriate for loose coupling is that of "streams" (Cohen and March, 1974). A stream can be thought of as a flow of "something" that travels through an organization as the Gulf Stream flows through the Atlantic Ocean.

Following Cohen and March, Birnbaum identifies three independent streams, involving problems, solutions, and participants, which interact to produce choices and decisions. It is only when a specific problem from one stream, a specific set of participants from another stream, and a specific solution from a third stream all just randomly happen to converge at the same time in a particular location (e.g., some administrator's office) that a decision can be made.[1]

Nevertheless, even though American research universities have many nonhierarchical tendencies, this perspective should not be overemphasized. The reason is simply that research universities, like most other large institutions, retain significant hierarchical features. For example, every university, whether public or private, has some kind of governing board in which authority over institutional management is legally vested.[2] While the members of the governing boards usually delegate much of their authority to a president (or whatever the chief administrative officer is called), they generally select who this president will be. While the president in turn usually delegates major responsibility for academic matters to a provost, the president usually decides who the provost will be. While the provost in turn usually delegates substantial responsibility to the deans of the colleges and schools, the provost generally plays a major role in selecting these deans.

And in fact, despite the substantial delegation that occurs, each of these administrative officials retains substantial authority over critical aspects of university decision making. At Michigan State University, for example, the authority of the president, of the provost, and of the deans is officially described as follows:

• "The President, as the principal executive officer of the University, shall exercise such powers as are inherent in the position in promoting, supporting, or protecting the interests of the University and in managing and directing all of its affairs; may issue directives and executive orders not in contravention of existing Board policies; shall be responsible for all business policies as heretofore enacted or modified or hereafter established subject to the general policies established by the Board; shall instruct the proper administrative officers to prepare an annual budget which upon approval, shall be recommended to the Board; shall be responsible for the preparation of the annual reports of the Board; shall exercise such other powers, duties, and responsibilities as are delegated or required by the Board of Trustees."[3]

• The Provost shall be the principal academic officer of the University and administer the various colleges, special units and academic support facilities; shall be responsible for assembling and administering the academic budget; shall be responsible for faculty personnel administration including procedures for faculty appointments and terminations, salaries and promotions, working conditions, and tenure; shall be responsible, with advice from the faculty, for development of new academic programs and for keeping existing programs updated and in conformity with University educational policies; shall be responsible for insuring that administrative procedures preserve academic freedom and insure academic responsibility; shall be responsible for supervising procedures and policies related to the admission of students, and liaison with high schools and community colleges; shall be responsible for supervising the registration process and for the orientation of new students; shall be responsible for administering academic facilities and support units such as Libraries, Computer Laboratory, Instructional Development and Telecommunication Services, and the Museum; shall be responsible for liaison with State Department of Education.[4]

• "Deans and directors of other academic units separately reporting to the Provost are responsible for educational, research, and service programs of the respective college or separately reporting unit. This responsibility includes budgetary matters, physical facilities, and personnel matters in his or her jurisdiction taking into account the advisory procedures of the college or separately reporting unit."[5]

Of course, the deans further delegate responsibility for many aspects of departmental management to the department chairs, and it is primarily at the departmental level that this relatively hierarchical structure begins to break down. For example, while selection of a department chair is sometimes solely a faculty responsibility, but sometimes officially the responsibility of the dean and provost, the choice of a chair is usually heavily influenced by the faculty members of the department. Even so, the department chair often retains substantial powers. At Michigan State, for instance, the powers of the chair are officially described in the following terms:

• "A department chairperson or school director serves as the chief representative of his or her department or school within the University. He or she is responsible for educational, research, and service programs, budgetary matters, physical facilities, and personnel matters in his or her jurisdiction, taking into account the advisory procedures of the unit. The chairperson or director has a special obligation to build a department or school strong in scholarship, teaching capacity, and public service."[6]

In sum, the administrators at Michigan State are given broad, significant, and clearly specified authority over many important matters, and there is no reason to think that administrators at Michigan State are at all unique in this regard. And most importantly for our purposes, this authority is not just a formality: on a yearly basis, it is these administrators who allocate the budget, approve new positions, reallocate vacant positions, approve or reject new program proposals, and approve—and occasionally reject—candidates for promotion and tenure.

It is presumably for these reasons that some of the literature on universities does refer to a hierarchical ranking of the authority of the president, provost, deans, and department chairs (see, e.g., Clark and Youn 1976, 16–18). For the same reason, it is easy to construct a traditional organization chart for a university (an enterprise that Birnbaum implicitly criticizes, as quoted earlier) from these descriptions of formal authority; indeed, most universities probably have such a chart.[7] In other words, universities are not quite the "organized anarchies," and higher-level administrators are not quite the organizational weaklings, that some of the higher-education literature alleges them to be. Trow (forthcoming) makes this same point in a study of the extensive reforms in the organization of the biological sciences at the University of California at Berkeley in the 1970s and 1980s, noting that these reforms were led and implemented by top-level administrators despite the fact that Berkeley has a quintessentially powerful faculty.

But while American research universities do retain significant hierarchical features, there is some variation in the characteristics of their hierarchies. To illustrate some of the possible variations in formal organizational structure among research universities, consider two kinds of structural differences between the University of Michigan in Ann Arbor and Michigan State University in East Lansing. At the University of Michigan the Department of Physics is separate from the Department of Astronomy, whereas at Michigan State University these two fields of study are combined in a single Department of Physics and Astronomy. Hence, we might ask, for the two universities' decisions involving physics and astronomy, does it matter that the physicists and astronomers are grouped together in one department (as at Michigan State) or separated into two departments (as at the University of Michigan)? More generally, does it matter for university decision making how the most basic organizational units—the "departments"—are defined?

These kinds of structural-design issues emerge at higher administrative levels as well. At the University of Michigan there is a College of Literature, Science, and the Arts which includes most of the non-professional schools, colleges, and programs, whereas at Michigan State University many of these same programs and activities are distributed among a College of Natural Science, a separate College of Social Science, and a separate College of Arts and Letters. Hence, we might ask, for the two universities' decisions involving natural scientists, social scientists, and students of the humanities, does it matter whether these faculty members are grouped together in one college (as at the University of Michigan) or separated into several colleges (as at Michigan State)? More generally, does it matter for university decision making how the basic organizational units are grouped together into "colleges" and "schools"?

The questions just posed are neither trivial nor obscure: at one time or another, every university has had to make decisions as to what its basic organizational units would be and how these basic units would be grouped together. Those who made these decisions presumably had some reasons for making them. That is, the decision makers presumably expected the consequences from some structural choices to be more desirable than the consequences from other structural choices. One would thus guess that decision making on these organizational issues would have attracted substantial scholarly attention.

Indeed, such fundamental questions about how the basic organizational units are defined and how these basic units are grouped together to form the organizational hierarchy lie at the heart of many theories of organization in both the public and the private sector. These questions have certainly been critical to organization theorists at least since publication of Luther Gulick's classic essay "Notes on the Theory of Organization" in 1937.[8] And Alfred Chandler's classic study of the organization of business firms, *Strategy and Structure: Chapters in the History of Industrial Enterprise* (1962), likewise made clear to economists and students of business administration that a firm's structure has a critically important impact on its decision-making processes.[9]

Rather surprisingly, however, while academic researchers on universities have extensively probed the reasons for, and impact of, the nonhierarchical relationships within the universities, remarkably little research seems to have been conducted on how the different ways in which the universities are hierarchically organized might affect the universities' decision-making processes and the decisions that result.[10] It seems unlikely that a university's hierarchical structure is completely irrelevant to its decision-making processes and outcomes, but essentially no such research seems to have been reported in the literature on the institutions of higher education.[11]

Thus we have an anomaly. On the one hand, the hierarchy of the research university—how the basic units are defined and how these basic units are grouped together—virtually defines the administrative context within which faculty members and administrators conduct their work. But on the other hand, researchers on the institutions of higher education seem to have developed essentially no understanding of the impact of this administrative hierarchy. The purpose of this chapter is thus to stimulate thinking and research on the following question: how do the hierarchical structures of American research universities affect their decision-making processes and the outcomes that result?

The next section describes some of the most basic aspects of university hierarchies: what the basic units are, why they have become the basic units, and how these basic units are assembled into the larger administrative hierarchy we call "the university." The following section examines a university's hierarchy as a dependent variable; that is, why does a university have a particular structure? The next four sections examine in more depth the university hierarchy as an independent variable, discussing how a university's formal structure can affect how top-level administrators perceive problems that may need attention, how a menu of possible choices is constructed for the top-level administrators, and how their final choices are implemented. The subsequent section then characterizes the nature of the choices that the designers of university hierarchies might be expected to face. The final section concludes the essay.

## The Basic Building Blocks of a University's Hierarchy

Two fundamental aspects of a hierarchy are what the basic units are (i.e., what the building blocks are), and how these basic units are clustered together to form the hierarchy. In a university, these basic units are generally referred to as "departments," and these departments are then usually grouped together into "colleges" or "schools." Let us consider each in turn.

### *The Basic Units: "Departments"*

What the basic units of any university are or should be is only rarely given much consideration. For the most part, these basic units are simply seen as a constant whose most basic features do not change much from one year to the next, or even from one decade to the next. However, the initial definition and creation of these basic units appears to involve some interesting conceptual, historical, and organizational issues.

In theory, grouping faculty members into "departments" could be based on many different principles of organization. Some of these organizing principles might reflect some aspect of the topic the faculty members are studying; for example, the faculty members could be clustered into groups that focus on various kinds of societal problems (e.g., there could be a "health-care department," an "urban problems" department, an "environmental problems" department, and so forth). Other organizing principles might reflect how the faculty members conduct their studies; for example, the faculty members could be clustered into groups based on "theoretical research," "empirical research," and "normative or policy-related research." Still other organizing principles might reflect various personal attributes of humans such as gender, race, ethnicity, or religious affiliation, producing units that focus, for example, on women's studies, African American studies, Hispanic studies, or Jewish studies.

In fact, there is essentially an infinite number of different principles on which the grouping of faculty members could conceivably be based. But, of course, many academic departments are based on some kind of academic discipline, and Pahre (1995, 243–244) argues that academic disciplines are primarily defined by agreement on some general class of phenomena—what he refers to as a "dependent variable"—that the members of the discipline are trying to explain. Thus, political scientists are united in trying to explain political phenomena, and so are housed in a department of political science; economists are united in trying to explain economic phenomena, and so are housed in a department of economics; and psychologists are united in trying to explain psychological phenomena, and so are housed in a department of psychology. What the departments in a university are not based on, Pahre suggests, is a common interest in some independent variable; as he remarks, "It is . . . telling that groups of scholars clustered around anything other than dependent variables do not organize themselves as a discipline, or even a formal subfield of some discipline" (244).

However, what is defined as a particular dependent variable around which disciplinary discourse is organized is not completely constrained; "dependent variables" themselves are subject to definition and redefinition. For example, every academic discipline has come to include some kinds of subjects, concerns, and methodological approaches but not others, and it may be that a critical influence on how some kinds of faculty members come to be grouped together into "departments" in a university is simply how the academic disciplines evolved historically.

For example, in the late 1800s a national "social science" association was formed in the United States, but it quickly split into two separate associations, one involving "economics" and the other involving "political science." In the following century these two disciplines, each with its own national association (the American Economic Association and the American Political Science Association), evolved quite independently from each other.[12] A key distinction might seem to be that economists were primarily interested in explaining "private" behavior involving the functioning of private markets and that political scientists were primarily interested in explaining "public" behavior involving the function of governmental institutions. But given the intimate and unavoidable interactions between economic and political institutions, it was not clear whether some topics belonged in "economics" or "political science."

For instance, where did the study of interest groups belong, particularly those focusing on "economic" matters? Did it belong in economics, because the interest groups were trying to influence economic outcomes? Or did it belong in political science, because the interest groups were trying to use the political process to influence economic outcomes? And there were numerous larger questions, involving the legal foundations of private enterprise (e.g., private property rights, contract law, and the like) and the origins of governments, in which what caused what was not entirely clear. For example, did private business organizations exist because governments created the legal foundations required for their existence? Or did governments exist because private businesses demanded (and even helped create) the public institutions that could supply the public goods needed by the private businesses? It was not clear what the dependent variables here actually were, and so it was not clear in which department—economics or political science—the study of these kinds of problems belonged.

In recent decades, of course, some universities have created various kinds of interdepartmental "programs" in political economy (see, e.g., the program institutionally housed inside the Graduate School of Business at Stanford University), but there seems to exist no department of political economy at any major American research university.[13] Indeed, it is the dominance of the disciplines of economics and political science outside each university that would control the academic job markets. A student who receives a Ph.D. in political economy would risk falling between the cracks of the two disciplines, and graduate students in economics or political science who do specialize in political economy are well advised to define themselves along the lines of some disciplinary subfield (e.g., international economics or comparative politics).

In effect, then, even though political economy as a field of study antedated both political science and economics, as we see from the works of Adam Smith, David Ricardo, John Stuart Mill, and Karl Marx, a consequence of the subsequent split between economics and political science is that political economy did not end up with a clear institutional or disciplinary home. The same holds for many other fields of study such as urban studies, American studies, African American studies, women's studies, environmental studies, Asian studies, African studies, Latin American studies, European studies, and Russian studies: none of them has a clear institutional or disciplinary home either.

Not only are some legitimate fields of study not clearly included within any one discipline, but closer inspection also shows that relatively few disciplines, at least in the social sciences, are defined by any kind of integrated and coherent set of questions, concerns, and methodological approaches. Economics is perhaps the most integrated and coherent of the social sciences, but many economics departments are split between microeconomic theorists (who are sometimes accused of developing theory without data) and econometricians (who are sometimes accused of analyzing data without theory). The other social sciences—political science, sociology, psychology, anthropology—are even less integrated and coherent, and some disciplines are even divided between the social sciences and the natural sciences. For example, the field of geography is divided between geographers with a primary interest in the social world (e.g., geographers whose interests overlap those of sociologists and even urban planners, who are in turn usually housed in departments of sociology and departments of urban planning, respectively) and geographers with a primary interest in the physical world (e.g., physical geographers, whose research interests overlap those of geologists, who are in turn usually housed in departments of geology or earth sciences).[14] In each of these cases, one could imagine plausible alternative conceptions of what belongs in any one department. Many departments, supposedly based on a single discipline, are actually just conglomerates of only partly related fields of study.

Moreover, while Pahre's (1995) argument that what defines a "discipline" is the effort to explain some common dependent variable, it seems difficult to apply this to at least some academic disciplines in a university. For example, it is not clear how to classify fields such as mathematics or statistics in terms of some common dependent variable. Instead, one could argue that the discipline of statistics, for example, is organized around the development of a particular methodology for assessing the impact of an independent variable on a dependent variable. Furthermore, the dependent-variable conceptualization seems less applicable to the applied departments and professional schools in a university. At the least, we would have to amend Pahre's formulation by arguing that each of these applied departments and professional schools is oriented not around explaining some common dependent variable, but around improving, saving, designing, or redesigning some common object.

In general, then, how each field of study came to be considered a "discipline" and institutionally embodied in an academic "department" involves some complex conceptual, historical, and institutional matters.[15] Indeed, one could probably comb through academia and find a great many such fields of study that, for largely historical reasons, have not come to be defined as a particular dependent variable and thus failed to be included within the ambit of some academic "discipline." So when universities officially endorse the study of these particular fields, the fields often end up having to be organized as "interdisciplinary" or "cross-disciplinary" programs and run jointly by faculty members from two or more discipline-based departments. But whatever their origins, what came to be considered "the departments" clearly constitute the basic building blocks of the university's hierarchy, and so can be expected to structure how scholars interested in any particular field of study interact with other scholars at that university.

### Grouping the "Departments" into "Colleges" and "Schools"

The same wide range of principles that can be used to group faculty members into "departments" can also be used to group these "departments" into "colleges" and "schools." One common principle, followed by the University of Michigan, is to group together all departments and programs that do not involve "professional" training (i.e., they do not involve the granting of degrees for "applied" work in law, business, medicine, dentistry, engineering, nursing, social work, and so forth) in its College of Literature, Science, and the Arts. In effect, the fundamental organizational division is between the professional schools and the nonprofessional schools.[16]

A different principle breaks the nonprofessional schools into separate categories involving the natural sciences, the social sciences, and the arts and humanities. This is reflected, for example, in the College of Natural Science, College of Social Science, and College of Arts and Letters at Michigan State University.

Just as there is an infinite number of different principles on which the grouping of faculty members into departments and programs can be based, there is an infinite number of different principles on which the grouping of departments and programs into colleges and schools can be based. What follows in the remainder of this chapter is an analysis of how some of these grouping definitions and decisions might have originated and how they might affect a university's decision-making processes and the outcomes that emerge from these processes.

## University Structure as Dependent Variable

A university's structure can be seen both as something to be explained and as something that explains other things. For example, we can try to explain why the university has a particular formal structure; that is, we can treat the formal structure of a university as a *dependent variable*. We can also try to explain what impact the formal structure has on university decision making; that is, we can treat the formal structure of a university as an *independent variable*. This section focuses primarily on the university structure as a dependent variable, while the following four sections focus primarily on the university structure as an independent variable.

As a dependent variable, the university's hierarchy can be seen as the outcome of forces from both outside and inside the university. For example, a particular structure may have been chosen because social, political, and economic interests outside the university wanted something from it, and so worked with the legislature, the governor, the university's governing board, the university administration, or the faculty (or some combination of these) to ensure that the university supplied what these interests wanted. This meant, in effect, that the structure of the university—both in the definition of the basic units and in the grouping of these subunits into colleges and schools—had to be designed so as to facilitate the supply of what the outsiders wanted.

For land-grant universities such as Michigan State, one of the main reasons for the creation of the university was to generate and supply practical, useful knowledge to the state's agricultural communities. Indeed, Michigan State University's original name was Michigan Agricultural College, and the names of some land-grant universities still retain their original focus, as with Texas A&M (that is, Texas Agricultural and Mechanical). When the land-grant universities grew in size and expanded in scope, a continuing demand for the creation and dissemination of useful knowledge to the states' agricultural communities usually led to the creation of an internal college of agriculture so as to maintain the focus on agricultural problems. At Michigan State, the resulting college has thus come to include such departments as Agricultural Economics, Agricultural Engineering, Botany and Plant Pathology, Crop and Soil Sciences, Entomology, Food Science, Horticulture, and Forestry. When also associated with an Agricultural Experiment Station of the U.S. Department of Agriculture (as again is the case at Michigan State, for example), a college of agriculture continues to provide agricultural interests with an entrée into the university, and it also provides the university with an organizational means of communicating with (and, not incidentally, of trying to gain the support of) these interests.[17]

Any efforts to significantly reorient the teaching or research activities of a college of agriculture, or even to dismember it and reallocate its constituent parts to other colleges at the university (e.g., at Michigan State the Department of Agricultural Economics could plausibly be transferred to the College of Social Science, the Departments of Botany and Plant Pathology, Crop and Soil Sciences, Entomology, Food Science, Horticulture, and Forestry could all go to the College of Natural Science, and the Department of Agricultural Engineering could go to the College of Engineering) might thus be expected to arouse considerable concern on the part of the state's agricultural interests. These interests might then make their concerns known to the governor and state legislators, who control a significant portion of the budget of public research universities, and to members of the university's governing board.

From this perspective, then, one could interpret the university's hierarchy from the perspective of contingency theory, which argues that an organization's structure and procedures are designed to handle the critical political or economic uncertainties that the organization faces.[18] Thus, a university would design an internal structure (e.g., a college of agriculture) whose primary purpose is to handle these uncertainties regarding a critical constituency, such as the agricultural sector in the state.

Of course, other aspects of a university's structure, such as a college of social science or a college of arts and letters, probably have fewer critical external constituencies. Hence, it is less clear that contingency theory will have anything useful to offer here. In fact, the design of some aspects of a university's structure may even have been left up to some of the faculty members themselves. At Michigan State, for example, when the College of Social Science and the School of Business were created several decades ago, campus lore has it that the faculty members in the Department of Economics had some influence over where they would be located and that they chose to be located in the School of Business because they expected their salaries to be closer to the higher salaries earned by business school professors (who were also in some demand by industry) than to the lower salaries of the other social scientists (who were in much less demand outside the university).

In sum, it may be that in explaining why some university has the structure that it has, there will turn out to be different explanations for different parts of its structure.

University Structure as Independent Variable

We can also treat formal structure as an independent variable. That is, instead of trying to determine why a particular structure was chosen, we can try to determine what the impact of the chosen structure actually is. Indeed, because the impact of formal structures is not well understood, whatever the original *intentions* were in selecting some structure, it may well be that the structure's *actual impact* has turned out to be quite different. Hence, treating the structure as an independent variable makes considerable sense. In this section and the three sections that follow, I develop some ways of conceptualizing the impact of a university's formal structure on various kinds of decisions made by the university.

In previous work aimed at developing a political science of hierarchies (Hammond 1986, 1990, 1993, 1994; Hammond and Horn 1984, 1985; Hammond and Miller 1985; Hammond and Thomas 1989, 1990), I have made the argument that while much of organization theory takes a top-down perspective, construction of an adequate theory of organizational structure and organizational design first requires an understanding of the bottom-up flow of information, policy recommendations, and conflicts over policy implementation. Only when these bottom-up processes are understood will it be possible to develop an adequate top-down theory of why a particular structure would or should be chosen.

The policymaking process in an organization can be seen as involving three fundamental stages: I will call them *orientation*, *advising*, and *policy implementation*. "Orientation" refers to problem recognition and problem definition, that is, the processes by which the administrators become aware of the existence of a problem. Problem recognition and problem definition by administrators do not occur automatically.

Instead, the administrators must first perceive that there is a problem requiring attention. Moreover, the problem can usually be defined or understood in several different ways. The perception and definition of a problem depend in part on the collection and assessment of some body of data. For most large institutions (and large research universities would certainly qualify), no single administrator can possibly give due consideration to every piece of relevant data. My argument here will be that different formal structures can create different sets of information for the administrators, and these different sets of information can sometimes be expected to lead decision makers to different definitions of the problem, or even to lack of recognition that there is a problem at all.

"Advising" refers to the process by which the administrators gather advice from subordinates on what to do about the problem that has been identified. Addressing a problem requires consideration of the options that may be available, and the act of choice by an administrator involves a comparison of these options. My argument here will be that different formal structures will create different menus of possible choices for the decision-making administrator. Given different menus, the administrator can sometimes be expected to make different choices, and the more divergent the menus are, the more divergent the resulting choices are likely to be.

"Policy implementation" refers to the process by which some administrator puts into effect the policy that she has selected, given the menu of available options. While implementation is a complex and multifaceted process (as are orientation and advising), a key aspect of implementation involves the resolution of conflicts among subordinates over precisely what new policy the administrator actually intended. In fact, such conflicts can sometimes freeze implementation of the policy until the conflicts are resolved. The conflicts can be resolved in two different ways. A conflict can be resolved by "horizontal" compromise or concession among the individuals involved. Or the conflict can be resolved by referring it "vertically" upward to some common administrative superior; this administrative superior can then use her formal authority to impose a solution. My argument will be that different formal structures will route such conflicts to different administrative superiors, and if these administrative superiors have different policy preferences, the conflicts may be resolved in different ways in the different structures.

In the next three sections these three organizational processes of orientation, advising, and implementation will be discussed in greater detail.

The Orientation Process in University Hierarchies

A top-level academic administrator such as a provost cannot personally pay attention to all the problems that confront the university: she has limited time and energy, and she may not have the specialized knowledge that would allow her to recognize the existence of various kinds of problems. Hence she will have to rely on other people, including her subordinates in the colleges and departments, to keep her informed about the various problems her university faces.[19]

It is often the university's bottom-level employees—the faculty members, graduate students, and departmental staff members—who initially perceive and collect the raw data indicating that there is a problem to which the provost should pay attention. But many different bottom-level employees will be scanning their environments and sending messages upward—to their department chairs or program administrators, to the deans, or to the provost—about potential problems. If the provost tries to read all these messages and engage in the back-and-forth communications required to fully comprehend the issues under discussion, she will be overwhelmed—there will not be enough hours in the day to do what needs to be done. Hence, the middle-level administrators, such as the department chairs and the deans, will be expected to collect, collate, and aggregate the reports from the bottom-level employees into summary documents, which are then forwarded to the provost. So what the provost normally sees is not the *raw data* that the bottom-level employees see but a highly aggregated or condensed *interpretation* by the middle-level administrators of what the bottom-level employees see. The provost will then base her choices about what problems to attend to on these interpretations from the middle-level administrators. March and Simon (1958) refer to this process as "uncertainty absorption," and they note that

> Through the process of uncertainty absorption, the recipient of a communication is severely limited in his ability to judge its correctness. Although there may be various tests of apparent validity, internal consistency, and consistency with other communications, the recipient must, by and large, repose his confidence in the editing process that has taken place, and, if he accepts the communication at all, accept it pretty much as it stands. (165)

My central argument here is that the way in which the subordinates are clustered together in "departments" and other academic units such as "programs," how these academic units are grouped together into "colleges" and "schools," and how the responsibilities for assessing particular kinds of data are assigned to these various organizational units can affect what kinds of inferences the top-level administrators will draw from the raw data flowing into the university via the bottom-level employees. That is, the formal structure of the university can affect just how uncertainty absorption takes place. Indeed, even when the bottom-level employees are seeing and collecting exactly the same raw data and so are sending identical reports upward, different kinds of comparisons among different sets of aggregated information can be expected to take place in different kinds of organizational structures. The different problems that are identified or that fail to be identified, and thus the different things that the top-level administrators thereby learn or fail to learn, can have important consequences for the university.

*Different Inferences from the Same Set of Messages*

To illustrate these arguments, consider the following simple model involving how four departments—the Departments of Entomology, Agricultural Economics, Genetics, and Sociology—could be grouped into two colleges. The goal is to determine whether a shift from a structure based on a College of Natural Science and a College of Social Science to a structure based on a College of Agriculture and a College of Literature, Science, and the Arts (LS&A) can affect the inferences drawn by the provost about where to assign a new development officer whose task will be to help some college attract outside grants. The model focuses on what the provost infers from messages the four department chairs and the two deans send upward as to whether there are opportunities for advancement from investments in their respective departments and colleges.

Assume the following four messages are sent upward from the bottom in each structure:

• The chair of the Department of Entomology always sends the message that there are "many opportunities for advances in studies in entomology" (considering the research grants that are available for entomologists, the market for new entomological findings, and the job market for graduate students with degrees in entomology).

• The chair of the Department of Genetics always sends the message that there are "many opportunities for advances in studies in genetics" (considering the research grants that are available for genetics studies, the market for new genetics findings, and the job market for graduate students with degrees in genetics).

• The chair of the Department of Agricultural Economics always sends the message that there are "some opportunities for advances in studies in agricultural economics" (considering the research grants that are available for agricultural economists, the market for new studies in agricultural economics, and the job market for graduate students with degrees in agricultural economics).

• The chair of the Department of Sociology always sends the message that there are "some opportunities for advances in studies in sociology" (considering the research grants that are available for sociologists, the market for new studies in sociology, and the job market for graduate students with degrees in sociology).[20]

Now consider the structures in Figure 5.1. In the first structure, the Department of Entomology and the Department of Genetics are grouped into the College of Natural Science, while the Department of Agricultural Economics and the Department of Sociology are grouped into the College of Social Science. Assume that each dean—the dean of the College of Natural Science and the dean of the College of Social Science—must aggregate the information from the two subordinate departments before passing it up the hierarchy to the provost. Thus, when the Natural Science dean receives the messages that there are "many opportunities for advances in studies in entomology" from the Entomology chair and "many opportunities for advances in studies in genetics" from the Genetics chair, he might plausibly summarize these messages in a memo to the provost, which states that there are "many opportunities for advances in studies in the natural sciences." In contrast, the Social Science dean would receive the messages that there are only "some opportunities for advances in studies in agricultural economics" and "some opportunities for advances in studies in sociology." He might thus summarize these reports in a message to the provost which states that there are only "some opportunities for advances in studies in the social sciences." One conclusion the provost might draw from these two messages is that there is reason to think that by assigning the new development officer to the College of Natural Sciences, she can generate additional revenues for the university; however, fewer improvements are possible in the College of Social Sciences, so the new development official will not be assigned to it.

Now assume that these four departments are organized in a different way (see the second diagram in Figure 5.1): now the College of Agriculture contains the Departments of Entomology and Agricultural Eco-

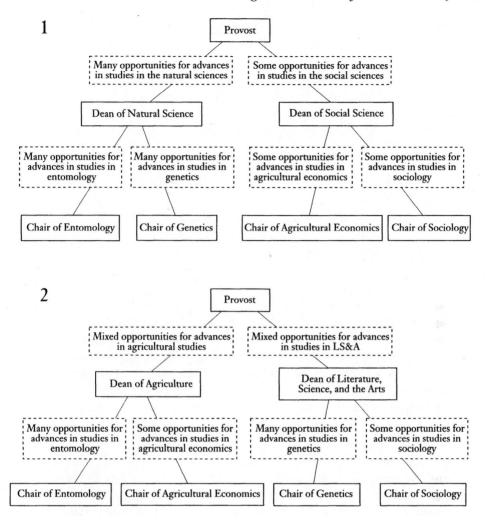

Figure 5.1. How the same information is processed in different ways in two different university structures.

nomics, and the College of Literature, Science, and the Arts (LS&A) contains the Departments of Genetics and Sociology. Assume that the same four department chairs send precisely the same messages as before upward to their deans, who now have the titles of dean of Agriculture and dean of Literature, Science, and the Arts. However, the Agriculture dean is now receiving mixed messages: from the Entomology chair he is receiving the message that there are "many opportunities for advances in studies in entomology," whereas from the Agricultural

Economics chair he is receiving the message that there are only "some opportunities for advances in studies in agricultural economics." Hence, the Agriculture dean might send a message that there are "mixed opportunities for advances in agricultural studies" to the provost. Similarly, the dean of LS&A is now receiving mixed messages as well: from the Genetics chair he is receiving the message that there are "many opportunities for advances in studies of genetics," whereas from the Sociology chair he is receiving a message that there are only "some opportunities for advances in studies in sociology." Hence, the dean of LS&A might send the message that there are "mixed opportunities for advances in studies in LS&A" to the provost.

In this second structure, then, the provost would receive messages that there are "mixed opportunities for advances in agricultural studies" and "mixed opportunities for advances in studies in LS&A." One conclusion she might draw from these ambiguous messages is that there is mixed evidence on whether there are opportunities for advancement in either college. She might then simply decide to retain the new development officer in her own office, and perhaps use this person on other projects not depicted here; meanwhile she could simply monitor the two colleges until more promising opportunities appear in the future.

In sum, it seems plausible to expect that the provost might draw different inferences from the same four messages being processed in the two different kinds of structures. So if the provost is dependent on others (such as the chairs and deans) to summarize and transmit information to her, the structure may affect what information she receives, what inferences she draws about her organization and the outside world, and thus how the organization's problems are framed and defined. In fact, even if precisely the same raw data come up from the bottom, as in our two structures in Figure 5.1, different structures may process and summarize these data in different ways for the administrator. We can summarize this as:

*Proposition 1*: Since different organizational structures may process the same raw data in different ways, the top-level administrator may draw different inferences from the messages sent upward by bottom-level employees.

Indeed, one can easily imagine a structure in which worrisome data never reach the top-level administrator at all. Not being alerted to the existence of a problem, especially in its early stages, allows the problem to grow in significance before its existence is recognized at top levels.

*What Role for Strategic Behavior?*

One noteworthy feature of the preceding analysis is that structure appears to affect information processing, and thus what the top-level administrator learns, even in the absence of self-interested or opportunistic behavior by subordinates. Of course, one can imagine a version of the Figure 5.1 example in which department chairs try to influence what the provost learns by deliberately distorting the information they send her. And one might reasonably guess that the particular kinds of distortions imparted would differ between the two kinds of structures. But even with completely "honest" department chairs who are interested only in what is "good for the university" and who thus attempt to "tell the truth" as they know it, the analysis suggests that biases can be expected in the information processing that is conducted via the hierarchy.[21]


The Advisory Process in University Hierarchies

Even when the top-level administrator does perceive a problem, how to solve it may remain unclear. She may realize that she needs to improve the academic performance of the university, for example, but she may not have specific ideas how to do this. For this reason she may solicit advice from subordinates on what goals the university should pursue—for example, "Should I cut the budget for one kind of academic program and add resources to other kinds of programs?"—and how to pursue them. With their recommendations in hand, she can then make her choices.

The university's structure can be expected to influence this policy-making process in four ways. First, the advice that reaches the top-level administrator will be a function of the university's structure: different structures may provide different sets of options—call them *choice sets*—from which she may choose. Given different choice sets, we can expect the top-level administrator to make different choices, depending in part on how different the choice sets are.

Second, the structure of the university may influence the basic characteristics of the options themselves. That is, *what kinds of options* end up in the top-level administrator's choice set may be influenced by the structure.

Third, the structure may influence what *criteria* the top-level administrator uses to evaluate and compare the options in the choice set. The kinds of options coming to her in one type of structure may suggest particular kinds of criteria by which the options might be evaluated and compared, while the different kinds of options produced by a different type of structure may suggest other kinds of criteria by which the options might be evaluated and compared.

Fourth, the structure will affect what the top-level administrator *learns about how to choose* among these options. Since a particular structure will routinely present a top-level administrator with particular kinds of options, she will, over time, learn more about what is involved in making these particular kinds of choices rather than what is involved in making other kinds of choices.

This section will address each of these matters in turn.

### The Impact of Structure on Choice Sets

For a top-level administrator to plan intelligently requires understanding what opportunities the university's departments and programs provide for advancing her goals for the university. Each top-level administrator with experience in the university will have accumulated a considerable store of knowledge about these opportunities. But since each top-level administrator necessarily follows some particular career path, she thereby gains less experience in some aspects of university life than in others. For this reason, she will be at least somewhat dependent on other employees for advice about how to solve the problems she has identified.

Much of this information and advice will come from lower-ranking subordinates since it is often these subordinates—the deans, program directors, department chairs, faculty members, and even graduate students and department staff members—who will discover and recognize these new opportunities. The subordinates' contribution to strategic planning will then take the form of advice to superiors on how to pursue these opportunities. So when a top-level administrator adopts a new program for the university, or decides to manage some old program in a new way, it is often because a subordinate has suggested this to her.

Now let us consider in detail how the university's structure may influence the set of options made available to the top-level administrator. To give the following illustration some bite (and even poignancy), it will be constructed as a question of promotion and tenure.

Each academic department will have its own standards, expectations, and practices involving promotion and tenure, and universities normally have at least two or more stages of review at higher levels as well (e.g., at the college or school level and at the level of the provost). Of course, a university may establish some minimum expectations that *all* candidates will have to meet. But at any one level of review (e.g., at the level of the department, the college or school, or provost), a tenure decision involving any one candidate may also depend, at least to some degree, on *who else* is being considered for tenure. That is, what the competition is will affect who succeeds and who fails. Thus, how a department is defined (e.g., is it a combined Department of Physics and Astronomy or is the Department of Physics separate from the Department of Astronomy?), and what departments are grouped together into a college or school, can be expected to affect who is on the menu of candidates for tenure at any one level of review.

Moreover, it is rarely the case that if a candidate is turned down for tenure at one level of review, he or she is reinstated for consideration at any of the higher levels. Thus, if how a department or college or school is constructed happens to lead to a negative judgment on one candidate at a relatively low level of review, this candidate is likely to be denied tenure at the provost's level. In contrast, an alternative construction of a department or college or school may allow the candidate's name to remain viable throughout the entire review process.

This all suggests that how the university is organized may affect who gets tenure and who does not. For example, consider the departments and colleges in Figure 5.2; they are the same departments and colleges as in Figure 5.1. In this example, each of the four departments will be assumed to have two candidates for tenure: the Department of Entomology has candidates $s$ and $t$, the Department of Genetics has candidates $u$ and $v$, the Department of Agricultural Economics has candidates $w$ and $x$, and the Department of Sociology has candidates $y$ and $z$. Assume that the chair of each department has authority to recommend no candidate, just one candidate, or both candidates, but to further simplify the example, assume that each chair recommends just one candidate.[22] Each dean will then take the two candidates forwarded by the chairs and (again to simplify) recommend just one to the provost. The provost will then take the two candidates forwarded by the deans and (again to simplify) recommend just one for promotion and tenure to the president and board of trustees; at this last stage, we may plausibly assume that the president and board just rubber-stamp the provost's recommendation, so we will treat the provost's decision as definitive. The question is, which of these eight candidates will receive tenure?

As shown in the list of preference orderings in Figure 5.3, the chair of Entomology judges $s$ to be a stronger candidate than $t$, and so

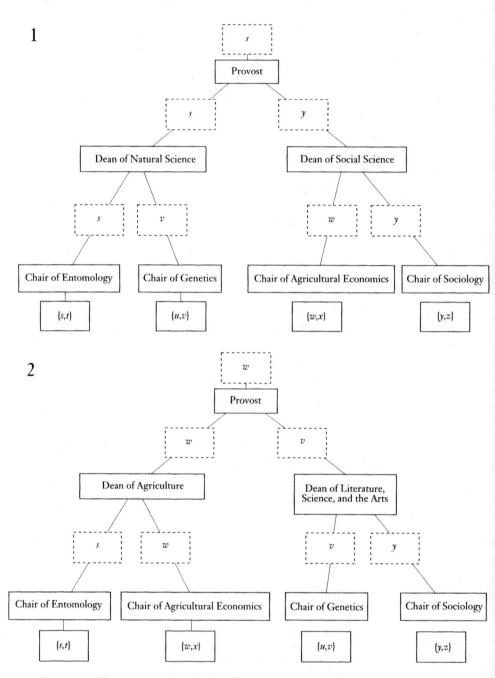

Figure 5.2. How university structure affects tenure decisions.

| Chair of Entomology | Chair of Genetics | Chair of Agricultural Economics | Chair of Sociology | Dean of Natural Science/ Dean of Agriculture | Dean of Social Science/ Dean of LS&A | Provost |
|---|---|---|---|---|---|---|
| $u$ | $z$ | $y$ | $x$ | $u$ | $v$ | $u$ |
| $x$ | $v$ | $t$ | $u$ | $x$ | $x$ | $s$ |
| $v$ | $u$ | $z$ | $s$ | $w$ | $y$ | $w$ |
| $s$ | $y$ | $u$ | $w$ | $s$ | $t$ | $y$ |
| $t$ | $t$ | $v$ | $y$ | $t$ | $u$ | $z$ |
| $w$ | $x$ | $s$ | $z$ | $v$ | $w$ | $v$ |
| $y$ | $s$ | $w$ | $t$ | $z$ | $s$ | $x$ |
| $z$ | $w$ | $x$ | $v$ | $y$ | $z$ | $t$ |

Figure 5.3. Preference orderings of chairs, deans, and provost over tenure candidates.

recommends $s$ to the dean of the College of Natural Science. Similarly, the chair of Genetics judges $v$ to be a stronger candidate than $u$, and so recommends $v$ to the dean of the College of Natural Science. The chair of Agricultural Economics judges $w$ to be a stronger candidate than $x$, and so recommends $w$ to the dean of the College of Social Science. And the chair of Sociology judges $y$ to be a stronger candidate than $z$, and so recommends $y$ to the dean of the College of Social Science.[23]

In the first structure in Figure 5.2, the dean of the College of Natural Science thus gets recommendations of $s$ and $v$ from his subordinate departments, Entomology and Genetics. Since he judges $s$ to be a stronger candidate than $v$, he recommends $s$ to the provost. Similarly, the dean of the College of Social Science gets recommendations of $w$ and $y$ from his subordinate departments, Agricultural Economics and Sociology. Since he judges $y$ to be a stronger candidate than $w$, he recommends $y$ to the provost.

Finally, the deans have created a choice set of $\{s,y\}$ for the provost, so she compares the promotion-and-tenure cases of candidates $s$ and $y$. Judging $s$ to be a stronger candidate than $y$, she decides to recommend candidate $s$ for promotion and tenure.

Now compare what happens to this promotion-and-tenure process in the second structure in Figure 5.2; note that the Entomology and Agricultural Economics Departments are both now in the College of Agriculture and that the Genetics and Sociology Departments are now in the College of Literature, Science, and the Arts. Assume that the same four department chairs make the same four recommendations as before; the chair of Entomology thus recommends $s$ to the dean of Agriculture, the chair of Agricultural Economics recommends $w$ to the dean of

Agriculture, the chair of Genetics recommends $v$ to the dean of LS&A, and the chair of Sociology recommends $y$ to the dean of LS&A.

The dean of the College of Agriculture receives recommendations of $s$ and $w$ from his subordinate departments; considering $w$ to be a stronger candidate than $s$, he recommends $w$ to the provost. Similarly, the dean of the College of LS&A receives recommendations of $v$ and $y$ from his subordinate departments; considering $v$ to be the stronger candidate than $y$, he recommends $v$ to the provost. The provost thus receives a choice set of $\{w,v\}$, and judging $w$ to be the stronger candidate than $v$, she recommends candidate $w$ for promotion and tenure.

Note that the two choice sets for the provost are *completely* different—in the first structure the choice set is $\{s,y\}$, whereas in the second structure the choice set is $\{w,v\}$—so she is virtually forced to make two different decisions in the two different structures.

Thus, despite the fact that the four department chairs made precisely the same four recommendations in each case, the different groupings of the departments into colleges produced completely different choice sets for the provost, and thus produced a completely different choice for tenure. So we can conclude with the following:

*Proposition 2*: Different formal structures can produce different sets of options for consideration by the top-level administrator, and thus can produce different final choices.

While this proposition is phrased in a relatively weak manner, it is actually possible to prove a much stronger result: it is *impossible* to design an organization (see Hammond and Thomas 1989) so that when the structure changes, the outcome is guaranteed not to change. In other words, "neutral hierarchies" cannot exist. It is also important to note that the proof of this result does not depend on any assumptions of self-interest or strategic behavior. Instead, it is the formal structure alone that drives the result, not the characteristics or behavior of the individuals in the structure. Indeed, even if the individual actors are complete automatons, with no conception of self-interest whatsoever, the structure can still affect outcomes.

In fact, not only can the structure, just by itself, have a crucial impact on what the outcome is from these promotion-and-tenure decisions, but the structure can also have an undesirable impact on the overall nature of the outcome. To demonstrate this, assume that the provost, each dean, and each department chair is able to make a judgment about the quality of all eight candidates for tenure: see these administrators' preference orderings in Figure 5.3. Note that all seven administrators prefer candidate $u$ to candidate $s$, the final choice in the first structure of Figure 5.2; all seven administrators also prefer candidate $u$ to candidate $w$, the final choice in the second structure. The reason the inferior candidates—$s$ and $w$—are chosen is that only the chair of Genetics could initially recommend candidate $u$, but his judgment was that candidate $u$ was weaker than candidate $v$; this eliminated candidate $u$ from further consideration. (Candidate $v$ was subsequently eliminated from further consideration by the dean of the College of Natural Science in the first structure and by the dean of the College of LS&A in the second structure.)

In other words, it is possible for the candidate ultimately recommended for promotion and tenure by the provost to be a Pareto-inferior choice; that is, the successful candidate might be judged *worse* than some other particular candidate by *all* administrators in the university. We thus see that departmental jurisdictions, while integral to specialization and decentralization in a university, can nonetheless have some undesirable side effects. In particular, individual specialization and organizational efficiency do not necessarily go hand in hand. So we also have:

*Proposition 3*: Organizational structures with department-specific and college-specific jurisdictions can produce Pareto-inferior choices for the top-level administrator.[24]

While the preceding analysis takes the departments as the basic building blocks for the hierarchy, and takes the department chair as speaking for the department, there is actually considerable variation in the governance structures and committee structures *within* departments.[25] In some departments, the chair makes the key tenure decisions and faculty members primarily play an advisory role; other departments have weak chairs and the important tenure decisions are primarily made by consensus or by some dominant departmental coalition. In the promotion-and-tenure process, then, what a chair reports may primarily reflect his own views, or his report may primarily summarize a broad consensus among the faculty. Quite different departmental recommendations could thus emerge from the same set of faculty members, depending on the departmental governance structure.

And while we are focusing here on the promotion-and-tenure process, the initial hiring process, which generates the candidates who will be considered for promotion and tenure several years hence, might also be affected by the departments' internal structures and incentive systems. For example, a search committee composed of members representing most of the fields in the department may invite a set of candidates that differs substantially from the set of candidates invited by a search committee consisting only of faculty members from just one field.

### The Strategic Provision of Advice

As previously noted, the structure can affect outcomes even if subordinates are not self-interested. Nonetheless, when a top-level administrator is dependent on subordinates for advice, this does give subordinates an opportunity to manipulate her choices by providing advice different from what they truly think is best. In general, we can state:

*Proposition 4*: Each subordinate may be able to improve organizational outcomes for himself by recommending an option different from what he most prefers.

Hammond (1986, 393–398) and Hammond and Horn (1984, 1985) illustrate some ways in which a subordinate in a multilevel hierarchy can improve outcomes for himself by recommending some option other than what he most prefers.

It is interesting to note that strategic behavior by subordinates can actually have a *positive* overall impact on outcomes for the university administrators. In the example in Figures 5.2 and 5.3, it was observed that the candidates recommended for tenure in the two structures— $s$ and $w$—were inferior in every administrator's eyes to candidate $u$, who was nonetheless rejected for tenure. These inferior outcomes can be avoided if at least one official behaves strategically. In the first structure in Figure 5.2, for example, if the chair of the Genetics Department forwards not candidate $v$ but candidate $u$ (whom he judges to be weaker than candidate $v$), then the dean of the College of Natural Science will receive recommendations of candidates $s$ and $u$. Since this dean prefers candidate $u$ to candidate $s$, he forwards candidate $u$ to the provost. The provost's choice set now becomes $\{u,y\}$, and she would choose candidate $u$ over candidate $y$. Thus, the Pareto-inferior choice, $s$, would be avoided here if the chair of the Genetics Department were to behave strategically. And note that the Genetics chair would himself benefit from acting strategically since he prefers candidate $u$ over candidate $s$. Hence, we can conclude that strategic behavior can have virtues not only for the strategizing individual but also for the whole university. For this reason we can advance:

*Proposition 5*: All the administrators may prefer the outcomes from strategic behavior to the outcomes that result when everyone behaves sincerely.

While no method of making social choices is completely immune to this kind of strategic manipulation (see, e.g., Gibbard 1973; Satterthwaite 1975), is it a phenomenon that we should expect to occur with substantial frequency? It is certainly the case that not all situations are ripe for manipulation by subordinates. Instead, how often situations are ripe depends both on the details of the university's advisory process and on the preferences of faculty members, chairs, deans, and provost. Sometimes there is nothing a subordinate can do to improve outcomes for himself by misrepresenting his views. For example, Hammond and Horn (1985) calculated the frequency with which a subordinate in a two-level hierarchy might find it profitable to engage in strategic behavior. The general lesson from this particular model is that strategic behavior is beneficial mostly when there are relatively few subordinates and relatively few options under consideration. In richer and more complex organizational contexts, strategic behavior by any one individual is less likely to be beneficial for that individual.

Moreover, even when a situation is ripe for manipulation, this does not mean that an individual will be able to discover or deduce a good strategy. One prime difficulty here is that strategizing requires accurate information about the likely choices of other actors when they are faced with various different choice sets. This information may not be easy to obtain in a hierarchy, and without it attempts at strategizing may be as likely to hurt the actor as help.

A second difficulty is that even when the necessary information about other actors' preferences is in hand, the calculations needed to use the information can be very complex. This is especially true if many other subordinates are simultaneously also attempting to behave strategically. Each subordinate may have to make some very subtle calculations of precisely how he should modify his advice, given that the advice of others may depend on what he does. This is a much more difficult computational problem than when only one subordinate is acting strategically.[26] Others have reached similar conclusions about the difficulty of calculating strategies. From a laboratory study of strategic manipulation, for example, Burton and Obel (1984, 174) concluded that "it is not obvious how to misrepresent advantageously even if one so desires. That is, an adequate procedural understanding of the process does not necessarily imply that one can game it." We can conclude that department chairs may be unable to determine what the equilibrium outcome would be (i.e., what candidate the provost would end up recommending for tenure), especially if *all* department chairs were to behave strategically in the promotion-and-tenure process. But if this equilibrium outcome cannot be accurately predicted, then this may lead the department chairs and other lower-level administrators to behave in a nonstrategic manner.

### What Kinds of Options?

In the most abstract terms, a budget request from a subordinate to an administrative superior constitutes a set of advice from the subordinate regarding what expenditures the superior should approve. If the budget of a large organization is to be comprehended by some top-level administrator, there must be some aggregation of expenditures. Otherwise the administrator would be inundated by so much detail that it could not be digested. One universal response to this problem is to give the budget a hierarchical structure consisting of nested categories of expenditures.

Of course, these nested categories of expenditures can be defined and grouped together in a wide variety of ways. For example, the budget format could be defined in terms of organizational units, most commonly the departments (each of which would then produce requests for salaries, benefits, and physical materials for itself). Alternatively, the budget format could be defined in terms of line items (such as salaries, benefits, travel, and the huge variety of physical materials ranging from paper for photocopiers to new flooring for the basketball arena to specialty reagents for biochemistry laboratories). Whatever format is adopted, how the administrator thinks about the budget and what the administrator learns about it will be structured, in good part, by what the budget's major categories of expenditures are.

The importance of this budget format can be seen by looking at the format from the viewpoint of what it tells the provost about the organizational units under her. Consider a budget format whose broadest categories are based on the academic units (e.g., the colleges, and the departments within each college): this format would draw the provost's attention to the sizes of, and requests for increases in, the budgets of the academic units. Comparisons of spending options would thus take place in terms of allocations across academic units. If this budget format were the only one available, it would be difficult and time-consuming for the provost to break the budget down and reaggregate the numbers in terms of line items. Her attention would thus be drawn away from questions involving comparisons of the various line-item categories.

In contrast, consider a budget format whose broadest categories are based on line items: this line-item format would draw the provost's attention to the sizes of, and requests for increases in, line items such as salaries, health benefits, travel, physical materials, and so forth. Comparisons of spending options would thus take place in terms of potential allocations across these line-item categories. If this budget format were the only one available, it would be difficult and time-consuming for the provost to break the budget down and reaggregate the numbers in terms of, say, the basic academic units. Her attention would thus be drawn away from questions involving comparisons of the budgets of the departments and colleges.

In other words, dealing with highly aggregated budget categories economizes on the top-level administrator's time and energy, but only at the cost of having the questions she raises, and thus what options can be formulated, structured by those budget categories. Of course, with a capable budget office, she could have the budget requests broken down and reaggregated in a large number of ways; this does happen. And if she somehow knows a priori what questions she would like to ask about proposed expenditures, she may be able to force the units under her to prepare a budget using a format that better suits the production of answers to the kinds of questions that she wants to ask. But she would somehow have to independently develop this understanding of what questions she should ask since the information organized in terms of the current budget format might not supply her with the necessary insights.

Furthermore, what kinds of choices any one administrator can make will be affected by the budget categories. For example, consider our initial observation that Michigan State University has a combined Department of Physics and Astronomy and the University of Michigan has a separate Department of Physics and Department of Astronomy. This suggests that the supervising dean at Michigan State—the dean of the College of Natural Science—will be presented with an aggregated request that combines expenditures for *both* physics and astronomy, whereas the supervising dean at the University of Michigan—the dean of the College of LS&A—will be presented with one request for physics and a separate request for astronomy. At Michigan State, the chair of the Department of Physics and Astronomy will thus play a major role within her own department in determining the balance between allocations to physics-related activities, on the one hand, and to astronomy-related activities, on the other. In contrast, at the University of Michigan it is the dean of LS&A who will play this major role of determining the balance between the allocations that go to the physics-related activities in the Department of Physics and the allocations that go to the astronomy-related activities in the Department of Astronomy. In this case, the chair of the Physics Department will have little impact on the budget for astronomy-related activities, and the chair of the Astronomy Department will have little impact on the budget for physics-related activities.

Similarly, at Michigan State the budget requests from political science, psychology, and sociology will go to the dean of the College of Social Science; the budget requests from mathematics, physics-astronomy, and chemistry will go to the dean of the College of Natural Science; and the budget requests from classical studies, English, and German will go to the dean of the College of Arts and Letters. The requests from the deans of Social Science, Natural Science, and Arts and Letters would then go to the provost for review, comparison, and decision, and it is the provost who would determine the allocations among the three colleges. In contrast, at the University of Michigan the budget requests from *all* of these departments would go to the dean of LS&A, and it would be this dean who would determine the allocations among all the departments. Unlike at Michigan State, then, the provost at the University of Michigan would be less directly involved in all these particular department-versus-department comparisons and allocations; it is the dean of the College of LS&A who would be making the key decisions.

On the other hand, the provosts in both of these universities would get heavily involved in matters involving allocations across the various professional schools (e.g., medicine, business). The reason is that at both universities the provost is the lowest common administrative superior for the professional schools. In general, then, we can state:

*Proposition 6*: Different organizational structures can produce different kinds of options for consideration by the top-level administrator.

### Learning and the Suggestion of Criteria for Choice

Whatever the nature of the choice set given to the top-level administrator (which options, what kind of options), a further aspect of policymaking—how she goes about deciding what advice to accept—can also be influenced by the structure. Choosing among options requires the selection of criteria by which to evaluate and compare the options. The nature of the options in the choice set will suggest *which particular criteria* will be most useful and appropriate for the administrator to use in evaluating and comparing the options.

For example, if budget requests from the College of Natural Science are to be compared by the provost against the budget requests from the College of Social Science, the proposals will tend to have one common denominator—the variable of the natural sciences versus the social sciences. Consideration of proposals in the choice set will thus tend to be conducted in terms of whether the provost expects increased funding for the natural sciences to be more helpful in meeting her goals than increased funding for the social sciences. But if the requests are from the College of Agriculture and the College of LS&A, the competing requests will have a different common denominator—the variable of agricultural benefits versus general disciplinary advancement—for use in making comparisons. In this case, consideration of proposals in the choice set will tend to be conducted in terms of whether the provost thinks that increased service to the agricultural community will be more helpful in meeting her goals than general disciplinary advances in letters, the sciences, and the arts. In either case, only with extra work will the provost be able to analyze a set of budget requests in terms of criteria for comparison that are different from those implied by the budget format, which in turn is likely to reflect the university's organizational structure. This yields:

*Proposition 7*: The organizational structure, and thus the characteristics of the top-level administrator's choice set, suggest some kinds of criteria (primarily *inter*college criteria) rather than other kinds of criteria (such as *intra*college criteria) on which to base comparisons of options.

Finally, since a structure exposes the top-level administrator to some kinds of proposals rather than others, and since some kinds of criteria for comparing proposals are more readily available than others, it seems reasonable to argue that what she *learns* about proposals and how to compare them will also be influenced by the structure. In different structures she will learn different things as she works at making her decisions. A provost at the head of the first kind of structure (involving the Colleges of Natural Science and Social Science) will, over time, become expert at making comparisons and choices among the natural sciences versus the social sciences, but she will learn less about making choices between agriculture and the general academic disciplines. On the other hand, at the head of the second kind of structure (involving the Colleges of Agriculture and LS&A) she would become expert at making comparisons and choices between agriculture and the academic disciplines, but would learn less about making choices between the natural sciences and the social sciences. So we can state:

*Proposition 8*: To the extent that a top-level administrator learns about different kinds of issues by making comparisons among different sets of options, the organizational structure will influence what is learned.

## The Policy Implementation Process in University Hierarchies

Even if a top-level administrator has been able to identify the key problems facing her university, and has been able to choose what response to make, the problem remains that her chosen policy must be *implemented*. It is difficult, however, for the top-level administrator to describe how to implement her chosen policy in such a way that *all* possible contingencies are covered by her instructions. Even if subordinates try in good faith to do what they have been told, unforeseen contingencies will arise for which her initial instructions will prove unclear.

Without clear instructions, subordinates with different responsibilities and concerns will often develop different views on how to solve these unanticipated problems. Since different solutions to these problems will affect how each subordinate does his work (and may also affect what happens to each subordinate's career in the long run), a subordinate may be inclined to press for one kind of solution rather than another.[27]

If subordinates cannot settle their differences of opinion among themselves, higher-level administrators may be called on to resolve them. Students of bureaucracy have occasionally remarked on this conflict-resolution role that administrators must often play. For example, the economist Kenneth Boulding (1964, 48–49) once suggested that

> The hierarchical structure of organizations can largely be interpreted as a device for the resolution of conflicts, with each grade of the hierarchy specializing in resolving the conflicts of the grade beneath it. The very structure of an organization can be regarded as a "constitution," a constitution being defined as a previously agreed method of resolving conflicts which have not yet arisen. We can go even further and argue that virtually all organizational decisions are the end

product of a process of conflict resolution between the points of view of various sections and departments.

Every administrator will thus have responsibility for settling conflicts among the subordinates beneath her. For each administrator, the contents of this class of conflicts will be influenced by the structure: some kinds of conflicts will be routed to the administrator in one kind of structure while other kinds of conflicts will be routed to her in another kind of structure. How the top-level administrator's policies are ultimately implemented will thus depend on the structure, and what the middle- and top-level administrators learn from this conflict-resolution process will also be influenced by the structure.

### Structure and the Routing of Conflicts

To illustrate the impact of the structure on the routing and resolution of conflicts, we will assume that there is substantial interdependence among the bottom-level faculty members and administrators; in effect, how one bottom-level employee does his or her job is presumed to affect how some other bottom-level employees do their jobs. For example, there might be some joint program in which two or more departments are required to carry out a particular task, and they cannot agree on how to do this. Or there might be some common resource that is in short supply, and the departments cannot agree on who gets to use how much. Or it might be that one department's activities impose costs (i.e., negative externalities) on another department and the second department objects to these costs being imposed on it.

When these conflicts cannot be resolved horizontally by the employees directly involved, they may consider referring their conflict upward to their mutual superior for resolution. Several factors affect this decision. For example, employees might sometimes find it in their mutual interest to resolve the conflict themselves. The reason is that the superior who settles the conflict might seem likely to impose a decision that neither employee likes. In this case, the employees would be better off settling their differences and never letting the superior get involved.

However, a horizontal settlement must appeal to *both* employees. If one employee prefers the solution likely to be imposed from above to what could be agreed on horizontally, he will be less likely to agree to a horizontal compromise. In general, then, we can state:

*Proposition 9*: For each employee involved in a conflict, the greater the value of the policy that would be imposed by a superior or superiors, compared to the value of the policy that could be agreed on horizontally, the more desirable it is to refer the conflict upward.

This kind of sophisticated behavior requires, of course, that subordinates be able to guess how their superior or superiors might resolve the conflict.

For her own part, the superior may not want to be drawn into subordinates' disputes: to do so would be time-consuming, might irritate one or both subordinates, and might be politically costly to her career. In general, taking no position at all is sometimes the safest thing to do. So the superior may threaten to impose penalties on subordinates who force her to get involved in their conflicts. Rational subordinates would then be more inclined to settle their own differences. Hence we have:

*Proposition 10*: The greater the penalties associated with referring a conflict upward, the more likely employees will reach a horizontal agreement.

Also affecting the subordinates' decisions to send a conflict upward is the severity of the conflict. An employee who feels especially strongly about some issue may find it worthwhile to risk the possibility of a penalty for bothering his superiors; he may also find it worthwhile to risk an adverse decision from some superior. So we can state:

*Proposition 11*: The greater the severity of conflict between two employees, the greater the probability they will refer their conflict upward for resolution.

If employees have perfect knowledge of each other's preferences as well as how a superior would resolve a conflict, no conflict should ever be referred upward. The reason is that if both parties to the conflict prefer a horizontal settlement to what the superior would impose, the conflict will be settled horizontally. And if at least one employee prefers what the superior would impose to what might be agreed on horizontally, the other employee would realize that he is in a weak strategic position and would agree to a compromise. In either case, a horizontal settlement should be expected. So if a conflict is in fact sent upward, the reason must be due to factors like subordinate misperception of, or uncertainty about, what solution a superior would be likely to impose. In what follows, the assumption is made that these latter conditions generally prevail, so that conflicts are generally sent upward for resolution.

If a conflict is sent upward, it will normally rise no higher than the lowest common superior of the employees involved; a subordinate relatively infrequently appeals a decision over the head of his superior (though appeals are probably made more often in universities than in institutions such as business firms and government agencies). For every pair of subordinates, then, the structure determines who their lowest common superior is. It follows that the grouping of employees in a structure affects how high in the structure the conflict might rise before resolution. Hence we have:

*Proposition 12*: For a conflict that is not horizontally resolved, the structure determines how high the conflict might have to rise before it is resolved by the lowest common superior of the employees involved.

For example, conflicts between department chairs over interdependent activities *within* the same college would normally rise to the level of the college's dean for resolution (e.g., for arbitration, mediation, or decision by fiat). In other cases, this mutual superior will be several levels higher in the structure and may, in fact, be the provost or even the president of the university. Thus, conflicts between department chairs over interdependent activities *between* two or more colleges will normally rise to the level of the provost for resolution.

To illustrate, consider the two structures in Figure 5.1. In the first structure, any conflict between the Entomology Department and the Genetics Department (perhaps over the features of some interdepartmental program on insect genetics) might rise to the dean of the College of Natural Science for resolution. Similarly, a conflict between the Agricultural Economics Department and the Sociology Department (perhaps over the features of some interdepartmental program on rural development) might rise to the dean of the College of Social Science for resolution. However, a conflict between any department in the College of Natural Science and any department in the College of Social Science (such as a conflict between the Entomology and Agricultural Economics Departments, or a conflict between the Genetics and Sociology Departments) would rise to the level of the provost for resolution.

In contrast, several of these conflicts would be handled differently in the second structure. For example, the conflict between the Entomology and Genetics Departments would now rise to the level of the provost for resolution; previously it would have been handled at a lower level, by the dean of the College of Natural Science. Similarly, the conflict between the Agricultural Economics and Sociology Departments would now rise to the level of the provost for resolution; previously, it would have been handled at a lower level, by the dean of the College of Social Science. But the conflict between the Entomology and Agricultural Economics Departments would now be resolved by the dean of Agriculture; previously, it would have been resolved by the provost. And the conflict between the Genetics and Sociology Departments would now be resolved by the dean of LS&A; previously, it also would have been resolved by the provost.

For these reasons, it should be apparent that how subordinates are grouped together in the hierarchy (e.g., how faculty members are grouped together into "departments" or "programs" and how these "departments" or "programs" are grouped together into "schools" or "colleges") can affect how high in the organization any conflict over implementation can be expected to rise. Some structures will resolve the conflict at a low level in the hierarchy, while other structures will route the same conflict all the way to the top. The critical variable is the location of the lowest common superior of the parties to the conflict. If the lowest common superior is a low-level manager, the conflict will be resolved at this low level. But if their lowest common superior is the top-level administrator, the conflict will be routed to the very top of the organization for resolution. We can thus pose the following corollary to proposition 12:

*Proposition 13*: For a conflict that is not horizontally resolved, structures based on some methods of grouping will resolve the conflict at low levels, while structures based on other methods of grouping may route the conflict to higher levels for resolution; the critical variable is the location of the lowest common superior to the parties to the conflict.

Proposition 13 also links questions about different methods of grouping to questions about "centralization" and "decentralization" in a university. If each structure resolves some conflicts at low levels and other conflicts higher up, a change in structure means that some conflicts previously resolved lower down will now be resolved higher up, and vice versa. That is:

*Proposition 14*: To structure an organization so that some kinds of conflicts rise to the top for resolution (i.e., they are "centralized") implies that other kinds of conflicts will be resolved at lower levels (i.e., they will be "decentralized").

Furthermore, it seems reasonable to think that conflicts resolved at lower levels will be resolved in terms of the preferences of the lower-level administrators, while conflicts resolved at higher levels will be resolved in terms of the preferences of the higher-level administrators. In other words, to the extent that the resolution of conflicts involves policymaking (i.e., decisions about precisely how the university's operational tasks are to be carried out), the structure can be expected to influence the university's policies. Hence we have:

*Proposition 15*: If the beliefs and preferences of the administrators at the lower levels are different from those of administrators at the middle and top, the structure will affect how conflicts are resolved and thus will affect what policies the employees in conflict at the bottom are ultimately told to implement.

## Learning from Involvement in Conflict Resolution

Since what a top-level administrator learns stems, in part, from her involvement in subordinates' conflicts, the way conflicts are processed in different kinds of structures has implications for what the top-level administrator learns. We begin by noting the following:

*Proposition 16*: The structure determines which kinds of conflicts come to each administrator for resolution and which do not.

In the first structure in Figure 5.1, for example, by getting involved in conflicts between the College of Natural Science and the College of Social Science, the provost will learn much about the activities of, and conflicts between, these two colleges. She will not learn as much about the activities of, and conflicts between, the different departments within the College of Natural Science or about the activities of, and conflicts between, the different departments within the College of Social Science. In the second structure, on the other hand, by getting involved in conflicts between the College of Agriculture and the College of LS&A, the provost will learn much about the activities and conflicts of these two colleges, but she will not learn as much about the activities and conflicts of the different departments in the College of Agriculture or about the activities and conflicts of the different departments in the College of LS&A.

From this perspective, then, the structure will have a systematic effect on what the top-level administrator learns and about what she remains ignorant:

*Proposition 17*: Because a top-level administrator learns about different kinds of issues in part by resolving conflicts among subordinates, the organizational structure will influence what she learns.


## Prescription and Contradiction in the Design of University Hierarchies

The structure of the university affects what information the top-level administrator sees, and so it affects what problems she perceives and how she defines these problems. It affects what options are made available to her, and it affects the criteria she uses in choosing among the options. Finally, it affects what disputes over implementation come to her for resolution.

Of course, this bottom-up perspective on structure and decision making might be criticized for treating the top-level administrator as an overly passive recipient of whatever the structure brings to her. Rounding out this bottom-up picture, then, requires attention to a more active role the top-level administrator might be able to play; rarely will she be a completely innocent victim of structural arrangements.

Given our bottom-up perspective, the obvious role for the top-level administrator is to design the structure in the first place. While there are probably substantial limits on what kinds of structural changes a top-level administrator can make, at least some kinds of structural changes may be feasible. For example, it may be feasible to split one department into two or more new departments; this may be a sensible strategy if she thinks some critically important scholarly perspectives or opportunities are being submerged within a larger departmental culture that is resistant to change. Alternatively, it may be feasible to aggregate several departments into one or two larger departments. This too may be a sensible strategy if she thinks that each of the original departments has too narrow a scholarly focus and is not aggressively moving into new areas of research; by aggregating the departments, she may be able to create a "critical mass" of certain kinds of faculty members who could influence the new department's direction better than they could as isolated individuals in their original departments.

One example of the latter strategy comes from Trow (forthcoming), who notes that in the 1970s and 1980s the University of California at Berkeley aggregated a large number of separate departments (e.g., Bacteriology, Virology) in the general area of biology, in part because the university was not producing major scientific breakthroughs.[28] The campus had many talented biology faculty members, but since they were distributed among twenty or so separate departments, it was impossible for administrators to create effective incentives for faculty to engage in more breakthrough research taking advantage of newer technologies; the intradepartmental incentive structures (e.g., what was the departmental reward structure, and who would be making the initial tenure decisions?) were difficult to overcome. There clearly existed the *potential* for a critical mass of faculty who wanted to move biological research at the university in different directions, but scattered as they were among numerous small departments, they were unable to exert sufficient influence anywhere, nor were their scattered voices, even in the aggregate, sufficient to overcome the voices of authority arising from the existing departments. The university's response was complex, as Trow makes clear, but one of the changes ultimately involved the aggregation of most of the small biology departments into just four large departments.

A more hypothetical example involves the study of political economy, as discussed earlier in this chapter. One might imagine that in some university as a whole, there is actually a substantial number of political economists, in the Department of Economics, in the Department of Political Science, in the School of Business, in the School of Public Policy, and so forth. But because the political economists are a small minority in each department or school, no chair ever sends a message like "We have a strength in political economy on which we could build," especially since it is all but impossible to build hiring coalitions across departments. Moreover, in hiring and promotions, a candidate who is a good fit for any one department or school will tend to look better on paper than a candidate who cuts across departments or schools; the latter type of candidate will tend not to get hired in the first place and run into trouble when he or she comes up for promotion. Creating a separate department for political economy could avoid at least some of these kinds of problems.

This discussion of strategy has focused on the characteristics of the basic organizational building blocks. What about the larger university structure? The problem here is that even if there is good reason to think that the overall structure affects policymaking, and even if the top-level administrator has the authority to select the structure, it remains unclear what structure she should choose. While the literatures on organizational design and on strategic management do contain some prescriptions, this bottom-up perspective on organizational structure leads to the conclusion that two of the major prescriptions are mutually incompatible. Even more importantly, it also clarifies the nature of the structural choices and trade-offs that this incompatibility poses for the top-level administrator.

At the heart of strategy formulation for a university is the matter of what the top-level administrator and her subordinate administrators *learn* about problems facing the university, about proposals for solving these problems, and about disputes over implementation of the solutions. The argument has already been made that the structure can affect this learning process. In particular, each structure leads the top-level administrator to learn some things and not other things; indeed, learning about some things *implies* not learning about other things. Thus, whatever colleges and departments define the organizational structure for the top-level university administrator, what she learns from this structure can be summarized in the following way:

*Proposition 18:* The orientation, policymaking, and implementation tasks all produce information for the top-level administrator relevant to *intercollege* perspectives, comparisons, and conflicts. Maintenance of the current structure is thus equivalent to a decision that she will remain ignorant about *intracollege* perspectives, comparisons, and conflicts.

Indeed, one might wonder if some top-level university administrators become prisoners of their university's structures, in the sense that while the outside world may change in significant ways, the internal information flows involving the orientation, advising, and implementation processes may not adequately reflect these external changes. This situation may, over time, produce increasingly dysfunctional decisions. Thus, instead of "structure following strategy," as Chandler (1962) recommended for the corporation, it may be that "strategy follows structure," which has potentially dire consequences for the university if the structure prevents top-level administrators from learning about problems that need to be solved.

If structure systematically affects what the top-level administrator learns and about what she remains ignorant, the key structural design question then becomes, What should the top-level administrator learn and about what should she remain ignorant?

One common prescription found in the strategic management literature on corporations, beginning with Chandler 1962, advances a prescription directly relevant to this question: since the top-level administrator's primary responsibility is to address the key strategic issues facing her university, it follows that she should design a structure that makes her as well informed as possible about the key strategic decisions she needs to make. If she believes that some decisions for her university are more critical than others, and if she wants to be the person who makes these critical decisions, then each possible structure should be evaluated in terms of the extent to which it brings to her what she needs to learn—the information, advice, and conflicts—so that she can effectively make these critical decisions. But how should she do this?

At this point a second common prescription might seem to be relevant. This prescription, advanced by the contingency theory and organizational design literatures, is to "match" the structure to the categories used to classify the objects or activities in the organization's environment: each important category of the environment should be assigned its own division or department within the university, presumably headed by its own administrator. A good "fit" between structure and environment, it is argued, will enhance the university's performance in the environment. In thinking about strategic issues for her university, the top-level administrator might thus create a set of organizational units and subunits (such as "departments" and "colleges") that match the most important categories in the environment. For example, these categories might correspond to the separate "markets" for the university's products (e.g., those who hire its students) or to important political constituencies of the university (e.g., the agricultural community in the state) or to the different governmental bodies that are important sources of government funding for the university (e.g., to the state legislature, or to federal funding agencies).

Moreover, by grouping together the activities that are most relevant to each critical category of the environment, the transaction costs of the administrators responsible for managing these critical programs will be minimized. That is, all the activities that must go on in order for any one organizational subunit to be successful in terms of that particular environmental category will be contained *within* the realm of authority and responsibility of that subunit's administrator.

But now assume—not unreasonably—that some organizational subunit contains activities that are more important for the university's survival than the activities in the other subunits. It would thus seem that the top-level administrator's strategic management responsibilities require her to be exposed to detailed information regarding the nature of these critical activities. However, a conflict between the "matching prescription" and the "strategic management prescription" now becomes clear: a structure whose subunits match those of the university's environment will cut the top-level administrator off from crucial sources of information, advice, and conflicts from *within* this subunit of greatest strategic interest to her. If there is a single consumer of the university's products (its students or its research) or some key government institutions, then it is the top-level administrator's *subordinate* (e.g., the program's administrator) who will deal with this most critical contingency and who will end up making the most critical decisions regarding the program's design and management; the top-level administrator will not be making these decisions herself. That is, the top-level administrator will not be able to perform the major role that the strategic management literature assigns to her, which is to make the most critical strategic decisions. This top-level administrator may decide *that* some critical decision will or should be made, but it will be the administrator's subordinate who actually makes the decision.

Ironically, then, it is only if the top-level administrator wants *someone else* in her university to become most knowledgeable about the most critical categories of the environment that she should select an organizational structure whose categories match those of the environment. If the categories embodied in the university's structure correspond to the categories of the environment, this means that the top-level administrator will remain relatively ignorant about what is going on *within* each category, including the most critical one. So it turns out that the strategic management prescription regarding proper structural design may directly contradict the matching prescription. That is, we now have:

*Proposition 19*: If the top-level administrator is to be well informed about the most critical category in her university's environment, the categories on which the university is structured should *cut across* the categories used for classifying (and matching) key elements of the university's environment.

It may only be in this fashion that the top-level administrator can design a structure which enables her to fulfill some of her most important strategic management responsibilities.

This argument also suggests that the prescriptions of transaction-cost minimization (see, e.g., Williamson 1985) may be incompatible with the continuing involvement of the top-level administrator in what she considers the university's most critical issues. In a structure that places interdependent academic units within the same department or college, so as to make it administratively easy for faculty members and administrators to work with each other in the design and management of some program, the top-level administrator might be able to play a strategic role in deciding *that* her university would do whatever the program is intended to do, and thus that there should be a department or college that does this. However, she would be unable to have nearly as much say in determining the particular features of the program that is ultimately designed and implemented; the selection of the program's features, and the making of trade-offs among the features, would largely be determined *within* the department or college. But if it is the particular mix of features and trade-offs that will determine the program's ultimate success, then she has, in effect, delegated that decision to others—she is entrusting to others (abdicating?) what may be her own strategic responsibility.

In other words, for all the undoubted costs of a structure that imposes a heavy burden of coordination on the university's top-level administrators, this structure would nonetheless provide the top-level administrator with an institutionalized opportunity to learn a great deal about the nature of her university's most critical products or activities, and thereby play a direct role in their definition and ultimate success. To choose a structure that makes it easiest for program administrators and faculty members to work with each other (i.e., which minimizes *their* transaction costs) is equivalent to cutting the top-level administrator off from intracategory debates about what should be the key characteristics of these critical activities; that is, this structure would maximize her transaction costs in finding out what she needs to know.

Moreover, while a structure that minimizes the transaction costs of the key program's administrators may enhance the top-level administrator's ability to judge the relative success of the program, compared to the success of other university programs (as the product-line organization is said to do for corporations—again, see Chandler 1962), this structural form tends to cut her off from information about *why* the various programs might have different success rates, and it does not put her in a position to learn what to do about any poorly performing programs.

In sum, it may be accurate to say that each possible structure reduces some administrators' transaction costs while increasing the transaction costs of other administrators. It follows that structural design may hinge on the question of whether the top-level administrator's transaction costs are more important, or less important, than those of her subordinates. Unfortunately, it is not yet clear whose transaction costs it is most important for the university to minimize.

While this analysis suggests that the top-level administrator faces an either-or choice of structural forms (e.g., should she minimize her own transaction costs or someone else's?), she may appear to have somewhat more flexibility than this; she may, for example, convene various kinds of committees whose members are selectively drawn from the departments on the basis of some common interest, concern, or perspective that may not be adequately represented by the department chairs. One can imagine committees on the status of women (consisting of women faculty members drawn from a wide variety of departments), or on the status of various kinds of minorities (consisting of minority faculty members drawn from a wide variety of departments), or on any of a large number of issues in which the top-level administrator may be interested but which the existing department-and-college structure is not representing very clearly or effectively. These kinds of committees, which institutionalize a viewpoint that is explicitly intended to cross-cut the existing departmental and college structure, can be a very useful device for informing the top-level administrator and providing her with options for choice and action which might otherwise never reach her level.

However, such a cross-cutting structure imposes two different kinds of costs on the top-level administrator. One kind of cost is that by bypassing the department chairs and the deans of the colleges, the top-level administrator may risk losing their support, especially if she frequently accepts advice from the committees that runs contrary to the interests of the chairs and deans. A second kind of cost is that these committees further increase the demands on the top-level administrator's time and energy: she must meet with them and listen to their advice. In either case, her transaction costs—the costs of what she must do to find out what she wants to know—will be further increased.

The overall thrust of these arguments is that the structural design of a university involves choices among imperfect, even unpalatable, alternatives: trade-offs have to be made. While the bottom-up approach advanced here cannot, by itself, tell a top-level administrator how to make the trade-offs, this approach to the formal structure of the university does suggest some ways of clarifying what the costs and benefits of each kind of structure might be. The approach may thus help in clarifying our understanding of the nature of the structural choices that a top-level administrator may face. It is only when the nature of the alternatives is better understood that an adequate theory of structural choice can be developed for the university.

Conclusion

In this chapter I have discussed a variety of ways in which the formal structures of American research universities might affect the universities' decision-making processes and outcomes. A university's formal structure, I am conjecturing, has extensive and systemic effects on what problems are perceived and how they are defined (the orientation process), on what options are made available for choice (the advisory process), and on how conflicts over the final choice are resolved (the implementation process). I am also conjecturing that by aggregating information in different ways, by presenting different kinds of options for choice, and by routing some kinds of conflicts but not others to the top-level administrator, the formal structure has an important impact on what the top-level administrator learns. Finally, I have suggested that organizational design necessarily involves trade-offs between strategic goal setting and involvement in the details of how any one strategic goal is pursued: no formal structure will easily allow the top-level administrator to do both herself.

There do exist some factors that are likely to dampen the impact and importance of the formal structure. For example, top-level administrators with a long history in a particular university will have had many opportunities over the years to learn about each department and program; hence, the formal structure may have a much smaller impact on this administrator's choices. In contrast, the formal structure may have a much greater impact on a top-level administrator who is new to the particular university or even new to higher education in general.

In addition, I have simply assumed the information the president, provost, and deans receive comes only from subordinates. However, it is undoubtedly the case that these administrators receive considerable information from outside the university, which may mean that the formal structure will have had relatively little filtering or aggregating impact on what these officials learn from these external sources. Nonetheless, unless the internally generated information is completely ignored by these top-level administrators, it seems reasonable to think that the internal structure might continue to play at least some role (albeit perhaps attenuated in some considerable degree for some kinds of problems). Only if the external information flows were to completely counteract the internal information flows would the structure be completely irrelevant, and for at least some important issues (such as tenure decisions and internal budgetary allocations) it seems unlikely that there will be external sources of information that would be able to play this counteracting role.

For these kinds of reasons, then, how much impact any given kind of structure actually has on any university's decision-making processes and outcomes is an empirical matter, as is the question of whether different kinds of structures in different universities actually lead to the different kinds of decision-making processes and outcomes that are hypothesized here. But by laying out a broad and reasonably coherent set of concepts and arguments about the possible impacts of formal structures, I hope to have put other researchers in a better position to conduct rigorous empirical investigations of these important matters.

# CHAPTER SIX

# Tiebout Competition versus Political Competition on a University Campus
## John Douglas Wilson

In an attempt to make their operations more efficient, large organizations can divide into units that engage in various forms of competition with each other. This competition can occur within private
firms or the public sector. For example, Tiebout's (1956) hypothesis
asserts that competition for households among local governments leads
to the efficient provision of public goods. In recent years, some universities in the United States have implemented a decentralized budgeting process called responsibility center management (RCM), under
which different academic units are induced to compete for students. In
its purest form, RCM essentially allows these units to keep the revenue
that they generate, but they must finance the costs of their operations
and pay fees to finance certain public goods, such as the library. Tuition
rates are set centrally, leaving units to compete for students by choosing the attributes of their educational services.[1] This system is similar
to a form of Tiebout competition where taxes are centrally set and local-
ities use their public expenditure policies to compete for households.
It is unlikely to satisfy the conditions required for an efficient Tiebout
equilibrium, but alternative methods of allocating resources can also be
expected to exhibit inefficiencies.

I have benefited from comments by Ronald Ehrenberg, Michael Waldman, and other
participants in the Cornell Higher Education Research Institute conference, "Governance
of Higher Education Institutions and Systems," and from comments by John Goddeeris.

This chapter compares the RCM method of decentralized budgeting with a form of centralized budgeting. In both cases, the issue is how to allocate resources across academic units, which are interpreted as schools or colleges within the university (rather than individual departments). In general, units can compete for several sources of revenue under RCM, including tuition revenue, alumni contributions, and research grants. In the case of a state university, units are also provided with a fixed share of the state appropriations, but most of my discussion will also apply to private universities. I focus on competition for undergraduate tuition revenue, thereby treating as exogenous the other revenue sources.

A purported strength of RCM is its visibility and simplicity as a resource allocation mechanism. Units are compensated for supplying credit hours, but this compensation does not vary to accurately reflect differences in the costs of these credit hours. To capture this simplicity, I assume that units are provided with a fixed fee per credit hour, which is the same for all credit hours and does not vary with the types of students taking the credit hours.[2] They may also receive a fixed base allocation. In general, this allocation may differ across units, allowing the central administration to distribute resources across units while utilizing the fixed compensation rate to elicit competition among units. Later in the chapter, I consider competition among units that differ in size, but to make my points most simply, the basic model assumes no asymmetries between units.

It would be easy to show that centralized budgeting is superior to RCM, simply by positing a central authority with the appropriate objectives, complete information, and the tools needed to take advantage of this information. However, this is not the position in which university administrators find themselves. Indeed, I am reminded of the comment by a former assistant dean that the position of department chair is preferable to anything in the dean's office, because department chairs have a greater ability to get things done. More generally, the importance of consensus building on a university campus is widely recognized, suggesting severe limitations on the power of central administrations. Accordingly, I construct a model in which a sizable amount of bargaining power resides with the academic units, rather than with the central administration, or "center." In other words, "Tiebout competition" is replaced by "political competition." The formal model assumes that the units present the center with proposed "budget schedules," which indicate how different levels of funding will be utilized. The center then compares the budget schedules of the different units and chooses how to allocate funds. It is the ability of the units to commit to these budget schedules that gives them a sizable amount of influence. On the other hand, the units are still competing among themselves for funds, which serves to limit this influence.

Despite this rather inefficient form of centralized budgeting, I find that it provides more powerful incentives for units to deliver educational services than RCM. The basic argument is presented in a nontechnical way in the next section, and the following section provides the formal proof. Another section discusses a variety of extensions of the analysis,[3] followed by a section that outlines an alternative view of RCM that may put it in a more favorable light.

## The Model and Basic Argument

In this section, I sketch a simple model and use it to provide the basic argument behind my comparison of centralized and decentralized budgeting, leaving details to the next section. The main idea will be that decentralized budgeting in the form of RCM insufficiently rewards the units on a university campus for improvements in their educational offerings. Under the form of centralized budgeting modeled here, the interaction between the center and units implies a system of rewards that places greater weight on such improvements.

The model, or illustrative example, consists of two units in a university, say, business and arts and sciences, which compete over a heterogeneous group of students. I assume a fixed number of students, but I later argue that the analysis can be extended to a variable student population, where each unit seeks to attract students who would either enroll in the other unit or undertake some alternative activity outside the university. For now, one may suppose that the admissions office has chosen how many students to admit, along with their attributes, and the units are competing for these students.

Students differ in their preferences about where to enroll. These preferences do not depend on tuition considerations, because the center collects a common tuition payment, regardless of where students enroll. Instead, each unit can influence enrollment decisions only by changing the "quality" of its educational offerings. Of course, student motivations are complex, and many of the attributes of a unit's educational offerings cannot be ranked from best to worst, from the viewpoint of all students. Some of these complications are discussed later, but for purposes of the basic argument, it is useful to consider a simple quality-competition game between the two units. In addition, I assume that each student completes all of his or her academic requirements within the chosen unit. To avoid distinguishing between credit hours and students, I assume that these academic requirements include a fixed number of credit hours. The formal model assumes that these credit hours are supplied at a constant cost per credit hour. There may also exist various fixed costs to operating the unit over the period of time under consideration, but they do not influence a unit's decisions and may therefore be ignored.

Following a typical RCM system, the central administration, or center, compensates units at a fixed rate per student, denoted $r$. The total amount of compensation provided in this way is assumed not to exceed the university's total tuition revenue. In other words, the university is not allowed to increase incentives to attract students without bound, simply by raising the compensation rate and financing it with fixed "taxes" on the units. This assumption accords with the practice of not distributing all tuition revenue in the form of the compensation rate, but rather withholding some funds for discretionary use by the center. Various fees may be collected from the units to pay for any costs that the unit imposes on the university as a whole (e.g., the university library), and the unit may also receive a fixed base allocation. But the units are assumed to be unable to influence the size of these transfers. Rather, the units respond to the incentives created by the compensation rate per student. With tuition rates beyond the control of units, this response takes the form of quality competition. In the language of game theory, the two units engage in a Nash game, with quality levels serving as the strategy variables, and a Nash equilibrium is reached when each unit's quality level is its most preferred, given the other unit's quality level. The formal model focuses on symmetric equilibria, where units pursue identical strategies because they face the same cost structures and student demands for their educational services. But the basic insights from this analysis hold more generally.

To determine what is most preferred, we need to specify a unit's objective. On a university campus, objectives are far from straightforward, owing to constraints on the ability of decision makers within units (e.g., deans) to distribute excess revenue to themselves and other members of the unit. Such constraints may be beneficial, but I leave this issue to later discussion and simply assume for now that a unit's objective is to maximize the excess of revenue over the minimum costs needed to provide educational services. In short, units seek to maximize "profits."[4] In the subsequent analysis, I shall sometimes refer to these profits as wasteful, in the sense that students could be provided with the same educational services at a lower cost.

The main conclusion that falls out of this model of RCM is that educational quality is inefficiently low in equilibrium. In other words, incentives to increase quality are not strong enough. The source of the inefficiency is a unit's need to raise quality to attract additional students. The unit keeps increasing quality to the point where the cost of attracting another student (or small group of students) equals the compensation received for this additional student. Increasing quality beyond this point would not be profitable and is therefore not undertaken. This marginal cost consists of two components. First, there is the cost of providing educational services with the prevailing quality to the additional student. I call this component the "social marginal cost," because it involves the use of labor and other inputs that are costly from the viewpoint of the economy as a whole. The second component consists of the increase in educational quality needed to attract the additional student. Since all students in a unit receive the same quality, this quality improvement increases the average cost of educating all students in the unit.[5] This is part of the unit's "private marginal cost," but it is not a social cost from the viewpoint of the entire economy, because it is offset by the benefits students receive from the quality improvement. As a result, the unit uses too high a value for the cost of educating an additional student, from the viewpoint of economic efficiency. By setting the private marginal cost equal to the compensation rate, it expands quality to the point where the social marginal cost still lies below the compensation rate. The level of profits in equilibrium depends on the extent to which fixed costs and any fees paid to the center eat into the earnings generated by this discrepancy, but there is no reason to expect these profits to disappear. In any case, we shall see that the discrepancy is reduced under centralized budgeting, thereby reducing any wasteful profits that do exist.

This inefficiency would not exist if units were perfectly competitive. As defined by economists, perfect competition would mean that the university consisted of many small units, each of which would have access to as many students as desired as long as it offered a particular quality level, namely, the one these students could obtain elsewhere. In other words, each unit would face a perfectly elastic supply of students. Since no unit would need to raise quality to obtain more students, the private and social marginal costs would be identical, as just defined. In equilibrium, quality levels would now be bid up to the point where the social (and private) marginal cost equaled the compensation rate, $r$, since only then would a unit be indifferent about attracting another student. If the center were also using $r$ as the tuition rate and setting it to efficiently control admission into the university, students would then enter the university until the marginal student's willingness to pay for education equaled the actual payment, $r$, and therefore equaled the social marginal cost of this education. In other words, students would enter the university until the marginal benefit equaled the social marginal cost, which is the classic condition for the efficient use of a facility. In the current case, the marginal benefit may exceed $r$, owing to non-price rationing associated with admissions standards, but we have seen that $r$ exceeds the social marginal cost. In other words, the marginal benefit exceeds the social marginal cost, implying that education is underprovided.[6]

The source of this imperfectness in competition is too few units chasing too many types of students. In models of local government behavior, or "Tiebout models," households sort themselves across communities so that each community contains a single type of household and can therefore tailor its taxes and public expenditure programs to the particular preferences of this type. In the present case, many types of students enroll in the same unit, and the unit has "market power" because some of these types strictly prefer to be there rather than in another unit. Expanding the number of units beyond two cannot be expected to eliminate this source market power, given the diversity of students that typically characterizes a university campus. The situation is somewhat exaggerated in the current model, because a unit does not offer different educational programs to different types of students, but the model does capture the reality that educational programs can never be perfectly tailored to each student's abilities and preferences.

This analysis points to the limitations of a budgeting system that rewards units based on the number of students taught, without consideration for how they are taught. In the current model, a unit is receiving additional funds when it teaches additional students, but there is no compensation for the fact that existing students are being made better off as a result of the quality improvements undertaken to attract these new students. As a result, education is underprovided.

Turn now to centralized budgeting, under which the central administration allocates resources across units. As noted in the introduction, we should recognize the limitations faced by administrators, including informational asymmetries and the relatively nonhierarchical command structures of universities. I next describe a model along these lines and argue that RCM is still inferior to central control of the budget.

The model retains the assumptions in the RCM model, except that the units now engage in what might be called "political competition," rather than competition for students.[7] Simply stated, they attempt to convince the center that they deserve a sizable share of the budget. This convincing consists of essentially bidding for funds by offering to deliver educational services in return for a funding level. In particular, each unit provides the center with a budget schedule, giving the relation between educational services and the funds the unit will need to provide these services. The center then chooses its budget allocation, and the units deliver the educational services dictated by their budget schedules. Students once again enroll in their most preferred units, and these choices must be consistent with the allocation of educational services. In the formal model, a unit's total supply of educational services is calculated by multiplying a measure of the quality of these services by the number of students enrolled in the unit.

I argue in the next section that each unit presents the center with a budget schedule under which the unit wastes a fixed amount of its budget, independently of the size of the budget provided by the center. In other words, an increase in the funding it receives from the center is spent on providing educational services at minimum cost, not on generating additional profits. In symbols, the budget schedules for the two units, A and B, take the following form:

$$b_A = \alpha E_A + K_A \quad \text{and} \quad b_B = \alpha E_B + K_B, \tag{1}$$

where $b_A$ is the center's chosen level of funding for unit A, or "budget," $E_A$ is its educational services that A then delivers in return for this funding, $\alpha$ is the minimum (variable) cost of each unit of these services, $K_A$ is a fixed payment that represents the money left over to finance any fixed costs (which do not depend on the level of education services) and provide profits, and the variables for unit B are similarly described. To maintain consistency with the RCM model, I continue to assume that a unit's objective is to maximize profits, which is equivalent to maximizing $K_A$ for unit A and $K_B$ for unit B.[8]

The units again engage in a Nash game, except that now their strategies are the budget schedules that they present to the center. Given the form of the budget schedules described earlier, the units are effectively competing through their choices of $K_A$ and $K_B$. The center's subsequent choice of a budget allocation is made with the goal of maximizing the total well-being of students, which depends on both the quality of educational services and the allocation of students across units (given their preferences for the two units). Thus, I am asking how well centralized budgeting can perform in delivering education to students, if this delivery is indeed the goal of the central administration. Centralized budgeting could obviously be made to look as bad as desired, simply by giving the center bad objectives. The current strategy is to ask whether centralization can perform better than RCM in delivering educational services, if the center does have student welfare as its objective. A separate issue is how to design incentives to induce the center to behave in a desirable way. The issue of other desirable objectives, including research activities, is addressed later. Note, finally, that my welfare comparison between RCM and centralized budgeting is using the students' own assessments of the quality of educational services. Thus, I am not viewing the center or units as being assigned the task of correcting the flawed choices made by students. The assertion that students don't know or do what is good for them provides an obvious argument against RCM, since an active central administration could exercise more control over student choices. The current chapter provides a case against RCM even without this argument.

Given the timing of events, I am granting the units a lot of power in their relation with the center; they effectively possess a first-mover advantage, in the sense that they are able to commit to their budget schedules before the center makes its budget decision. Nevertheless, in the case where the same level of funds is being competed over under RCM and centralized budgeting, I find that students are better off in the latter case. In this sense, moving to centralized budgeting reduces the wasteful use of educational resources. The proof relies on technical results from the theory of "common agency," which refers to cases where multiple agents (the units) attempt to influence the behavior of a single agent (the center).[9] But at least some rough intuition can be attempted here.

As noted earlier, the reason for inefficiencies in the RCM model is the imperfect competition associated with a small number of units competing for many types of students. In particular, quality levels are set below the levels that perfectly competitive units would choose. Similarly, imperfectly competitive private firms that sell a good at a single unit price usually supply an inefficiently low amount of this good, in an attempt to drive up the price. It is well known, however, that this inefficiency could be eliminated if these firms were able to perfectly price discriminate, selling each unit of the good at a different price, namely, the maximum price that consumers are willing to pay for each unit. In this case, supply would be expanded to the point where the price of the next unit equaled the cost of the next unit, which is the necessary efficiency condition.

Under centralized budgeting, something akin to perfect price discrimination is also occurring. At the margin, each unit is offering to "sell" another increment of educational services to the center in return for additional funds equal to the true cost of these services. In other words, the provision of additional services is generating no additional profits for the unit. This is what the budget schedules described by equation 1 are telling us. The units are able to generate positive profits, however, by collecting fixed payments from the center (denoted $K_A$ and $K_B$ in equation 1). In equilibrium, each unit is able to take advantage of its bargaining power by setting this payment at a level that makes the center indifferent between funding this unit and instead letting the other unit teach all of the students. Given that the center's concerns are with the well-being of students, it is willing to pay an amount equal to the welfare loss that students would experience if all of them had to enroll in the other unit. In other words, the payments are capturing the surplus benefit that students receive in their chosen units.

Thus, we have a situation that is similar to perfect price discrimination by a monopolist. Each unit is effectively selling its last unit of educational services at its true social cost. Recall, in contrast, that units under RCM bear the costs associated with raising the quality of these services to attract additional students, but are compensated only for these students, not the higher quality. Put simply, education is being efficiently priced at the margin in the centralized case, not under RCM. There may still exist waste in the form of excess profits going to units, but the use of efficient prices lowers it.

## The Formal Analysis

I now fill in some details for the models just described and provide the mathematical derivations of the results.

Consider first the RCM model. As already described, a heterogeneous group of students choose between two units, A and B. The total number of students is fixed for now, and a student's only decision is whether to enroll in unit A or unit B. With the center setting the same tuition rate for both units, students base their choices on the relative attractiveness of the educational offerings in the two units. The units control the levels of educational quality that students receive, denoted

$e_A$ and $e_B$. A type-$s$ student places a value of $e_A + 1 - s$ on an education from unit A and $e_B + s$ on an education from unit B.[10] The "preference level," $s$, is an innate attribute of students that varies between zero and one and measures the relative attractiveness of unit B over unit A. For simplicity, I use the approximation of a continuum of students, with $s$ treated as a continuous variable. Thus, students divide themselves across units, so that the marginal student possesses a preference level, $s^o$, that leaves him or her indifferent between units. In symbols,

$$e_A + 1 - s^o = e_B + s^o. \tag{2}$$

All students with preference levels below $s^o$ prefer to enroll in unit A, while those with levels above $s^o$ prefer B. For simplicity, I assume that students are uniformly distributed across preference levels, meaning that an equal number of students possess each preference level. Thus, $s^o$ represents the fraction of students enrolled in unit A, and $1 - s^o$ is the fraction in B. The assumption of a uniform distribution enables us to consider symmetric equilibria, where each unit chooses the same quality level.[11]

Under RCM, the center compensates units at a fixed rate per student, $r$, and the total compensation is $r(N_A + N_B)$, where $N_i$ is unit $i$'s enrollment level ($i = A, B$). As discussed earlier, each unit is assumed to treat as fixed any additional revenue that is distributed to it by the center.[12] Thus, any such revenue is irrelevant for a unit's choice problem. Costs depend positively on both the quality level and the number of enrolled students. In accordance with the constant-cost assumption in the previous section, the variable costs of educational services take the form $\alpha e_i N_i$, where $e_i N_i$ represents total educational services, and $\alpha$ is the minimum cost of a unit of services.[13] Subtracting these costs from revenue gives the profit expression that the unit seeks to maximize, $(r - \alpha e_i)N_i$.[14]

The variables $e_A$ and $e_B$ are the strategy variables in the Nash game under consideration. In equilibrium, unit $i$ chooses $e_i$ to maximize profits, given the other unit's chosen quality level. At the optimum, $e_i$ is set where the rise in $e_i$ needed to attract another student has a zero first-order impact on profits. Using calculus notation, the first-order condition is

$$r - \left( \alpha e_i + \alpha \frac{de_i}{dN_i} N_i \right) = 0, \tag{3}$$

where the derivative $de_i/dN_i$ represents the increase in $e_i$ needed to attract another student. The term in parentheses is the private marginal cost, as described in the previous section. Without loss of generality, let us normalize the total number of students to equal one. Then $N_A = s^o$, and differentiation of equation 2 gives $de_i/dN_i = 2$. Given the symmetry of the model, both units choose the same quality levels and split the student population between themselves. Thus, $N_i = \frac{1}{2}$. Substituting these equalities into equation 3 and rearranging then gives

$$e_i = \frac{r}{\alpha} - 1. \tag{4}$$

As discussed in the previous section, the excess of $r$ over $\alpha e_i$ represents the excess of the private marginal cost of a student over the social marginal cost. In the case of perfect competition, units would be able to attract as many students as desired by offering the quality level provided by other units to similar students. As a result, quality levels would be bid up to the point where each unit was indifferent about attracting additional students, or where $r = \alpha e_i$.

Turning to centralized budgeting, let us assume that the two units compete over a budget equal in size to the total compensation level under RCM, $r(N_A + N_B)$, again with the goal of maximizing profits. This comparison isolates differences in incentives from variations in the budgets that are up for grabs. As previously described, each unit offers the center a budget schedule described by equation 1, with educational services, $E_i$, now measured by $e_i N_i$. The explanation for this form of the budget schedule comes from the theory of common agency. First, common-agency problems have been found to possess a critical property, which in this case concerns the budget schedules: they satisfy a condition that may be called "local truthfulness." In particular, the additional funding that a unit demands in return for a small increase in its educational services from the equilibrium level leaves the unit indifferent about this increase. Since $\alpha$ is the cost of a unit of services, it follows that the budget schedules require the payment of $\alpha$ in return for another unit of services.

The common-agency literature has argued that reasonable strategies possess an even stronger property, "global truthfulness."[15] In the present case, this means that large changes in a unit's educational services result in budget changes that also leave the unit as well off as before. In particular, the unit requires a payment of $\alpha \Delta E_i$ in return for $\Delta E_i$ units of additional educational services. The budget schedules given by equation 1 possess this property.

Given these budget schedules, the two units are effectively playing a Nash game in their required profit levels, which are determined through their choice of the payments $K_A$ and $K_B$ in equation 1. Budget schedules are first presented to the center, and then the center chooses a budget allocation, which determines $E_A$ and $E_B$. Students then allocate themselves across units so that each student is enrolled in his or her most preferred unit, and the enrollment and quality levels are consistent with the chosen levels of $E_A$ and $E_B$. I again consider a symmetric equilibrium, where the center allocates funds equally between the two units. Again relying on agency theory, we can determine the common value of $K_A$ and $K_B$ in this equilibrium by noting that unit A raises $K_A$ until the center is exactly indifferent between providing funds to the unit and instead funding only unit B (according to its budget schedule). To calculate this $K_A$, recall that the center cares only about the total well-being of students. This well-being is measured by integrating (or "summing") $e_A + (1 - s)$ over all students in A and $e_B + s$ over all students in B (noting that $N_A + N_B = 1$ under our normalization):

$$W = e_A N_A + \int_0^{N_A} (1-s)ds + e_B(1 - N_A) + \int_{N_A}^1 sds. \tag{5}$$

Performing the integration yields the following expression for total welfare:

$$W = e_A N_A + e_B(1 - N_A) + N_A - N_A^2 + \frac{1}{2}. \tag{6}$$

With both units offering the same quality levels in a symmetric equilibrium, it is clear that $N_A$ must equal $\frac{1}{2}$ for this expression to be maximized, which is the case in the equilibrium. Starting from this equilibrium, if we then reduce $N_A$ to zero by moving all students to B, this expression falls by an amount equal to $\frac{1}{4}$ (which is the value of $N_A - N_A^2$ at $N_A = \frac{1}{2}$). Thus, the center can keep $W$ from changing only if it possesses the funds necessary to raise $e_B$ by $\frac{1}{4}$ (noting that all of the $N_A + N_B = 1$ students now receive $e_B$). According to B's budget schedule, the value of the required funds is $\alpha/4$. Thus, the center is indifferent about moving students to B only if it can obtain exactly these funds from the costs saved by eliminating the fixed payment $K_A$. Thus, $K_A = \alpha/4$, and similarly for $K_B$. Since each unit teaches half of the students ($N_i = \frac{1}{2}$) and receives half of the total revenue, $b_A + b_B = r(N_A + N_B) = r$, the budget schedules given by equation 1 yield $\alpha e_i/2 = r/2 - \alpha/4$. I have shown that the equilibrium quality levels satisfy

$$e_i = \frac{r}{\alpha} - \frac{1}{2}. \tag{7}$$

Comparing equations 7 and 4 proves the claim that educational quality is higher under centralized budgeting than under RCM.

I discuss a number of extensions of the analysis in the next section, but two issues concerning specific assumptions in the model are addressed here. Consider first the assumption of a constant cost of educational services per student, $\alpha e_i$ for unit $i$. Alternatively, RCM could be made preferable to centralized budgeting by positing capacity constraints on the production of education, whereby the center would encounter much higher educational costs per student if it moved a sizable number of students out of one unit and into a rival unit. Such constraints would effectively increase the bargaining power of the units by limiting the alternatives available to the center if it shut down a unit. However, the relevance of such capacity constraints in this context is debatable. If RCM is exercised over a long enough time period, then such constraints become less important. In addition, an important issue is how various types of infrastructure in the university are allocated between units. Under RCM, units might effectively rent buildings from the center, in which case one unit's buildings could expand relative to the other unit's buildings as it attracted students away from the other unit. While it would certainly be useful to explore alternative cost structures, the one used for the current analysis seems like a useful benchmark case.

Second, a variable student population can be introduced into the model by assuming that students are indexed not just by the preference level, $s$, but also by an "outside opportunity," $v$. In other words, all students with a given $s$ possess a range of possible outside opportunities, described by an interval of $v$'s, the location of which may vary with $s$.[16] Given quality levels $e_A$ and $e_B$, $s$ determines the unit in which all type-$s$ students within the university choose to enroll, whereas a type-$s$ student's $v$ determines whether this particular student enters the university. If, for example, type-$s$ students enroll in unit B, then these students must have $v$'s where $e_B + s$ is at least as high as $v$. Otherwise, they would prefer opportunities outside the university to enrolling in unit B. Note that the distribution of the $v$'s and $s$'s across students may reflect admission requirements set by a central administration. In other words, there may exist students where $e_B + s$ is greater than $v$, but these students are not included in the set of students under consideration, because they are denied entrance. For this extension of the model, these admission requirements are treated as exogenous, as are the tuition fees paid by students. Given these exogenous variables, improvements in quality levels $e_A$ and $e_B$ increase the attractiveness of the university to students, thereby raising enrollments. Higher quality levels would allow admission levels to be tightened, producing another equilibrium where the student population is unchanged but the existing students are left better off. If units anticipated this tightening, however, then we would be back to the model with a fixed student population. So the basic difference in models is that units do not anticipate an offsetting tightening of admission requirements. Given this variable student population, measures of student welfare should now include not only actual students but also potential students.

With this setup, the previous comparison between RCM and centralized budgeting remains intact. Adding a variable population tends to increase the elasticity of the supply of students to a given unit. In other words, it reduces the rise in quality $e_i$ needed to increase $N_i$ a unit. From equation 3, this fall in $de_i/dN_i$ increases the equilibrium $e_i$ under RCM, because it lowers the marginal private cost of a student. As a result, the units choose greater quality levels than before under RCM. On the other hand, the existence of a variable population increases the center's bargaining power under centralized budgeting, because it reduces the welfare loss from the elimination of a unit. Whereas students could previously only enroll in the other unit, some students can now choose activities outside of the university as a substitute for the unit that has been eliminated. These additional opportunities cushion the welfare loss from eliminating the unit, and the center is able to use the effective increase in its bargaining power to obtain greater quality levels. With quality levels rising under both RCM and centralized budgeting, it can be shown that centralized budgeting remains superior to RCM.

Extensions

This section discusses a number of ways in which the analysis can be extended. A message that emerges is that the benefits of centralization survive and, in some cases, are enhanced. I also indicate instances where additional research is needed to sort out the relative merits of RCM and centralized budgeting.

## Multidimensional Services

In the discussion of RCM, I have observed that there are two components to the cost of an additional student: the cost involved in providing education to that student (denoted $\alpha e_i$ in the previous section), and the cost of the quality improvement that must be implemented to attract the student (a rise in $e_i$). Quality is increased to the point where the sum of these two costs equals the revenue from another student, denoted $r$. But this means that the compensation rate exceeds the cost of servicing another student: $r - \alpha e_i$ is positive.

A critical implication of this finding is that a unit always benefits if another student takes credit hours in it. Under RCM, units can therefore be expected to continually explore new and cheaper methods for attracting students and then exploit them to the point where they no longer have a cost advantage over the existing methods. Such exploration is ignored in the basic model, where units choose only a one-dimensional quality variable. In practice, however, quality is multidimensional, and educational programs possess multiple attributes that cannot be ranked from lowest quality to highest quality (e.g., curriculum issues or grading policies). Thus, units choose among multiple methods for generating credit hours. For example, a unit's grade policies are optimized only when a change in these policies that attracts another student to the unit imposes a cost on the unit that equals the cost of attracting a student by some other method. Such costs might include reduced teaching effectiveness. The incentive to attract students in the least-cost way under RCM is likely to lead to important misallocations of resources, particularly if students differ in more ways than considered to this point.

## Heterogeneous Students

In the basic model, students differ according to their relative preferences between the two units. At the end of the last section, I extended the model to encompass a variable population, with students possessing different opportunities outside the university. But students differ in many other ways, including abilities and educational preferences over the courses and programs offered within a unit. As a result, the cost of providing a credit hour may depend on which student takes the credit hour, giving units incentives to compete more vigorously for low-cost students. In addition, units will naturally place more weight on the preferences of the students who are more mobile across units, as represented by their responsiveness to changes in a unit's expenditures on different educational activities. In both cases, the unequal treatment of different types of students is unlikely to coincide with reasonable objectives for the university. If the more mobile students are also the relatively less-able students (e.g., less-able students lack strong preferences about their choice of majors), then an RCM system could erode academic standards.

Krause and Wilson (2000) present a model of RCM that focuses on this unequal treatment of different types of students. In particular, units offer different fields of study, and students possess different preferences for these fields. In their efforts to compete for students, units put the most resources into fields they offer that are most similar between the units (e.g., "business economics" and "arts-and-sciences economics"), since these fields matter the most for attracting students. As a result, resources are misallocated across fields, causing students to misallocate themselves across fields. In other words, an inefficiently large number of students choose fields that are most similar between units, since this is where the educational resources are going.

This competition may also affect the fields that are offered. If some fields are too similar between units, then competition for students may bid up the resources devoted to them to the point where the units are not compensated enough to cover the full costs of operating these fields (including fixed costs). If units anticipate this form of "ruinness competition," then they may respond by eliminating these fields (e.g., no economics departments), or funding them at minimal levels to meet accreditation requirements. Once again, resources are clearly misallocated across fields within a unit.

There does not seem to be similar incentives for units to misallocate resources under centralized budgeting. If we incorporate Krause and Wilson's internal structure of units into the current model of centralized budgeting, then the budget proposals presented to the center would need to include not just the total supply of educational services, but also the allocation of these services within the units. But if units care only about the maximization of some measure of total profits, then neither the units nor the center should have an incentive to try to force a deviation from the efficient internal allocation.

On the other hand, the absence of competition for students as an incentive device gives departments within units more freedom to pursue their separate objectives. In other words, the assumption that units possess a single well-defined objective becomes even more questionable, and competition among departments can lead to types of inefficiencies that might not be present under RCM. More work needs to be done on the decision making within units under centralized budgeting.

Once the student population is allowed to vary for the university as a whole, another issue arising from student heterogeneity is whether the university should seek to attract particular types of students, perhaps with differential tuition levels, and what implications this goal has for RCM.[17] For example, state legislatures typically behave as though in-state students contribute more to state welfare than do out-of-state students.[18] Such preferences, along with the practice of charging relatively high tuition rates to out-of-state students, suggest that the RCM system should be modified in a way that provides differential compensation rates to units for these two groups of students. But Wilson (2002) argues that it is not clear how these compensation rates should differ, suggesting that attempts to improve on the simplest RCM systems can quickly require the kind of information that reduces its purported informational advantages. Owing to this lack of information, the prices attached to different activities under any feasible RCM-type system are likely to produce large inefficiencies in university behavior.[19] Note, however, that the unequal treatment of different types of students in my model of centralized budgeting would require that units offer the center a vector of educational services in return for funding, with each element denoting the services going to a particular type of student. This extension also raises complications that deserve further research, including potential differences in the relative preferences of the unit and center for teaching different types of students.

### Restrictions on the Behavior of Units

One common attribute of RCM is that few restrictions are placed on the behavior of units, at least relative to centralized budgeting systems. But this relative lack of restrictions can clearly lead to additional waste. One way to understand such restrictions is that they limit the ability of a unit to engage in expenditures that have little or no relation to the provision of educational services. In this case, additional educational services now benefit the unit by allowing it to more easily undertake wasteful activities. In other words, educational services lower the "cost" of waste to the unit. In an attempt to circumvent behavioral restrictions and increase waste, the unit may therefore increase quality levels beyond those in the absence of restrictions. To the extent that RCM removes such restrictions, it may encourage additional waste.

A problem with this conclusion is that attempts by the university to eliminate waste run the danger of inadvertently restricting activities designed to improve the delivery of educational services. Indeed, an argument for RCM is that the center lacks the information needed to directly control the behavior of units in desirable ways. The form of political competition described here might be subject to restrictions on how the units can spend their funds, but the removal of some of these restrictions might be welfare-improving. It would be useful to investigate how to design restrictions on the behavior of units, given the informational asymmetries between the center and units. Once again, agency theory is likely to be useful.

### Asymmetric Units

Allowing units to differ in size introduces another potential source of inefficiency into the basic model of RCM. Size differences can be introduced by assuming that more students prefer to enroll in unit A than in unit B when the two units offer identical quality levels. In this case, unit A has an incentive to set its quality level below the one chosen by B. Raising its quality level to attract additional students is more costly, because a greater number of existing students must be provided with this higher quality. This difference in equilibrium qualities is another source of inefficiency, because it distorts a student's decision about where to enroll. Since tuition rates do not vary across units, an inefficiently large number of students choose unit B. To see this, hold quality levels fixed, and move a small number of students from unit B to unit A. Since the marginal student is indifferent between units (as described by equation 2), this move does not significantly affect the movers' welfare levels. However, it does lower the total cost of educating students on campus, since more students are being educated in the low-quality unit, namely, unit A. This cost saving could then be devoted to either making the units better off (more wasteful profits) or making the student better off (higher quality levels).

Thus, we can expect too many students to enroll in small units within a university, with too few remaining in large units. This result parallels the conclusion from the public economic literature that small countries have an advantage when they compete with large countries for internationally mobile capital: they face stronger incentives to lower their taxation of capital, making them relatively attractive to investors. See, in particular, Wilson 1991 and Bucovetsky 1991.

A surprising result is that there is no similar tendency for quality levels to differ under the centralized budgeting system discussed here. Under the budget functions given by equation 1, the cost of another unit of educational services is $\alpha$, regardless of whether this unit is obtained from A or B. With these services having equal value to students, the center has no incentive to tolerate any inequality in quality levels. Hence, they are equalized. For this reason, the superiority of centralized budgeting extends to the case of asymmetric units.

Another issue is how size affects the internal workings of units. The basic model treats units as though they are controlled by a set of decision makers with a single objective. But this assumption becomes less reasonable as unit size increases. With increased unit size, there exist greater opportunities to support money-losing activities through cross-subsidies within the unit. Academic departments recognize such opportunities and may therefore devote resources to trying to obtain subsidies, rather than trying to increase credit hours. In other words, the departments of larger units are more immune to the incentive effects of RCM. This is an additional reason why large units compete less vigorously for students.

It is not clear whether similar disadvantages of largeness carry over to centralized budgeting. In fact, one might argue that an increase in size raises the effective bargaining power of a unit by making it more indispensable to the functioning of the university. The conjecture here is that small units should view RCM more favorably than large units, but this issue deserves further investigation.[20]

### Externalities

The only source of inefficiency in the basic model of RCM is the lack of perfect competition among units. But the units that constitute a university typically exhibit interconnections that give rise to externalities, where the choices made by one unit impose costs or benefits on other units, in ways that are not efficiently priced under an RCM system. One example is reputation effects. A unit's reputation with the potential employers of its students depends in part on the reputation of the entire university, which is based on the collective reputations of all units.[21] Thus, efforts by one unit to improve the quality of its academic programs are likely to benefit other units. For example, students in a business program may find it easier to obtain high-quality jobs if the school of arts and sciences offers rigorous, high-quality programs. The existence of positive externalities of this type may lead to "free-riding," whereby a unit underinvests in its academic programs because it is able to rely on high-quality academic programs elsewhere on campus to mask the deterioration in its own programs, at least for a period of time.

This reasoning presumes that individuals located outside the university are imperfectly informed about educational activities inside the university. The students themselves may also lack important information about the quality and types of educational programs offered by various units in a university. Such informational asymmetries are another potential source of inefficiency. For example, a unit might engage in extensive marketing activities to induce students from high schools to enroll in its programs, although some of these students might be better suited for other units. Once the students are on campus, the unit might design its degree requirements to make it difficult for its students to change majors at a later date.

Under centralized budgeting, the central administration would presumably attempt to internalize such externalities. In this respect, centralized budgeting appears to have a distinct advantage over RCM, but informational asymmetries remain a problem.

### Majors versus Nonmajors

One major source of externalities under RCM is the ability of students to take courses in different units within the university. In particular, students major in one unit while taking distribution requirements in other units. In this case, the academic programs offered by different units become interdependent, leading to a host of welfare-reducing externalities not captured by the basic model developed here. For example, a unit may design the curriculum of its courses to cater more to the students majoring within the unit, at the expense of students majoring elsewhere, if doing so tends to increase total credit hours within the unit by generating more majors.

The ability of units to independently control the programs taken by their majors provides another source of inefficient competition among units. In particular, credit hours can be increased by forcing majors to take more credit hours within the unit, if doing so does not substantially reduce the attractiveness of the major. This behavior is similar to the use of "tied sales" by private firms. In particular, a firm can increase profits by packaging goods together and selling them at a single price, so that a customer is induced to buy more than desired. Similarly, an academic unit can confront a student with the choice of majoring in the unit and taking most of his or her courses there, or not majoring in the unit. Limiting choices in this way is a means of raising profits.

Other forms of RCM might be used to counteract these problems. One possibility is the University of Michigan system, where each academic unit is compensated for the number of students that major within the unit, rather than credit hours.[22] In this case, however, units have an incentive to send their majors to other units for coursework. A mixed compensation system, based on both credit hours and number of majors, might be a solution.

A common problem with centralized budgeting is that units typically face insufficient incentives to teach students. As we saw, however, central administrators can restore these incentives by rewarding units that teach a lot of students with large budgets, but not in the form of a flat rate per student. In a sense, the menu-auction approach described earlier represents a nonlinear pricing scheme that seems to improve on RCM. This interpretation is pursued further in the final section of this chapter.

### Research

One complaint about RCM is that it places too much emphasis on teaching relative to research. This concern is perhaps overdone, for several reasons. Although RCM may generate more wasteful profits for units than a centralized budgeting system, I have observed that the center can seek to place restrictions on the use of profits. One potential use is for research. To the extent that RCM frees up additional resources, it has the potential to increase research activities.[23] In addition, the forms of research that are complementary to teaching may be particularly encouraged by RCM.

Note also that a full RCM system rewards units not only for generating credit hours, but also for other activities that raise revenue, including research grants and alumni contributions. A common complaint about centralized budgeting is that it reduces research incentives by distributing a portion of research grants away from the units that generate them. By eliminating this cross-subsidization, RCM can encourage research.

Still, if we do view RCM as encouraging both research and teaching, then it is not completely clear how much one of these activities is encouraged relative to the other. There is at least some cause for concern that research gets shortchanged. This is another issue that deserves further research.

## An Information-Based Approach to RCM

The formal model of centralized budgeting that I have presented does not explicitly deal with informational asymmetries. Units know each other's strategies, consisting of budget schedules, and the only role for the center is to allocate resources based on these schedules. However, the setup of the model is motivated by the center's lack of information about the internal functioning of units. If the center did possess complete information, then it could regulate the behavior of the units in a way that eliminated wasteful expenditures (assuming it had the incentive to do so, which is also an important issue). The surprising result of this study has been the finding that student welfare is higher despite the center's inability to directly influence the internal workings of units.

An alternative view of centralization is that the center obtains information from the units and bases its budget decisions on this information. The problem here is that many of the messages that units might wish to send to the center are difficult to verify (e.g., the relative importance of faculty recruiting in different fields). Moreover, individual units and the center clearly possess different preferences about the allocation of resources within the university, giving the units incentives to lie.

There is a sizable literature on this type of information transmission problem. See, in particular, Crawford and Sobel 1982, and Grossman and Helpman's (2001) applications of their work to special interest politics. In Grossman and Helpman's model, a special interest group sends a message to a policymaker about the "state of the world," and the policymaker uses this information to choose its policy. Since the truthfulness of the message cannot be directly verified, the message will be truthful only if it is in the interest of the special interest group to make it truthful. One of the main results from this model is that truthfulness is possible, but only for messages that are coarse to the extent that they reveal a range of possible states, but not the specific state. Moreover, these truthful messages necessarily become less informative (i.e., more coarse) as the difference between the preferences of the special interest group and policymaker grow.

This framework suggests a possible role for RCM: to bring the preferences of the center and units closer together, thereby facilitating the transmission of information. The presumed benefit of RCM is that it forces units to place greater weight on the delivery of educational services to students. In so doing, it might better enable units to communicate information to the center that can then be used by the center for allocating resources that are not part of RCM. This reasoning suggests a mixed system, whereby units compete for students in an effort to receive some funds from the center, but the center exercises discretion over other funds. Perhaps some mixture of RCM and centralized budgeting is preferable to either extreme. It would be useful to develop formal models of various mixed systems, recognizing the importance of informational asymmetries on a university campus.

## Conclusion

In this chapter, I have provided an argument for why centralized budgeting is superior to RCM, even though my depiction of centralized budgeting has severely limited the power of the central administration. My explanation for this result has rested on the crude way in which RCM compensates units for teaching students, with a fixed payment for each student (or credit hour). In effect, I have argued that this scheme still does not provide sufficient incentives to raise educational quality.

One approach to this problem would be to implement a more complex compensation scheme. In particular, we might consider schemes that do not treat all credit hours identically. In the basic model, a nonlinear compensation scheme under which the compensation rate rose as more students were taught could provide more powerful incentives to improve quality, without increasing total compensation costs. But this solution has problems. First, it eliminates the simplicity of RCM, raising the question of whether there exists sufficient information to design the required degree of nonlinearity. Second, such a scheme is likely to introduce problems not present in the basic model, particularly the tendency of RCM to create incentives for units to pay too much attention to the preferences of the most mobile students. It seems unlikely that an RCM system could be designed that would adequately substitute for the active involvement of central administrators in resource allocation decisions on a university campus.

# GOVERNANCE
# IN PRACTICE

# CHAPTER SEVEN

# How Academic Ships Actually Navigate
## Gabriel E. Kaplan

Institutional governance lies, if not at the heart of the academic enterprise, then at its origin. Before today's universities or colleges began to operate, they received a charter from the state, established bylaws, and appointed trustees or directors of the enterprise. Colleges and universities pursue their activities under the auspices of and with the support of the state because they are understood to be public trusts and to be pursuing the advancement of the public's general welfare (Hall 1997). Governance is the means by which the public trust can be monitored and its general welfare implemented.

The concept of governance encompasses explicit and, occasionally, implicit arrangements by which authority and responsibility for making decisions concerning the institution are allocated to the various parties who participate in it (Hirsch and Weber 2001). In higher education, the governance system consists of "the written and unwritten policies, procedures, and decision making units that control resource allocation within and among institutions" (Benjamin 1993, 5). Among colleges and universities, authority and *de jure* control over the institution ultimately rest with the board of trustees, but the trustees often delegate components of this authority to others within the institution such as administrators, faculty, and committees that frequently are composed of students, staff, and alumni.

All organizations must solve the challenge of governance. How they address this challenge will depend on their legal status—whether they

I thank Harvard's Hauser Center for Nonprofit Organizations, the American Association of University Professors, and Professor Emeritus Otway Pardee, whose assistance and support made this project possible.

are public or private, whether they operate for profit or not—and on the legal requirements placed on them by their charter and the contracts into which they enter (Weeks and Davis 1982). In the for-profit corporate setting, the analysis of governance is often confined to the study of the governing board and its relations with top executives (Fama and Jensen 1983a, 1983b; Lorsch 1989). In higher education, the delegation of the board's authority to parties such as faculty, students, alumni, and others requires that the analysis be much broader and encompass the formal and informal interrelations of these parties. The academic practice of shared governance characterizes the complex managerial character of higher education institutions and helps to distinguish them from other organizations in other industrial sectors. While the patterns of delegation and practices of shared governance are neither absolute nor uniform in American higher education, understanding how governance is defined and implemented on college campuses constitutes an essential project for understanding the behavior of higher education organizations. Despite the importance of this project and growing interest in governance, broad and systematic study of governance practices in higher education has been a neglected area of research.

This chapter describes the findings of a recent national survey of higher education governance practices and the implementation of shared governance concepts at a large number of colleges and universities. It examines the kinds of systems employed for enacting shared governance and their incidence. It attempts to analyze how power is distributed among organizational participants and the factors that might account for variation in these distributional patterns. The chapter also presents some preliminary findings concerning the relationship between particular governance practices and institutional outcomes and performance. Some of the questions used in this survey were drawn from past studies of academic governance in the hope that by comparing answers from the present with those from the past, we could learn something about how governance has changed since these studies were last conducted. The survey also included questions developed in the context of the current challenges facing institutions in order to subject some of the current governance literature to preliminary evaluation. The findings presented here and the study discussed on these pages are not the definitive word on the current state of higher education governance in the United States, nor do they pretend to be. Scores of questions about governance and its practice remain unanswered, but the evidence presented here marks a first step in a long series of necessary strides toward the understanding of academic governance. One clear conclusion that can be drawn from these findings is the need for continued examination of the issues raised here and for sustained inquiry concerning the formal and informal processes that surround decision making and institutional action.

## Background

Understanding and attending to the implementation of governance among colleges and universities is an essential project for scholars of higher education everywhere, but it is particularly important in the context of U.S. higher education because the United States does not have a centralized system of postsecondary education. The sector's achievement of the public good is understood to emerge from a plurality of autonomous activity set within a federalist political framework and embedded in a market context that places primacy on the consumer's sovereignty. The absence of centralized planning over the system, the broad range of conceptualizations of the public good, and the variety of ways in which these concepts are pursued is a uniquely American phenomenon and has been a prime strength of the system, endowing it with rich financial resources, freeing the institutions for innovation, and generating responsiveness to social and economic needs. But, as with any investment tool, past performance is no guarantee of future returns. Even if society feels it cannot control each institution, it does expect that the sector's output and functions will conform to social expectations, attain at least minimal social objectives, and employ resources efficiently.

What do we know of shared governance today? Unfortunately, not nearly enough to attend to the policy challenges at hand. The salience of public concern for higher education issues has made academic governance a central issue in policy debates and provoked much public discussion about the relationship between institutional performance and current governance practices. Nevertheless, much that gets written about higher education rests on anecdote or, at best, a handful of case studies of governance at a small number of institutions. The various criticisms of governance—that it has become too corporate and capitalistic or that it is too arcane in its traditions and unresponsive to the demands of the modern world—circulate in an environment distinguished by a dearth of systematic and comprehensive information.

The early 1970s witnessed a flurry of scholarly work on academic governance, with much of this interest coming from sociologists.[1] Between 1969 and 1971 the American Association of University Professors (AAUP) conducted a national survey of institutions with AAUP chapters and asked faculty and administrators to rate faculty participation in a variety of decision areas (American Association of University Professors 1971). Around that time sociologists Seymour Lipset, Everett Ladd, Talcott Parsons, Gerald Platt, and Martin Trow were compiling their own studies of decision processes (Ladd and Lipset 1975; Parsons and Platt 1973; Trow 1977). Much of this research provided the foundations for many of the central ideas and contributions of modern organizational sociology. No major comprehensive study of governance practices among both private and public institutions of higher education has been conducted since that time. There have been a few smaller-scale studies of decision making in small subgroups of the higher education population but nothing on so broad a scale that it cuts across the sector and across ownership types (see Chaffee 1984, 1985; Schuster et al. 1994). No study has facilitated a comparison of public and private institutions or provided insight into the functioning of governance at all levels, including the interface of students and administrators, faculty and administrators, boards and presidents.

## Issues of Interest

The 2001 Survey of Higher Education Governance was conceived as an effort to close this information gap. It revisited and replicated some of the earlier surveys while developing new questions that would shed light on current implementation. The goals of this survey were multifold. The prime objective was to provide an assessment of the state of governance today. What are the relationships among the groups involved in governance on a campus? What institutions or decision processes are used to implement governance, and do they fall into particular types? How are the institutional structures of decision making distributed across the higher education sector, and do particular organizational traits account for any pattern in this distribution? How broadly diffused are particular governance practices and suggested innovations or reforms in shared governance?

The survey instrument also sought to provide data on the distribution of power among various parties on a campus. Power can lie in formal structures that grant authority, but it can also stem from one's social position in the broader milieu, access to alternative employment opportunities, ability to produce resource flows for the institution, or the professional authority and expertise one wields (Pfeffer and Salancik 1978; Emerson 1962; Dahl 1957; French and Raven 1968). Scholars can use participants' perceptions of how power is allocated to determine whether the locus of power coincides with the kinds of decisions and resource allocation patterns that an institution favors.

By incorporating questions from past studies of governance, such as the AAUP's 1970 survey, the new survey made an effort to facilitate comparisons across time, in order to identify which institutions experienced changes in their governance, the direction of those changes (who gained and who lost influence), and what institutional traits or market circumstances may have accounted for these developments. The expansion of information, the explosion of knowledge in the sciences, the development of new fields such as computer science, and the increasing professionalization of the undergraduate curriculum pose numerous challenges for higher education institutions. How do organizations that face particular environmental pressures respond with changes in their decision structure? How does their response influence the relationship of parties on the campus? Which institutional types have been successful at meeting the challenges thrust before them? Have they been able to contract effectively and reallocate resources? The survey paid particular attention to the question of change and adjustment.

## Problems in Studying Governance

Perhaps one reason for the dearth of large-scale survey work in higher education governance stems from the particular challenges involved in using questionnaires to gain a picture of decision practices from campus to campus. All surveys must surmount the common problems of sampling work, but what would a survey of governance need to remain cognizant of before it began? The most obvious challenge facing any study of governance is the problem of specification error: attempting to measure a concept or phenomenon that is ill defined or not measurable. The study of higher education governance is prone to specification error for five essential reasons.

First, governance on a college or university campus is difficult to study systematically because decision making may not appear to function as a systematic process (Cohen and March 1974). Governance structures and decision processes are rarely delineated with the same clarity and precision as political systems operating at a national or local level. Before questions about governance can be developed, all the permutations by which a decision can be reached must be considered.

Second, even when rules of decision are clearly specified, they may differ from the actualities of power's exercise. Questions that ask respondents to specify the written rules regarding a decision process, and the procedures that need to be followed in decision making may miss the reality of campus government.

Third, it may be difficult to separate the board's legal authority over all decisions from the assigned responsibilities over particular decisions. The concept of academic governance embraces the notion that power, governance, and decision making are shared tasks and responsibilities which can be allocated in various ways, but in legal terms, lawful authority and responsibility for all decisions ultimately rest with the board. Specifying where responsibilities for budgets, degrees, curriculum, and other decisions lie may prove difficult for those who understand the board's formal responsibility but recognize the role of other groups in particular decisions.

Fourth, groups in higher education may not carry the clear and contradictory objectives of political models. Even if power over long-range budget planning rests with the faculty governing body in one institution while it rests with the administration in another, each institution can develop identical goals if faculty and administrators share common interests or values. Although faculty and administrators frequently do clash over some decisions, they often share similar values and goals and also can possess common beliefs about what actions or policies are unacceptable. Even governing boards may take their cues about goals and values from the faculty, making it difficult to utilize the beneficiaries of institutional decisions to distinguish between institutions with strong governing boards and those without.

Finally, any efforts to gauge shared governance and determine faculty influence must make clear how faculty power will be recognized. The case of tenure illustrates this problem. Political models might suggest that a campus where all faculty members receive tenure when eligible is a campus captured by the faculty. However, some of the most elite institutions rarely grant tenure to junior faculty, yet the faculty still possess a great deal of authority and power over decisions. Faculty power in governance is often difficult to assess because most faculty members remain uninterested in the powers that have been delegated to them under the rules of governance on the campus, and reserve their authority merely for cases in which they feel the administration or board overstepped their bounds.

## Survey Methodology

Reliability, accuracy, validity of the data, and consistency of responses within an institution depend, in survey work, on whether respondents have accurate information to respond to the questions asked, have the same understandings of the questions as the survey author, and are not influenced in their responses by the survey instrument. To assess the quality of the instrument and verify the value of the collection methodology, the survey instrument was pretested at a handful of institutions in an urban area by administering cognitive interviews to a small sample of administrators. Such site interviews are a recommended way of protecting against measurement error in survey work (Biemer and Fesco 1995; Light, Singer, and Willett 1990). Fifteen administrators and senior faculty at five different institutions were consulted and asked to provide answers to each survey question in an oral interview. This small sample consisted of the same kinds of individuals who would be responding to the survey nationally. Discussions involving each question were used to develop clarifying language that matched a question's aim with the understandings of the concept expressed by administrators. The responses that were provided in these interviews were then tabulated to see whether they were consistent across the administrators at the same institutions (did people see things in the same way?) and whether the answers given were accurate (did responses match the information about the institution that was publicly available?). The answers proved consistent over 90 percent of the time. By checking answers with what could be learned by reading information about the institution available in campus publications, bylaws, and published on Web sites, it appeared that the consulted group possessed accurate information about governance at their institution.

Getting accurate data is always difficult when one relies on one individual or several to report on the characteristics of a social collective as complex as a university or college. Nevertheless it is a standard method in the study of large organizations to rely on one "expert" respondent (Knoke, Kalleberg, and Marsden 2002). The findings from the on-site cognitive interviews generated a high level of confidence that this technique would yield valuable institutional data.

In order to generate confidence that the data produced are truly representative of the sample population, a survey must obtain an adequate response rate and protect against sampling bias. The 2001 survey was more of a census than a sample, since every four-year institution accredited to grant bachelor's degrees in the liberal arts was sent a survey. Special efforts were made to obtain a high response rate by following the Tailored (or Total) Design Method (TDM) for survey research recommended by Dillman and colleagues (Dillman 2000; Paxson, Dillman, and Tarnai 1995).[2] By inviting all institutions, and verifying that the response population matched the sample population in various ways, the survey sought to avoid the methodological pitfall of sampling error.

The 2001 survey used the National Science Foundation's CASPAR database to generate a listing of the four-year institutions in the United States that were accredited to grant bachelor's degrees in the liberal arts.[3] Matching this list against an address list from Higher Education Directory Publications, Inc. generated a survey population of some thirteen hundred institutions.[4] To encourage participation by institutions, several prominent groups in higher education were approached for sponsorship and support.[5]

Following the TDM protocols, members of the survey population received an introductory letter informing them of the survey, a packet with a copy of the survey, a return envelope, and an instruction letter, and two email reminders before the survey deadline. Respondents had the option of a Web-based reply. All correspondence was personally addressed to survey participants. Letters were sent to campus presidents and AAUP chapter heads. The president was asked to fill out the survey or pass it on to a senior and trusted member of the administration whose views corresponded to the president's and whose knowledge of governance matched that of the campus president. The letter also asked the president to identify a faculty member with seniority and knowledge about governance and to pass along the survey packet and request that the faculty representative fill in his or her part of the survey.[6]

Survey Findings

These efforts resulted in a successful survey project with an institutional response rate of almost 70 percent. Table 7.1 shows how closely the population of survey respondents matched the universe of possible respondents. The results presented here are drawn from a survey population of 1,321 four-year institutions. The survey consisted of two

Table 7.1. Response to 2001 Survey of Higher Education Governance

|  | Respondent Population | Total Survey Population |
|---|---|---|
| Total number | 903 | 1,321 |
| Institutional response rate | 68.4% | |
| Institutional characteristics | | |
| Public | 350 (38.8%) | 494 (37.4%) |
| Private | 553 (61.2%) | 821 (62.6%) |
| Has a medical school | 84 (9.3%) | 112 (8.5%) |
| Mean SAT score | 965 | 958 |
| Proportion of tenured faculty | 56.2% | 55.9% |
| Average faculty salary | $40,786 | $40,364 |
| % revenues from tuition | 46.3 | 46.5 |
| Breakdown by Carnegie classification* | | |
| Research I | 69 (7.6%) | 88 (6.6%) |
| Research II | 33 (3.7%) | 39 (3.0%) |
| Doctoral I | 28 (3.1%) | 44 (3.3%) |
| Doctoral II | 41 (4.5%) | 55 (4.2%) |
| Comprehensive I | 282 (31.2%) | 419 (31.7%) |
| Comprehensive II | 57 (6.3%) | 86 (6.5%) |
| Liberal Arts I | 121 (13.4%) | 160 (12.1%) |
| Liberal Arts II | 272 (30.1%) | 430 (32.6%) |
| Regional breakdown | | |
| New England | 76 (8.4%) | 114 (8.6%) |
| Mid-Atlantic | 172 (19.0%) | 255 (19.3%) |
| Great Lakes | 156 (17.3%) | 215 (16.3%) |
| Great Plains | 96 (10.6%) | 147 (11.3%) |
| Southeast | 238 (26.4%) | 335 (25.4%) |
| Southwest | 58 (6.4%) | 100 (7.6%) |
| Rocky Mountains | 28 (3.1%) | 36 (2.7%) |
| Far West | 79 (8.8%) | 119 (9.0%) |

* From Carnegie Foundation for the Advancement of Teaching 1994.

parts. The first section consisted of questions about the institution's administrative structure and governing board and was to be completed by campus administrators. The second section concerned the implementation of shared governance and was to be filled out by both faculty representatives and administrators. A total of 903 institutions submitted at least one reply, with the vast majority of institutions supplying responses from both faculty and administrators. The overall response rate was 68.4 percent.

The breakdown of responses from public and private institutions matched the general population of institutions quite well. Three hundred and fifty public institutions and 553 private institutions are included among the respondents. Public institutions comprise 37.4 percent of the population of institutions surveyed and 38.8 percent of the institutions that responded. The participant institutions' general characteristics also mirrored those of the overall population, with similar percentages of Carnegie-classified research institutions, liberal arts colleges, and comprehensive institutions (Carnegie Foundation for the Advancement of Teaching 1994). Regional breakdowns also supported the finding that the survey population matched that of the general population of schools. The mean combined SAT score of participating schools was slightly higher than the full population, as was the likelihood that the institution had a medical school. But the average faculty salaries and the proportion of tenured faculty on the payrolls at both sets of institutions were strongly similar.

Nonrespondents, however, could not be described as entirely random or nonsystematic. In other words, even though the responding institutions mirrored the general population, the likelihood that an institution did not respond to and participate in the survey was not the same as the likelihood that an institution did choose to participate. Nonrespondents were not similar to the general population of institutions. For instance, the fraction of Liberal Art II colleges among nonrespondents was almost 38 percent, but they comprised only 32 percent of the population of institutions. Institutions from the Great Plains and from the Southwest regions were slightly less likely to participate than their counterparts in other regions, while those in the Great Lakes area were slightly more likely to respond.[7] Furthermore, while the institutional characteristics of the general and sample population were highly similar in most cases, it may be the case that the populations are not identical along some unmeasured dimension.[8] In spite of these concerns, the sample population appeared highly representative of the general population.

### The State of Shared Governance

The picture painted by the survey findings is generally more favorable than either critics of shared governance or defenders of shared governance usually admit. Most critics of shared governance tend to complain that it rarely functions well in practice, slows decision making, and impedes necessary reorganizations and strategic change. Advocates who defend shared governance often voice concern that it faces increasing pressures for centralization and for more top-down, bureaucratic and corporate forms of organization. The evidence produced here does not invalidate the claims of critics or advocates, but it does indicate that problems associated with encroachments on the traditions of shared governance or with its unresponsiveness represent a minority of cases or situations. The survey found scant evidence that shared governance poses widespread problems to effective management and found no broad consensus around this idea among any group, including administrators.

Respondents also expressed a positive view of relations between faculty and administrators and, if few respondents rated the faculty's participation in governance enthusiastically, neither did they express great concern. Table 7.2 summarizes some basic questions that highlight the state of relations on campus. On a scale from 1 to 5, respondents rated faculty participation 3.3 on average, with 1 indicating low levels of participation and 5 indicating enthusiastic participation. This score was lowest among public institutions and highest among private liberal arts colleges. The high scores among the smaller schools are likely due to the closer relations between faculty on such campuses and the manageability of smaller decision groups. Administrators were slightly more positive about faculty participation, and AAUP chapter members tended to be the most negative. Despite the insistence of critics that the faculty stymies administrative action and is unwilling to make tough decisions, administrative respondents tended to view the implementation of shared governance more positively than did faculty.

The same patterns in attitudes emerged when respondents were asked to categorize relations on campus between faculty, governing boards, and administrators. Fifty-three percent of respondents rated the governance environment between faculty and administration as cooperative and another 41 percent characterized relations as having some conflict but still collegial. Only 6.5 percent of respondents expressed concern that the governing environment could be best categorized as suspicious and adversarial. These numbers were consistent across several different institutional types, with the large private institutions indicating the least cooperative environment and the liberal arts colleges appearing to have the most cooperative relations, but the difference between these extremes was not large. When these characterizations of campus relations are broken down by respondent group, there are some discrepancies between the sanguinity of the faculty and that of the administration. Sixty-two percent of administrators were apt to see relations as generally cooperative, while only 47 percent of representatives from the faculty shared this view. Among survey respondents from AAUP chapters, only 28.5 percent of respondents felt relations were cooperative. Clearly, AAUP representatives possessed the dimmest view of relations on campus, and this could be

Table 7.2. State of Shared Governance

| Survey Question | All | Public | Private | Large Private | Liberal Arts (private) | Administration | Faculty Representative | AAUP Chapter Member |
|---|---|---|---|---|---|---|---|---|
| Rating of faculty participation* | 3.3 | 2.9 | 3.5 | 2.7 | 3.7 | 3.4 | 3.3 | 2.9 |
| Campus relations | | | | | | | | |
| Cooperative | 52.9% | 50.4% | 54.5% | 49.4% | 57.9% | 62.1% | 46.9% | 28.5% |
| Conflict but collegial | 40.6% | 41.7% | 39.9% | 41.9% | 38.6% | 35.0% | 43.8% | 57.8% |
| Adversarial | 6.5% | 7.9% | 5.6% | 8.7% | 3.5% | 2.9% | 9.3% | 13.8% |
| Number of presidents over last 30 years | 4.2 | 4.6 | 4.0 | 3.7 | 4.0 | NA | NA | NA |
| Unionized faculty | 15.9% | 32.2% | 5.7% | 8.8% | 3.8% | NA | NA | NA |

Note: NA, not applicable.
* See text for scoring system.

either because people with concerns about relations between faculty and administration are drawn toward participation in the AAUP or because the AAUP often finds itself in conflict with campus administrations.

Other indicators of relationships on campus also revealed relative stability. The number of presidents in the last three decades was similar across institutional types. On average, campuses reported having had about four presidents over the last thirty years, for an average tenure of 7.5 years. Some campuses reported more turmoil at the top, but only a small minority. Eighty-two percent of campuses reported fewer than five presidents and 92.5 percent reported fewer than six. While faculty unions are quite common among public institutions, most public institutions remain nonunionized. Despite the limitation on organizing among faculty at private institutions, 6 percent of private institutions continue to recognize faculty unions. Most unionization activity occurred prior to 1990, with 90 percent of collective bargaining units beginning before then. Since then, unionization has persisted at a steady but low annual rate.

Respondents were asked to evaluate how the relative formal powers of a number of participant groups had changed in the last two decades. Table 7.3 reports the average evaluation of how power changed for each of the groups by institutional type. Despite fears among some faculty that the practice of shared governance is ebbing, few institutional types reported significant deterioration in the power of any group. Although department chairs and faculty governance bodies were judged to have lost the most power, faculty governance bodies were also identified as the most significant gainers of power after deans and other division heads. Table 7.4 reports information from the same set of questions but breaks down answers by respondent group. Faculty respondents were more likely to see their authority as deteriorating in recent years, particularly those individuals who were responding to the survey on behalf of an AAUP chapter. Although only 26.4 percent of AAUP representatives felt faculty authority had deteriorated in the last two decades, this compared with 11.5 percent of faculty governance body representatives and 2.1 percent of administrators. While faculty tended to be more pessimistic than administrators in this regard, few of the survey responses indicated widespread faculty concern about their authority in governance.[9] Faculty respondents were more likely than administrators to view boards and presidents as having assumed more power in the last twenty years. Faculty were more likely to see faculty governance bodies as having less authority; however, approximately 90 percent of respondents from faculty governance bodies rated their

Table 7.3. Changes in the Distribution of Power (%) over Last Two Decades

| Participant Group | All | Public | Private | Liberal Arts (private) |
|---|---|---|---|---|
| Governing board | | | | |
| More | 21.4 | 29.7 | 16.1 | 16.5 |
| Same | 74.3 | 65.9 | 79.6 | 80.6 |
| Less | 4.3 | 4.5 | 4.2 | 2.9 |
| President | | | | |
| More | 21.3 | 26.0 | 18.3 | 16.0 |
| Same | 74.4 | 68.4 | 78.3 | 80.0 |
| Less | 4.3 | 5.6 | 3.5 | 3.9 |
| Deans and other division heads | | | | |
| More | 37.9 | 33.5 | 40.8 | 39.8 |
| Same | 56.6 | 60.0 | 54.4 | 55.8 |
| Less | 5.5 | 6.6 | 4.8 | 4.4 |
| Department chairs | | | | |
| More | 23.5 | 23.5 | 23.5 | 22.9 |
| Same | 67.8 | 68.8 | 67.1 | 66.9 |
| Less | 8.7 | 7.7 | 9.4 | 10.3 |
| Faculty governance bodies | | | | |
| More | 35.5 | 32.3 | 37.5 | 34.4 |
| Same | 56.5 | 59.1 | 54.9 | 57.8 |
| Less | 8.0 | 8.6 | 7.6 | 7.8 |
| State coordinating board | | | | |
| More | | 30.8 | | |
| Same | NA | 58.1 | NA | NA |
| Less | | 11.1 | | |

*Note*: NA, not applicable.


Table 7.4. Perceptions of Change in the Distribution of Power (%) over Last Two Decades

| Participant Group | Administrators | | | Faculty Representatives | | | AAUP Chapter Members | | |
|---|---|---|---|---|---|---|---|---|---|
| | Less | Same | More | Less | Same | More | Less | Same | More |
| Governing board | 4.1 | 76.8 | 19.1 | 4.2 | 72.1 | 23.6 | 6.4 | 69.1 | 24.6 |
| President | 2.9 | 80.6 | 16.6 | 4.9 | 70.1 | 25.0 | 9.9 | 58.6 | 31.5 |
| Deans and other division heads | 2.1 | 61.1 | 36.8 | 8.6 | 52.0 | 39.4 | 10.9 | 51.8 | 37.3 |
| Department chairs | 4.4 | 70.8 | 24.7 | 12.2 | 64.4 | 23.4 | 17.4 | 66.1 | 16.5 |
| Faculty governance bodies | 2.1 | 63.1 | 34.8 | 11.5 | 49.9 | 38.6 | 26.4 | 50.0 | 23.6 |
| State coordinating board | 12.1 | 60.5 | 27.4 | 8.8 | 53.7 | 37.6 | 13.66 | 65.3 | 18.4 |

Table 7.5. Chief Executive Backgrounds

| Background | All | Public | Private | Liberal Arts I Colleges | Liberal Arts II Colleges |
|---|---|---|---|---|---|
| % with a Ph.D. (% listing other doctorate) | 72.8 (14.2) | 77.4 (10.4) | 69.9 (16.6) | 77.1 (11.4) | 64.1 (19.6) |
| Field of degree (%) | | | | | |
| Liberal arts | 47.1 | 49.5 | 45.7 | 61.5 | 39.0 |
| Education | 25.9 | 23.9 | 27.2 | 17.3 | 35.7 |
| Business | 4.4 | 4.2 | 4.5 | 0.0 | 5.5 |
| Law | 5.2 | 6.9 | 4.1 | 6.7 | 2.2 |
| Theology | 6.2 | 0.4 | 9.9 | 6.7 | 9.9 |
| Other (includes engineering) | 11.2 | 15.2 | 8.6 | 7.7 | 7.7 |
| Served as tenured professor (%) | 61.4 | 77.1 | 51.4 | 54.8 | 44.3 |

faculty as having either more or as much power as they had twenty years ago.

One fear often expressed by the defenders of shared governance is that executives from outside of academia, from both the military and the business world, are being brought in to run colleges and universities with a more business-like focus and bureaucratic orientation. By choosing executives who lack academic experience, governing boards may be seeking to instill a business acumen in the management of the institution or to build links to communities outside the college walls. Despite some expressed concerns that the boards of many institutions have recruited chief executives with little experience in academia, most colleges and universities continue to be headed by individuals with a substantial academic background. Table 7.5 shows that the chief executive at 72.8 percent of institutions has a doctorate degree. Forty-seven percent of college presidents have a Ph.D. in a liberal arts field. Another 26 percent have advanced degrees (either a Ph.D. or an Ed.D.) in education. Six percent have a Ph.D. in theology. This distribution of backgrounds was consistent across both public and private ownership forms. Liberal arts colleges also had roughly a similar distribution of degree experiences among their chief executives. However, the figures from liberal arts colleges hid a cleavage among two classes of such colleges. The small colleges categorized as Liberal Arts II by the Carnegie Commission on Higher Education (Carnegie Foundation for the Advancement of Teaching 1994) were the least likely to report a president with a Ph.D. Furthermore, while 61.5 percent of Liberal Arts I colleges were headed by someone with a Ph.D. in the liberal arts, only 39 percent of the Liberal Arts II institutions were headed by someone with a similar background. If nonacademic executives are migrating anywhere, it is to those smaller private colleges that currently face some of the most severe economic challenges (Brenneman 1994).

Many of the executives, in addition to their scholarly education, served as faculty members themselves prior to assuming their leadership positions. Over 61 percent of college and university presidents served as tenured, full professors prior to becoming a chief executive. However, the presidents of public institutions (77 percent) tended to be drawn from faculty ranks more often than were the presidents of the private institutions (51.4 percent). Among the liberal arts colleges this number dropped even more. A weighted average of the two categories indicates that less than 50 percent of the presidents of such institutions came from the academic ranks. Again, the institutions in the Liberal Arts II category were the least likely to have a chief executive who previously had a tenured faculty position.

### The Locus of Authority

Shared governance, although it takes a variety of forms and is expressed through different kinds of governing structures, seems to function well at many of the institutions surveyed. Respondents expressed a belief that faculty governance bodies had a significant impact on the policymaking process on campus, and participation in decisions seems to be fairly well distributed among all of the different groups except for students. Table 7.6 records responses to several questions about influence and decision making broken down by institutional type. Eighty-four percent of respondents indicated that they felt the main representative body of the faculty either influenced or directly made policy at the institution. Faculties at public institutions were judged slightly less influential than those at private institutions. Faculties at the liberal arts colleges were reported to be the most influential. Faculty senates at private research institutions were seen as less likely to make policy and more likely to have advisory powers than at public research institutions.

Table 7.6 also indicates that the locus of budget activity is generally seen as resting with the president and the deans. Almost 70 percent of respondents saw the president as playing a major role in budget making, and 81 percent of respondents felt that the deans participated a great deal in the budget process. Faculty might play some role in budget

Table 7.6. Influence of Different Groups in Decision Making (%)

| | All | Public | Private | Liberal Arts (private) | Private Research | Public Research |
|---|---|---|---|---|---|---|
| **Influence of faculty senate** | | | | | | |
| Advisory | 16.2 | 19.8 | 13.8 | 11.4 | 25.6 | 18.3 |
| Policy influence | 68.1 | 66.3 | 69.3 | 67.1 | 72.1 | 63.5 |
| Policy making | 15.8 | 14.0 | 17.0 | 21.5 | 2.3 | 18.3 |
| **Roles in budget making** | | | | | | |
| *Governing board* | | | | | | |
| Not much | 38.1 | 52.5 | 29.0 | 26.1 | 48.8 | 54.9 |
| Somewhat | 37.9 | 27.0 | 44.8 | 46.4 | 34.9 | 19.7 |
| A lot | 24.0 | 20.5 | 26.2 | 27.6 | 16.3 | 25.4 |
| *President* | | | | | | |
| Not much | 5.6 | 8.8 | 3.6 | 2.6 | 8.9 | 12.6 |
| Somewhat | 27.3 | 28.1 | 26.8 | 24.1 | 33.3 | 29.9 |
| A lot | 67.1 | 63.1 | 69.7 | 73.4 | 57.8 | 57.5 |
| *Deans and other division heads* | | | | | | |
| Not much | 0.9 | 0.6 | 1.2 | 1.2 | 0.0 | 0.0 |
| Somewhat | 18.0 | 21.4 | 15.9 | 11.6 | 17.8 | 17.3 |
| A lot | 81.0 | 78.0 | 83.0 | 87.2 | 82.2 | 82.7 |
| *Department chairs* | | | | | | |
| Not much | 12.5 | 12.0 | 12.8 | 8.8 | 29.6 | 10.5 |
| Somewhat | 58.6 | 61.5 | 56.7 | 60.6 | 43.2 | 59.7 |
| A lot | 28.9 | 26.4 | 30.5 | 30.6 | 27.3 | 29.8 |
| *Faculty at department level* | | | | | | |
| Not much | 46.8 | 53.4 | 42.6 | 37.7 | 72.1 | 59.4 |
| Somewhat | 48.4 | 42.7 | 52.1 | 56.7 | 27.9 | 38.2 |
| A lot | 4.8 | 3.9 | 5.3 | 5.7 | 0.0 | 2.4 |
| *Faculty at institutional level* | | | | | | |
| Not much | 44.5 | 45.4 | 43.8 | 44.3 | 55.8 | 43.2 |
| Somewhat | 46.7 | 47.5 | 46.3 | 45.8 | 37.2 | 48.0 |
| A lot | 8.8 | 7.1 | 10.0 | 10.0 | 7.0 | 8.8 |
| *Students* | | | | | | |
| Not much | 78.9 | 75.3 | 81.2 | 80.1 | 90.5 | 78.2 |
| Somewhat | 20.1 | 23.6 | 17.8 | 19.1 | 7.1 | 20.2 |
| A lot | 1.0 | 1.1 | 1.0 | 0.8 | 2.4 | 1.6 |

making, but at almost half the institutions they were not identified as having much influence. In budgeting, the faculties at private research institutions were again seen as having the least amount of influence after students. Faculty influence in budget matters tended to be expressed at the institutional level, most likely through the governance bodies, rather than at the departmental level. Department chairs play an important role in the budget process and appear to be even more prominent than the governing boards, but they assume a role that is secondary to higher-level administrators. The boards of private institutions are often singled out for being less proactive and supervisory than the governing boards of public institutions (Ehrenberg 2000a). Interestingly, the governing boards at public institutions were rated as having less influence over budget matters than were those of private institutions. Governing boards were judged to be most active among the smaller colleges. Their participation in budgetary decisions among the private research institutions seemed to mirror that of the public institutions.

Once again, administrators were more likely to judge faculty participation and influence in budget matters more optimistically than were faculty. Table 7.7 shows that compared to AAUP chapter respondents, administrators rated the influence of the faculty governing body as greater, saw boards and presidents as having less of a budgetary role, and saw faculty as having more of a role in budgeting. Compare the responses of the AAUP chapter respondents with those of administrators concerning the role of department chairs and of faculty at the department level. Faculty members were twice as likely as administrators to see the role of faculty at the department level as having little influence in budget matters. Administrators were more likely to see faculty at the institutional level as having some role in budget making.

Still, when asked to characterize faculty participation in a number of decision areas, faculty and administrators tended to ascribe similar distributions of authority to faculty across fifteen major decision areas. Table 7.8 reports summary statistics from responses to the survey questions borrowed from the 1970 survey of the AAUP. Respondents were asked to classify the faculty's participation in fifteen different issue areas according to a system of five categories—determination, joint action, consultation, discussion, and none—by estimating the percentage of faculty whose participation took each of the five forms.[10] Two of the five categories reflected a significant role for faculty—full determination by the faculty over a matter and joint action between administration and faculty. The percentage of faculty respondents supplied for these categories were combined for each respondent and then averaged by institution to yield the faculty participation scores shown in Table 7.8.

Faculty authority appears to be concentrated in the areas that both faculty and the AAUP have traditionally felt were the domain of academics—degree requirements, curriculum, tenure, appointments, and degree offerings. Faculties appear to play a much smaller role in deci-

Table 7.7. Perceptions of Influence of Different Groups in Decision Making (%)

|  | Administrators | Faculty Representatives | AAUP Chapter Members |
|---|---|---|---|
| **Influence of faculty senate** | | | |
| Advisory | 14.8 | 16.1 | 24.6 |
| Policy influence | 70.3 | 66.1 | 64.9 |
| Policymaking | 15.0 | 17.8 | 10.5 |
| **Roles in budget making** | | | |
| Governing board | | | |
| Not much | 44.7 | 31.6 | 30.9 |
| Somewhat | 37.2 | 38.4 | 40.0 |
| A lot | 18.1 | 30.0 | 29.1 |
| President | | | |
| Not much | 6.1 | 5.5 | 2.6 |
| Somewhat | 30.4 | 24.6 | 22.6 |
| A lot | 63.5 | 69.9 | 74.8 |
| Deans and other division heads | | | |
| Not much | 0.3 | 1.9 | 0.0 |
| Somewhat | 12.5 | 22.6 | 28.7 |
| A lot | 87.3 | 75.6 | 71.3 |
| Department chairs | | | |
| Not much | 7.4 | 15.9 | 25.9 |
| Somewhat | 55.8 | 61.5 | 59.8 |
| A lot | 36.8 | 22.6 | 14.3 |
| Faculty at department level | | | |
| Not much | 34.2 | 54.8 | 80.5 |
| Somewhat | 58.7 | 42.0 | 19.5 |
| A lot | 7.0 | 3.1 | 0.0 |
| Faculty at institutional level | | | |
| Not much | 38.2 | 49.3 | 56.6 |
| Somewhat | 50.6 | 43.2 | 41.6 |
| A lot | 11.2 | 7.5 | 1.8 |
| Students | | | |
| Not much | 73.7 | 82.3 | 92.0 |
| Somewhat | 24.9 | 17.0 | 7.1 |
| A lot | 1.3 | 0.7 | 0.9 |

sions regarding the size of disciplines, the setting of budgets, determining salaries and salary scales, and planning for construction projects. Faculty are described as playing a somewhat greater role in decisions about teaching loads, in the selection of deans and department chairs, and in the shape that faculty governance will take. Still, even here, the proportion did not reach 50 percent, meaning most of the authority over these areas of decision resides with either the administration or the governing board. These answers are relatively consistent across institutional types with only a few exceptions. According to the responses to question 10, the faculties of liberal arts colleges participate less often in the appointment of department chairs. The faculties at

Table 7.8. Percentage of Faculty with Determinative Authority or Joint Authority with the Administration in Different Decision Areas

| Decision Area | All Institutions | Public | Large Private | Liberal Arts Colleges | Administrators | Faculty Representatives | AAUP Chapter Members |
|---|---|---|---|---|---|---|---|
| Faculty status | | | | | | | |
| 1 Appointments of full-time faculty | 69.9 | 69.0 | 71.7 | 69.8 | 74.0 | 65.8 | 65.8 |
| 2 Tenure promotions for faculty | 66.1 | 66.0 | 67.8 | 65.0 | 68.5 | 62.7 | 68.5 |
| Academic operation | | | | | | | |
| 3 Decisions about the content of the curriculum | 89.9 | 88.6 | 88.8 | 92.0 | 91.5 | 89.3 | 83.0 |
| 4 Setting degree requirements | 87.5 | 84.4 | 87.1 | 91.2 | 89.8 | 86.5 | 79.5 |
| Academic planning and policy | | | | | | | |
| 5 Types of degrees offered | 73.4 | 70.9 | 74.6 | 75.3 | 75.5 | 73.0 | 63.0 |
| 6 Relative sizes of the faculty of various disciplines | 35.0 | 31.8 | 35.1 | 38.3 | 39.9 | 31.3 | 24.0 |
| 7 Construction programs for buildings and other facilities | 8.6 | 8.8 | 7.5 | 9.0 | 11.1 | 6.6 | 3.0 |
| 8 Setting of the average teaching loads | 38.7 | 41.4 | 40.0 | 37.0 | 44.5 | 33.0 | 32.8 |
| Selection of administrators and department chair | | | | | | | |
| 9 Appointing the academic dean | 31.2 | 33.3 | 31.3 | 28.8 | 36.5 | 26.5 | 23.0 |
| 10 Appointing department chairs or heads | 51.6 | 56.2 | 52.7 | 45.8 | 55.4 | 49.1 | 41.1 |
| Financial planning and policy | | | | | | | |
| 11 Setting faculty salary scales | 19.2 | 24.1 | 17.2 | 15.2 | 21.2 | 17.5 | 15.5 |
| 12 Decisions about individual faculty salaries | 17.1 | 23.3 | 15.4 | 11.5 | 19.4 | 15.0 | 13.8 |
| 13 Short-range budgetary planning | 17.6 | 17.1 | 17.2 | 18.6 | 21.6 | 15.2 | 6.3 |
| Organization of faculty agencies | | | | | | | |
| 14 Decisions that establish the authority of faculty in campus governance | 60.4 | 62.7 | 58.6 | 59.1 | 61.5 | 61.5 | 48.7 |
| 15 Selecting members for institution-wide committees, senate, and similar agencies | 77.6 | 77.1 | 78.0 | 77.8 | 78.2 | 77.8 | 72.3 |

*Note:* The 1970 survey categorized five decision-making styles or approaches to governance in higher education, ranging from faculty determination over an issue to no faculty participation in governance (see n. 10, p. 293). It recognized that on some campuses some of the faculty might be in departments characterized by a good deal of faculty participation in governance, while in other divisions the faculty would have little say. The survey asked respondents to estimate the percentage of faculty whose participation in governance could be categorized by these governance forms in each of a number of critical decision areas. The 2001 survey used a subset of the same questions.

public institutions play a greater role in financial planning and policy matters (note the averages for questions 11 and 12).

The responses provided by faculty representatives and administrators corresponded fairly closely, and once again AAUP chapter members took the dimmest view of faculty participation in each of these decision areas. Faculty and administrators provided similar characterizations of the faculty's role in setting degree requirements. Administrators on average estimated that 90 percent of the faculty on their campus either had sole determinative authority over degree requirements or shared this authority jointly with the administration. This corresponds with the appraisal of faculty representatives, who estimated on average that 87 percent of the faculty played such a role in setting degree requirements. Faculty governance representatives and AAUP chapter members who responded to the survey tended to give similar estimates of faculty participation in the areas of faculty appointments, appointments of the dean, decisions about salaries, and selection of faculty representatives to governance bodies. Faculty representatives and administrators tended to provide similar estimates for the percentage of faculty involved in the appointments of department heads, setting of degree requirements, establishing faculty authority in governance, and curriculum decisions. The sharpest disparities between the responses of faculty members and administrators appear to be in the area of appointments, campus construction projects, appointments of the academic dean, and the setting of teaching loads.

*Institutions of Governance: Board Practices*

Neither the fondest hopes of governance efficiency advocates, such as the Association of Governing Boards (AGB), nor the worst fears of shared governance champions, such as the AAUP, seem to be realized at this time. Such groups make frequent prescriptions for effective governance practice, with the AGB focusing on practices of governing boards and the AAUP attending to institutions of faculty governance and the relations between administrators and faculty. A series of questions relating to the practice of institutional governing boards and concerning the institutions of shared governance were included in the survey questionnaire and are discussed here and in the next section.

Proponents of reforms in the area of governing boards often call for shrinking the size of boards to make them more effective and for stocking them with individuals who do not have direct participatory connections to the institution. A particular policy recommendation is that

186    *Gabriel E. Kaplan*

Table 7.9. Governing Board Practices

|  | All | Public | Private | Liberal Arts Colleges (private) | Private Comprehensives |
|---|---|---|---|---|---|
| Board meeting frequency (per year) | 4.9 | 7.4 | 3.3 | 3.2 | 3.5 |
| Executive committee meeting frequency (per year) | 3.9 | 3.3 | 4.3 | 4.1 | 4.2 |
| President votes in the board | 38.2% | 2.7% | 60.7% | 57.7% | 66.7% |
| Average number of members | 24.8 | 13.2 | 32.1 | 31.1 | 32.1 |
| Number of members prescribed | 83.9% | 77.9% | 87.6% | 85.7% | 88.2% |
| Faculty or student members | 28.8% | 53.9% | 13.2% | 14.5% | 13.7% |
| Change in faculty/student membership policy* | | | | | |
| Decrease | 1.4% | 1.4% | 1.4% | 1.1% | 2.3% |
| Increase | 12.2% | 20.5% | 7.0% | 7.0% | 7.8% |

* Change in last 10 years.

faculty and students not serve on governing boards. Table 7.9 reports summary statistics from several questions about board practices. Almost 30 percent reported that faculty or students serve as voting members of the governing board, and this number rises to 54 percent among public institutions. Private institutions appear to be more reluctant to allocate board seats to either faculty or students. When board seats are reserved for inside members, it is most often for students, and typically these are seats reserved for student representatives from the student governing association. Only 1.4 percent of respondents reported that their institution had scaled back either student or faculty representation in recent years. Boards of private institutions tend to meet quarterly (an average of 3.3 board meetings a year) and those of public institutions more often. Private institutions appear to do more business through the executive committees since these appear to meet more frequently, most likely because these groups are smaller and represent a more tractable number of individuals. Presidents of public institutional boards rarely participate with voting privileges in board meetings; however, they are active members on 61 percent of governing boards of private institutions. Table 7.9 also indicates that presidential voting rights are more common among the larger private institutions. Sixty-seven percent of the institutions classified as Comprehensive by the Carnegie coding system report that the president serves as a voting member of the board.

Other proposals regarding the promotion of effective governance by boards concern minimizing board size and controlling the appointment process. Public institutions appear to be more closely adhering to the admonition of board efficiency advocates to keep board size small. The average size among public boards (thirteen members), however, is still larger than what proponents of effective board practices call for (typically eight to ten board members). The average size of governing boards across the higher education sector is twenty-five members, and this number derives from the significant size of private boards. Some private boards can grow quite large; one, in fact, has over one hundred members. The average size of private institutional governing boards is about thirty-two members. Such boards appear to fulfill a dual purpose, functioning both as fund-raising tools and as governing apparatuses. Board seats can be used to reward large donors and they can be used as donor recruitment tools, to build connections to funding communities or individuals and invest particular parties with a strong interest in the welfare of the institution.

However, proponents of effective board practice also call for strict rules fixing the board's size. Appointments to the governing board can be used to maintain control over decision making. When board size is not prescribed and regular rules for appointment are not in place, a voting bloc can maintain its influence by appointing board members sympathetic to its views. Eighty-four percent of institutions report that the number of members is prescribed either in the institutional charter, in the by-laws, or by state statute. Table 7.10 reports data concerning the appointment process. Here there are clear differences between private and public governing boards. Ninety percent of public institutions report that board members are appointed by state officials. Among the private institutions, about 90 percent of appointments are actually made by the board. The other significant designators of board members are church bodies, which play a significant role in the appointment of board members among private liberal arts colleges.

Public institutions can range in their degree of publicness. Some can resemble state agencies in the way they handle resource allocation and compensation. Others may look more like their private institutional counterparts. Table 7.11 reviews some of the characteristics of governing boards and their authority at public institutions. Nineteen percent of institutions reported that they were overseen by a statewide board, and 46 percent reported that the president dealt most frequently with

Table 7.10. Governing Board Selection Methods (%)

| Method | All | Public | Private | Liberal Arts Colleges (private) | Comprehensive I and II (private) |
|---|---|---|---|---|---|
| Selected by governing board (self-perpetuating) | 56.9 | 5.72 | 89.2 | 87.5 | 91.4 |
| Selected and confirmed by governor or state bodies | 35.8 | 90.2 | 1.5 | 1.0 | 1.4 |
| Alumni election | 12.2 | 6.4 | 15.9 | 20.1 | 5.8 |
| Internal election (e.g., campus election for student representative) | 5.7 | 4.7 | 6.4 | 9.0 | 2.9 |
| Outside election (e.g., state election) | 3.5 | 3.4 | 3.6 | 4.8 | 1.4 |
| Selected by president | 4.2 | 0.3 | 6.6 | 6.2 | 8.6 |
| Selected by church body | 10.6 | 0.0 | 17.2 | 22.2 | 11.5 |
| Other | 4.4 | 4.0 | 4.7 | 3.8 | 5.8 |

*Note*: Respondents could select more than one response, so percentages do not add to 100%.

Table 7.11. Characteristics (%) of Public Institution's Governing Boards

| | |
|---|---|
| President deals most often with | |
| Statewide board | 18.7 |
| System board | 45.9 |
| Campus-based board | 35.4 |
| Faculty are employees of | |
| State or commonwealth | 48.1 |
| Institution | 51.9 |
| Tuition levels set by | |
| Institution or governing board | 35.8 |
| System board | 33.5 |
| State board | 12.7 |
| Legislature or governor | 14.3 |
| Other | 2.6 |
| Revenues from tuition | |
| Retained by institution | 73.5 |
| Retained at state board level | 5.5 |
| Deposited in state tuition accounts | 12.4 |
| Deposited in state general funds | 5.5 |
| Other | 3.1 |

a governing board that oversaw a system of state institutions. Campus-based boards are most involved in governance at 35 percent of the public institutions, and in a similar number, tuition levels are set by the institution's governing board. Faculty members are considered to be employees of the state at 48 percent of the public institutions

Table 7.12. Administration–Faculty Interactions in Governance (%)

| | All | Public | Private | Liberal Arts Colleges |
|---|---|---|---|---|
| Union leaders allowed to serve in governance | 92.3 | 88.5 | 93.4 | — |
| Administrator chairs faculty governing body | 26.6 | 9.8 | 37.4 | 48.5 |
| Administrator votes in faculty governance body | 40.3 | 32.5 | 45.3 | 51.8 |

responding. Tuition revenues are most often retained by the institution for its own use, but a significant proportion reported that such monies are deposited into state accounts and must be reallocated by either a state board or the legislature.

### *Institutions of Governance: Administration–Faculty Relations*

If governing boards have yet to realize the goals of efficiency advocates, governing bodies of the faculty seem to adhere closely to some of the recommended guidelines in the AAUP Redbook.[11] Table 7.12 indicates that 60 percent of institutions reported that administrators do not have a vote in the faculty governance body, and 73 percent reported that an administrator or chief executive does not chair the governing body meetings. Note also that these figures were somewhat depressed by the responses from the smaller institutions such as the liberal arts colleges, where administrators are more directly involved with faculty governance and work more closely with the faculty in governing matters. Administrators are active in the faculty governance bodies of such institutions, both chairing them and serving with voting rights, about 50 percent of the time. Among the larger institutions, administrators tend to be much less involved in the functioning of governance bodies. Contrary to the recommendations of groups such as the AGB, faculty leaders in the bargaining unit are also allowed to serve on campus faculty governance bodies in about 90 percent of all institutions where faculty are unionized.

In many instances, both private and public institutions appear similar in terms of the nature of faculty authority. As Table 7.8 showed, the governance bodies are perceived as having similar kinds of influence on policy. Among public institutions, the faculty's authority in areas such as budgeting, academic matters, and strategic planning essentially mirrors that of the private institutions. The first part of Table 7.13 indicates that the modes by which faculty express influence are similar in

Table 7.13. Means of Faculty Representation in Governance

| | All | Public | Private |
|---|---|---|---|
| Primary point at which faculty influence is felt | | | |
| Department level | 12.6 | 16.0 | 10.3 |
| Division level | 10.5 | 7.8 | 12.2 |
| Institutional level through governing body | 72.3 | 69.0 | 74.4 |
| Faculty bargaining unit | 3.2 | 5.6 | 1.7 |
| None of the above | 1.5 | 1.7 | 1.3 |
| Selection methods for faculty governing body | | | |
| Central administration | 2.3 | 1.1 | 3.1 |
| Full faculty vote | 49.8 | 25.7 | 65.4 |
| College or division vote | 30.6 | 47.3 | 19.7 |
| Department chair | 0.2 | 0.2 | 0.2 |
| Department vote | 9.0 | 19.0 | 2.6 |
| Other | 8.1 | 6.8 | 9.0 |
| Full voting rights in governance awarded to | | | |
| Faculty above a certain rank | 2.9 | 4.3 | 3.0/1.8* |
| Faculty who have tenure | 0.7 | 1.1 | 0.8/0.2* |
| Tenure-track or tenured faculty | 16.4 | 26.1 | 18.7/5.9* |
| Full-time faculty | 57.9 | 43.7 | 63.1/68.9* |
| Faculty in bargaining unit | 2.6 | 4.8 | 2.6/0.2* |
| All faculty voting rights in governing | 19.6 | 20.0 | 11.9/23.0* |

* First number is for private universities and second number is for private liberal arts colleges.

both public and private institutions. Faculty influence, however, is felt most often at the institutional and division level among private institutions and at the departmental and institutional level among the public institutions. As the middle part of Table 7.13 shows, appointments to the faculty governance bodies occur according to this pattern as well, with most of the action occurring at the division or institutional level in private institutions and greater activity occurring at the departmental and division level among the public institutions. Private institutions, according to the last part of this table, have the broadest enfranchisement polices for faculty. Private institutions are more likely to award voting rights to all full-time instructional faculty, while public institutions tend more toward granting such rights to tenured and tenure-track faculty members only.

How do the structures of faculty governance differ across public and private institutions? Table 7.14 indicates that faculty governance structures take different forms at public and private institutions. Among private institutions, faculty influence is less structured, while governance among the public institutions appears to be more formalized. Academic senates composed of faculty, students, and staff are twice as

Table 7.14. Institutions of Governance (%)

| | All | Public | Private | Private Universities | Liberal Arts Colleges |
|---|---|---|---|---|---|
| Regular meetings of the full faculty | 72.5 | 45.9 | 89.6 | 78.9 | 96.7 |
| Institution-wide faculty senate | 58.6 | 72.3 | 49.6 | 65.3 | 39.0 |
| Institution-wide academic senate | 16.2 | 23.3 | 11.5 | 14.5 | 9.5 |
| Division-level units of governance | 45.6 | 49.4 | 43.1 | 53.1 | 36.0 |
| Systemwide faculty senate | 29.0 | 37.7 | 10.7 | 19.4 | 4.4 |
| Systemwide academic senate* | 3.3 | 3.0 | 4.0 | 4.2 | 4.4 |
| Faculty sit on major policy committees (e.g., budget, promotions, academic policy) | 98.0 | 96.5 | 98.9 | 99.1 | 98.8 |

*Note*: Numbers do not add to 100% because multiple responses were possible.

\* An academic senate is distinguished from a faculty senate by having senators elected from among the administration, faculty, students, and staff.

likely on a public campus as they are in a private institution, and senates composed of faculty alone are almost 50 percent more likely at public institutions. The holding of full faculty meetings occurs on half the fraction of public campuses as on private campuses. The faculty serve as members on key campus committees involving academic policy, budget, promotions, and employment policies on 98 percent of campuses, a figure that is roughly similar across both private and public institutions. Faculty members appear to have a significant role in major decision areas at most institutions.

### The State of Governance Reforms

The challenges facing higher education today are much discussed, and reforms in the area of academic and management policy are commonly proposed. The professionalization of the role of president is apparent in the high incidence of training that presidents receive. Table 7.15a shows that the presidents of public and private institutions received some kind of further and formal training after assuming the presidency almost 90 percent of the time. An interesting finding from this table is seen in the incidence of training among the leaders of institutions that the Carnegie Commission classifies as Research I. The heads of these large, complex, and multipurpose institutions are most often drawn from the ranks of the professorate (see Table 7.5), but they are also the least likely to receive any kind of formal training for their role as pres-

Table 7.15a. Major Policies and Reforms (%)

|  | All | Public | Private Universities | Liberal Arts Colleges | Research I |
|---|---|---|---|---|---|
| Presidential training | 86.9 | 88.5 | 84.7 | 86.7 | 56.5 |
| Performance review relative to a peer group | 87.4 | 87.7 | 89.3 | 86.0 | 93.8 |
| Merit pay | 56.2 | 72.6 | 51.9 | 42.0 | 94.9 |
| Tenure | 90.2 | 97.6 | 89.4 | 83.3 | 98.0 |
| Post-tenure review | 63.0 | 75.3 | 55.2 | 55.0 | 67.3 |
| Formal academic freedom statement | 97.3 | 96.2 | 98.3 | 97.9 | 98.0 |

ident. Most institutions also report that they monitor and compare their performance relative to that of a peer group of institutions, indicating that competitive and social pressures may lead institutions to closely mimic the behavior and decision patterns of like institutions (DiMaggio and Powell 1983).

What is the status of two current hot-button issues in governance and administration—post-tenure review and merit pay? Fifty-six percent of institutions have instituted some scheme of merit pay. Sixty-three percent have implemented some kind of system for conducting post-tenure reviews. These two policy innovations in academia appear to be quite widespread, perhaps surprisingly so given faculty opposition and resistance to these ideas, but they are still not pervasive. Tenure is quite common, employed by 90 percent of the institutions that responded to the survey, but is least likely among the liberal arts colleges. Formal statements concerning academic freedom are nearly universal.

The diffusion of merit pay and post-tenure review policies (Table 7.15b) makes for an interesting display of the kinds of social differences that seem to exist across geographic areas of the United States. Merit pay and post-tenure review are least likely in the Northeast and the Great Plains, regions where the older land-grant colleges and more traditional institutions are quite common. The policies are most common in the South and the Rocky Mountain region. This pattern is a likely indication that in these regions the traditions of academia are least diffused and that concerns about performance and minimizing expenditures are greatest. Since the private higher education sectors in these states are also smaller, and public institutions comprise a larger share of the institutional population, taxpayer concern over the spending of tax dollars probably creates more apparent pressure for policies that facilitate monitoring of the faculty.

Table 7.15b. Diffusion of Major Policies and Reforms (%), by Regions

| | New England | Mid-Atlantic | Great Lakes | Great Plains | Southeast | Southwest | Rocky Mountains | Far West |
|---|---|---|---|---|---|---|---|---|
| Presidential training | 76.6 | 81.6 | 90.5 | 93.8 | 91.0 | 83.0 | 88.0 | 83.3 |
| Performance review relative to a peer group | 94.0 | 92.2 | 85.5 | 87.7 | 84.7 | 83.0 | 84.0 | 86.6 |
| Merit pay | 47.8 | 47.6 | 55.6 | 40.5 | 65.0 | 76.6 | 70.8 | 56.7 |
| Tenure | 81.2 | 95.1 | 89.4 | 93.8 | 88.7 | 85.4 | 88.0 | 93.9 |
| Post-tenure review | 50.7 | 53.5 | 54.9 | 66.2 | 66.0 | 72.9 | 84.0 | 81.8 |
| Formal academic freedom statement | 97.0 | 95.6 | 97.6 | 97.5 | 98.0 | 97.9 | 100.0 | 97.0 |

Table 7.16. Response to Challenges: Faculty Recruitment (%)

| | All | Public | Private | Private Universities |
|---|---|---|---|---|
| Would the department recruit faculty at salary higher than others in department? | | | | |
| Yes, regularly do that | 14.5 | 23.63 | 7.9 | 14.2 |
| Occasionally do that | 52.6 | 55.13 | 51.0 | 54.1 |
| No we rarely do that | 33.3 | 21.3 | 41.1 | 31.7 |
| Would there be pressure to raise others' salaries? | 54.5 | 59.7 | 50.8 | 51.7 |
| If yes, would the institution raise salaries? | | | | |
| Very likely | 2.6 | 1.4 | 3.6 | 3.8 |
| Somewhat likely | 15.0 | 13.6 | 16.1 | 15.7 |
| Hard to say | 32.3 | 31.0 | 33.4 | 34.1 |
| Somewhat unlikely | 28.3 | 31.0 | 26.2 | 26.5 |
| Not likely at all | 21.7 | 23.0 | 20.6 | 20.0 |

*Meeting the Challenges Facing Liberal Arts Colleges and Universities*

Data discussed earlier indicate that nonacademic presidents were most common among the smaller liberal arts colleges. The turn toward nonacademic presidents underscores the financial concerns that often face these less well-known colleges (Brenneman 1994). This finding generated the hypothesis that the executives of such institutions were brought in to help meet these challenges with alternative leadership. How have institutions managed the complexities of a rapidly evolving world of knowledge and a challenging economic environment? Has outside leadership positioned smaller institutions so that they can face these threats and has it spurred significant policy change among these institutions?

The survey indicated that a significant proportion of institutions appear to be able to flexibly adapt to changing circumstances and successfully reorganize departments or recruit high-quality faculty, even if the result is salary disparities within departments. Table 7.16 shows that efforts to transform the faculty and improve quality in particular areas were most common among universities. Surprisingly, public universities were more likely than private universities to report that they would recruit outside faculty, even if it meant paying a higher salary. The budget constraints that face public institutions because of their reliance on public funding and their external control by state legislatures do not result in weaker efforts at recruitment than those of the private institutions. Table 7.16 also implies that the liberal arts colleges are the least likely to engage in activity aimed at improving their academic standing or enhancing faculty quality: since the numbers for the private sector as a whole reported in the third column are lower than those for the subset of private universities in the fourth column, the liberal arts college group must be pulling the overall private figures downward. Fifty percent of institutions report that bringing in outside senior faculty at higher salary levels would generate significant pressure to increase salaries for existing faculty and to reduce any resulting disparities. Respondents from public institutions report greater pressure for faculty salary equalization than those from private institutions, but at least half of all responding institutions indicated that faculty recruitment could generate pressure for across-the-board raises. Perhaps the small size of faculties at liberal arts colleges and the importance of collegiality in governance at such a scale make these institutions reluctant to invite any turmoil associated with competitive faculty recruitment.

Closing and merging departments offers institutions a way to get a handle on changing student demands, developments in disciplinary knowledge, and the need to transfer resources from one subject area to another. Almost half of all institutions reported that they had closed a department in the last five years. Data from the survey shown in Table 7.17 indicate that private universities were the most likely to have closed a department. Surprisingly, despite whatever challenges they face, liberal arts colleges were the least likely to have closed a department, closing on average only 1.2 departments. Again, this may be a function of their size, as they have fewer departments to close. Given that this group of institutions was also less likely to participate in the survey, this evidence might be cause for some concern. If a reluctance to respond to the survey is indicative of particular tensions over governance and the economic pressures that beset these institutions in the current economic climate, their reluctance to close departments is troubling. The small size of the faculty and the fear of upsetting any collegial balance may also play a role here.

What reasons do institutions give for closing departments and what factors do they report make this task most difficult? The survey asked institutions that had closed a department to select from a number of choices some reasons why such change was most necessary and most difficult. The findings were particularly informative with regard to the barriers that stand in the way of reorganization. Despite the common claim that tenure presents significant challenges for colleges that want to strategically reorient themselves, administrators were actually less likely than faculty to feel that tenure posed a significant challenge to reorganization strategies and to department closures. Even among

Table 7.17. Response to Challenges: Department Closures

| | All | Public | Private | Private Universities | Liberal Arts College |
|---|---|---|---|---|---|
| Was a department closed in last 5 years? | 43.2% | 44.7% | 42.2% | 51.4% | 36.2% |
| Average number of closures or mergers | 2.2 | 2.9 | 1.7 | 2.4 | 1.2 |
| Reasons that made decision difficult | | | | | |
| Institution-wide faculty concerns about the closure | 37.3% | 37.2% | 37.3% | 38.0% | 36.6% |
| Faculty resistance in that department | 47.9% | 51.2% | 45.8% | 49.1% | 42.6% |
| Student concerns about the closure | 33.2% | 28.9% | 36.2% | 30.4% | 41.5% |
| Alumni concerns about the closure | 11.1% | 8.4% | 13.0% | 11.7% | 14.2% |
| Concerns that closure might violate tenure or academic freedom provisions | 5.4% | 4.2% | 6.2% | 7.0% | 5.5% |
| Concerns about the public perception of this closure and damage to the institution's reputation | 26.5% | 24.7% | 27.7% | 25.7% | 29.5% |
| Reasons that made decision necessary | | | | | |
| Enrollment levels in the years preceding the decision | 74.2% | 71.6% | 76.0% | 71.3% | 80.3% |
| Direction from the board or an administrator that the institution should re-orient itself | 32.2% | 31.4% | 32.8% | 29.8% | 35.5% |
| Other institutions had closed or scaled back activities in this area | 3.4% | 2.5% | 4.0% | 4.1% | 3.8% |
| Declining numbers of department faculty members and a deficiency of replacements | 18.4% | 18.8% | 18.1% | 19.9% | 16.4% |
| Faculty demands for resources in other fields and departments | 29.2% | 27.6% | 30.2% | 27.5% | 32.7% |
| Student demands for resources in other areas of the institution | 13.3% | 17.2% | 10.7% | 11.1% | 10.4% |

faculty, less than 7 percent felt that tenure made closures or reorganizations more difficult. However, most respondents agreed that faculty opposition to such a change posed the most significant barrier. Student concerns also appear to play a role in making such change difficult, particularly among the private institutions. Despite their large size and the strong influence of outside political pressure on their behavior, the public institutions were more likely to report that faculty resistance would make such change difficult. Of course, they were also slightly more likely than private institutions to have undertaken department closures. However, this may be a function of size or mission, since private universities report roughly similar numbers of department closures. Faculty resistance was less likely to be reported by the liberal arts colleges as a significant factor impeding change. The incidence of faculty resistance among public institutions, then, may result from the more common experience of closure among universities and the preponderance of institutions of this size in the public sector. Of course, it may also be the case that the external control over these institutions creates more acute pressures for closure and attendant resistance on the part of faculty to this policy.

Enrollment pressures and direction from a governing board are the most common reasons for departmental closures and reorganizations. Liberal arts colleges that closed departments or programs were more likely than their larger counterparts (both public and private) to do so as a result of enrollment pressures or under direction from the board, highlighting the particular circumstances that challenge such institutions. While faculty resistance was less likely to be a significant factor preventing closures on such campuses, student opposition was more often seen as an obstacle at the smaller institutions. Among the reported reasons that made such change most necessary, however, student concerns were listed least often by respondents from liberal arts colleges. Boards also appear to be more actively involved in such decisions at the smaller institutions.

How and why do institutions respond to student concerns and stated needs? The survey included a question on this subject, and the findings listed in Table 7.18 highlight that market pressures are keenly felt among institutions of higher education. Almost 50 percent of all institutions and over 50 percent of private institutions reported that they accommodate felt student needs most often in response to pressures communicated to them through the marketplace. Public institutions are more likely to make such accommodations in response to demands from the student representative body. In sharp contrast to what the experi-

Table 7.18. Response (%) to Challenges: Responding to Student Needs and Demands

|  | All | Public | Private | Private Universities |
|---|---|---|---|---|
| Major institutional change to meet student needs results most frequently from response to | | | | |
| The student representative body | 24.3 | 28.9 | 21.3 | 19.6 |
| Student protest or petitions | 3.7 | 3.6 | 3.8 | 3.1 |
| The marketplace | 48.7 | 43.9 | 51.8 | 54.1 |
| None of the above | 23.4 | 23.6 | 23.2 | 23.2 |

ence of institutions thirty years ago must have been, schools rarely make changes in response to student protest or petition. About a quarter of institutions answered that attempts to meet student demands were in response to none of the three listed possibilities. Cognitive interviews conducted to test the survey instrument prior to sending it out indicated that most administrators who chose the option "None of the above" felt their institutions made such changes out of consideration for what they believed to be in the best interests of students.

What, then, do colleges and universities set as their major goals, and what policies emerge from these governing structures? The survey asked administrators to report on the three main goals of the mission statement or most recent strategic plan. Each of these responses was read and categorized among thirty-five different policy goals.[12] Among the thirty-five categories, three goals occurred far more frequently than the other identified institutional objectives: raising academic quality, encouraging enrollment growth, and improving facilities and technology. Academic quality was twice as likely to be mentioned as the other two and almost three times as likely to be mentioned as the next most popular goal.

These thirty-five categories were then reviewed to detect any commonalities among them. Despite the large number of categories generated, six thematic areas of concern that cut across all of the categories emerged from this effort: quality, enrollment, financial performance and efficiency, responsiveness to the demands of the market (management), traditional academic values, and public service–oriented policies. Table 7.19 lists the breakdown of these themes by institutional type. Of the thirty-five categories compiled in the first pass through the data, improving the quality of the institution and attracting more students to the campus were the most commonly described institutional objectives.

Table 7.19. Response (%) to Challenges: Setting Missions and Policy Goals

| Policy Goal | All | Public | Private | Liberal Arts I & II | Private Research I & II, Doctoral I & II |
|---|---|---|---|---|---|
| Enrollment | 26.4 | 26.2 | 26.4 | 29.5 | 13.2 |
| Finance | 39.2 | 28.4 | 46.0 | 48.1 | 34.2 |
| Management | 47.9 | 41.7 | 51.7 | 54.1 | 47.4 |
| Public service | 25.8 | 39.9 | 17.0 | 17.2 | 23.7 |
| Quality | 78.9 | 84.5 | 75.4 | 73.9 | 81.6 |
| Traditional values (academic or spiritual) | 23.8 | 12.2 | 31.0 | 31.7 | 23.7 |

*Note*: Percentage of institutions indicating category as a top 3 goal or mission.

This broad consensus seems to cut across all the institutional types in the sample, but quality concerns were most pronounced among the public institutions and the private research and doctoral granting universities.[13] Private research institutions were the least likely to report enrollment as an institutional objective. Public institutions were far more likely than private institutions to report concerns for and objectives pertaining to public service. Liberal arts colleges and private comprehensive universities were the least likely to include public service–type objectives among their listed goals. Financial and management concerns were, as might be expected, most commonly listed by these smaller institutions. Such schools were also more likely to include traditional values, of either an academic or a spiritual nature. The concern for the traditional study of the liberal arts is an inherent mission of such institutions, but the large proportion of religiously affiliated institutions among this group also explains the concern for traditional, spiritually oriented values.

### Changes since 1970

The survey included questions from the 1970 AAUP survey in order to see how governance has evolved and, in particular, to see whether shared governance had deteriorated in the face of a more challenging economic environment. Market pressures are said to be eroding the institutional commitment to shared governance and the willingness of administrators and boards to include faculty in tough decisions, to either wait for them to make decisions or be confident that they can make choices that are in the institution's best interest (Nelson 1999). The increasing mobility of faculty and their tendency to award their

Table 7.20a. Changes in Faculty Participation since 1970

| | Faculty Control in 1970, mean (%) | Faculty Control 1970 (matched institution), mean (%) | Faculty Control 2001 (matched institution), mean (%) |
|---|---|---|---|
| Faculty status | | | |
| 1 Appointments of full-time faculty | 30.7 | 30.6 | 72.8 |
| 2 Tenure promotions for faculty | 35.4 | 35.1 | 68.1 |
| Academic operation | | | |
| 3 Decisions about the content of the curriculum | 81.8 | 83.3 | 90.3 |
| 4 Setting degree requirements | 81.2 | 83.0 | 88.2 |
| Academic planning and policy | | | |
| 5 Types of degrees offered | 71.3 | 72.4 | 73.5 |
| 6 Relative sizes of the faculty of various disciplines | 10.0 | 9.0 | 33.2 |
| 7 Construction programs for buildings and other facilities | 7.1 | 7.1 | 8.1 |
| 8 Setting of the average teaching loads | 23.7 | 24.0 | 38.6 |
| Selection of administrators and department chair | | | |
| 9 Appointing the academic dean | 13.5 | 13.3 | 29.7 |
| 10 Appointing department chairs or heads | 21.9 | 21.4 | 53.2 |
| Financial planning and policy | | | |
| 11 Setting faculty salary scales | 6.2 | 5.1 | 19.1 |
| 12 Decisions about individual faculty salaries | 6.9 | 6.5 | 17.5 |
| 13 Short-range budgetary planning | 4.4 | 4.3 | 16.3 |
| Organization of faculty agencies | | | |
| 14 Decisions that establish the authority of faculty in campus governance | 45.9 | 44.7 | 62.1 |
| 15 Selecting members for institution-wide committees, senate, and similar agencies | 59.8 | 59.3 | 78.7 |

*Note*: Faculty control is the sum of responses for joint action and faculty determination (see n. 10 for definitions).

loyalty to their discipline rather than to an institution is said to have eroded faculty commitment to shared governance (Lodge 1984). Did the survey uncover findings to verify these claims? Not at all.

Table 7.20a lists the mean responses to the fifteen questions that correspond to the categories and responses described earlier in Table 7.8. The last two columns of Table 7.20a compare the mean responses concerning faculty participation at a matched set of institutions whose responses were available from both the 1970 and the 2001 survey. Comparing responses from Table 7.8 and the first column in Table 7.20a, it is apparent that the matched schools merely verify that the differences in means from 2001 and 1970 are not a function of different survey samples. Several areas draw immediate attention. The most striking finding is that the mean level of faculty participation in all fifteen decision categories has increased.[14] Striking increases in faculty control and authority over decision areas are evident in the area of appointments and promotion, setting the size of the disciplines, appointment of academic deans and department heads, and deciding on the authority and membership of faculty governance agencies. The faculty role in financial planning and policy also increased since 1970; however, only a fraction of faculty appear to be involved with much authority in these areas even today. Change did not seem to occur in two areas. The percentages of faculty reported to have authority over academic operations appear to be roughly similar across the three decades. In 1970, 83 percent of faculty played a determinative or joint role with administrators in the setting of degree requirements and deciding on the curriculum. This number rose modestly to about 90 percent in 2001. Decisions regarding the types of degrees offered seem to be made in a fashion similar to the approach employed thirty years ago. Faculty played almost no role in decisions about building and facility construction then, and they continue to play a small role today.

Table 7.20b provides a breakdown by each decision-style category for faculty participation for each of the fifteen questions. The table also compares estimates provided in 1970 with those provided for the most recent survey. Recall that respondents were given a list of fifteen decision areas and asked to estimate the fraction of faculty at their institutions whose participation in the decision took each of five possible styles. The five categories of decision style ranged from full faculty determination to no participation whatsoever. In some cases faculty might share authority jointly with a board or with the administration. In others, these groups might consult with the faculty prior to taking action or might merely discuss agreed-on policies with the faculty post-hoc.

The patterns revealed in Table 7.20a are confirmed by this more detailed analysis of the ratings provided by survey respondents. Faculty authority appears to have increased in the last thirty years. The categories are arranged in columns in descending order from the most faculty authority on the left to the least on the right. Moving from the left, cells are shaded to the point where the sum of percentages reaches at least 50 percent. That is, at least 50 percent of the faculty participate with at least the amount of authority indicated by the right-most shaded cell.

Table 7.20b. Distribution of Responses from 1970 to 2001

| | | Faculty Determination (%) | Joint Action (%) | Consultation (%) | Discussion (%) | None (%) |
|---|---|---|---|---|---|---|
| **Faculty status** | | | | | | |
| 1 Appointments of full-time faculty | 1970 | 4.5 | 26.4 | 27.7 | 29.5 | 11.7 |
| | 2001 | 14.5 | 58.2 | 24.2 | 2.3 | 1.0 |
| 2 Tenure promotions for faculty | 1970 | 5.7 | 30.2 | 30.7 | 17.1 | 16.4 |
| | 2001 | 13.2 | 57.7 | 26.1 | 1.4 | 1.5 |
| **Academic operation** | | | | | | |
| 3 Decisions about the content of the curriculum | 1970 | 45.6 | 36.4 | 11.4 | 5.6 | 1.0 |
| | 2001 | 62.8 | 30.4 | 5.4 | 0.9 | 0.4 |
| 4 Setting degree requirements | 1970 | 48.1 | 33.1 | 11.4 | 5.2 | 2.0 |
| | 2001 | 54.6 | 36.6 | 6.8 | 1.5 | 0.6 |
| **Academic planning and policy** | | | | | | |
| 5 Types of degrees offered | 1970 | 20.8 | 51.1 | 15.6 | 7.1 | 5.2 |
| | 2001 | 22.9 | 54.0 | 17.6 | 4.0 | 1.5 |
| 6 Relative sizes of the faculty of various disciplines | 1970 | 1.4 | 8.7 | 19.5 | 31.2 | 39.2 |
| | 2001 | 6.2 | 30.5 | 40.2 | 17.5 | 5.6 |
| 7 Construction programs for buildings and other facilities | 1970 | 0.5 | 6.7 | 26.8 | 39.6 | 26.5 |
| | 2001 | 1.3 | 7.6 | 40.7 | 38.0 | 12.4 |
| 8 Setting of the average teaching loads | 1970 | 4.7 | 19.3 | 23.7 | 29.8 | 22.5 |
| | 2001 | 6.7 | 34.0 | 30.8 | 22.4 | 6.3 |

## Selection of administrators and department chair

| | | | | | | |
|---|---|---|---|---|---|---|
| 9 Appointing the academic dean | 1970 | 0.7 | 13.0 | 33.0 | 24.6 | 28.7 |
| | 2001 | 2.8 | 29.7 | 53.7 | 9.1 | 4.7 |
| 10 Appointing department chairs or heads | 1970 | 6.5 | 15.5 | 28.0 | 26.5 | 23.5 |
| | 2001 | 16.5 | 37.5 | 36.2 | 6.3 | 3.5 |

## Financial planning and policy

| | | | | | | |
|---|---|---|---|---|---|---|
| 11 Setting faculty salary scales | 1970 | 0.2 | 6.1 | 24.2 | 19.6 | 49.9 |
| | 2001 | 1.9 | 18.4 | 30.5 | 34.0 | 15.2 |
| 12 Decisions about individual faculty salaries | 1970 | 1.3 | 5.7 | 15.7 | 26.0 | 51.3 |
| | 2001 | 2.8 | 15.3 | 24.0 | 30.0 | 28 |
| 13 Short-range budgetary planning | 1970 | 0.5 | 3.9 | 21.5 | 30.5 | 43.6 |
| | 2001 | 2.1 | 16.3 | 37.9 | 31.2 | 12.4 |

## Organization of faculty agencies

| | | | | | | |
|---|---|---|---|---|---|---|
| 14 Decisions that establish the authority of faculty in campus governance | 1970 | 9.3 | 37.4 | 27.9 | 7.8 | 17.6 |
| | 2001 | 12.6 | 50.6 | 22.2 | 11.1 | 3.5 |
| 15 Selecting members for institution-wide committees, senate, and similar agencies | 1970 | 32.1 | 28.4 | 14.1 | 9.7 | 15.7 |
| | 2001 | 52.9 | 27.7 | 12.6 | 4.0 | 2.7 |

*Note:* See n. 10, p. 293, for definition of each category of decision-making style. The numbers are average percentages. Figures may not add to 100% because of rounding.

The numbers of shaded cells and of white cells provide a visual representation of the balance of authority over issues in this area over time. A measure for faculty authority can be visualized as the length of the white area in each row, and the degree of administrative or board control over an issue is indicated by the length of the shaded area in each row. For instance, for the two questions concerning academic operations—decisions about curriculum (3) and setting degree requirements (4)—faculty authority in 2001 is quite significant; more than half of faculty are classified as having full determinative authority over these issues. Correspondingly, faculty authority in financial planning issues is quite minimal, and the shaded gray cells indicate the strength of board or administrative authority in this area. In a comparison of the shaded area representing 1970 and 2001 for all items, the 50 percent mark was reached under a greater level of faculty participation in 2001 than in 1970. Most faculty are classified under either the joint action category, meaning they share joint authority with administrators and boards, or under the consultation category, meaning the faculty is consulted before major decisions but the decision may or may not reflect faculty views. In both the previous and current surveys faculty appear to be rarely involved in matters grouped under academic planning or financial planning. Decisions regarding faculty status and academic operation seem the primary responsibility of the faculty in 2001, just as they appear to have been in 1970. The overall picture is one of stability, with some change in the direction of greater faculty authority. Whether this represents a diminution of the situation fifteen years ago, in the mid-1980s, is not clear. But by looking over a longer term, it does appear that faculty participation in decisions has expanded.

## Conclusion

Despite much current concern among both faculty and observers of higher education about the state of shared governance, the data collected here depict an image neither as cumbersome and unloved as some critics seem to believe, nor as threatened and supplanted as some advocates seem to fear. Faculty seem to have a significant role in governance at many institutions, and their participation appears to be valued. Few administrators suggested that faculty governance presented a significant obstacle to effective governance. The data indicate that faculty have significant authority in the decision areas where they claim the greatest expertise and tend to demand that their voice be preeminent: the curriculum, degree requirements, appointments and promotions, and determining the arrangements of shared governance. Budget making, strategy, and construction planning seem to remain the realm of administrators and boards.

While the faculty's role seems healthy, faculty respondents were clearly less satisfied with matters than were administrators, or at least they expressed less sanguine appraisals of their participation. Faculty respondents tended to grade their participation and influence more conservatively than administrators rated faculty influence. Of course, administrators also seemed to feel that they had less influence than faculty tended to ascribe to them. These perceptions are consistent with the common observation made of higher education that all groups ascribe to others more influence than those groups ascribe to themselves. No one seems to think they have enough influence, and everyone seems to feel other groups possess more influence than they may actually have.

In assessing perceptions of power, the important question becomes "power relative to what?" Without a clear standard or measure of power, it is difficult if not impossible to conclude whether individuals or groups have sufficient or appropriate levels of power and influence. Those who have high standards for the degree of power they want to wield may express low assessments of their influence and dissatisfaction with the system.

One conclusion that is possible from this analysis is that relative levels of power have changed over time. Data from the survey indicate that the sector is not without disturbance or transformation. Some institutions have seen significant turmoil at the executive position. Efforts to impose management tools that assess performance and outcomes have made headway. Among the public institutions, the epicenter of influence appears to have shifted somewhat in the direction of boards and executive officers. Still, comparisons of the 2001 survey data with the data gathered thirty years ago suggest that faculty participation in a number of decision areas has expanded. What is more, despite a great deal of talk in policy circles about change, many of the traditions and practices of shared governance continue as they have in the past. The survey uncovered little evidence that proposed changes in governance or suggested policies regarding participation and voice have made much headway. Liberal arts colleges, despite facing some of the most significant challenges in the sector, also appear to have avoided rapid or drastic change. Despite their importation of nonacademic leadership, the survey data indicate that these colleges shied away from efforts to attract better faculty and improve their competitive position and have had the least experience with reorganizations and department closures.

While governance clearly affects the kinds of choices an institution faces and the decisions it makes, the survey also highlighted that other factors can matter as much or more. Among them, mission, size, market pressures, and a school's market niche shape the adoption of particular policies. The similarity of responses from private and public research universities suggests the importance of mission in determining the choice and decision structure. While some academics continue to resist treating higher education as a market good, market pressures appear to be real factors that affect institutional decision making and that account for variation in institutional approaches. The survey data reviewed here point out clear differences in policy and in governance structures among institutions that found themselves in different markets, serving different clientele, and having different kinds of market opportunities.

None of this should be surprising for economic analysts of the sector. However, the survey did produce a number of findings that might upset some of the presuppositions an economist might bring to an analysis of governance. For instance, we might expect to observe more faculty control at private institutions, because the public's ownership of state institutions should provide incentives to situate strong powers with governing boards, institute systems of monitoring, and impose rules that shift the locus of power away from faculty and toward the public. This did not appear to be the case. Control mechanisms and structures for faculty participation took different forms, but the ascribed levels of faculty influence were not significantly different between private and public institutions. While dependence on the market for tuition-paying students may reduce faculty influence and account for a narrowing of discrepancies between public and private institutions, even those institutions with strong market positions such as the Research I and Liberal Arts I institutions did not distinguish themselves by having extraordinarily strong faculty governance structures.

We might also expect that faculty would more successfully resist the importation of new management techniques like post-tenure review and merit pay if the governance structure granted them significant powers or if the faculty's reputation afforded them significant options in the faculty labor market. The data did show that in some cases faculty power, both structural and market-based, is correlated with a lower incidence of adoption of policies such as merit pay. However, private research universities, which we might think would be associated with the most faculty power and the greatest labor market flexibility for faculty, were among the most eager adopters of such management methods. Perhaps this apparent atrophy of collective efforts in faculty governance at research universities confirms that when markets provide exit power to organizational participants, their interest in the expression of power from voice deteriorates (Hirschman 1970).

The increasing competition for students, the demand from students for training that prepares them for twenty-first-century job opportunities, and the budget constraints that often limit the growth opportunities of public institutions might also suggest that private institutions would be more aggressive in their pursuit of quality. Whether in fact a rank divergence between public and private institutions has appeared is a question for another study, but from the data reported here, it does not seem that public institutions have been less aggressive in their pursuit of faculty or in their concern for quality. The respondents from private institutions certainly expressed greater sensitivity to market factors in their responses; think of how respondents characterized their reaction to student needs. Public institutions, though, appeared more aggressive in faculty-hiring policies. To ascertain whether the differences indicated here among ownership forms and institutional types persist would require analysis that controls for other sources of variation among institutions, but the survey does suggest such an investigation would be worthwhile.

A number of reasons may explain this convergence over the pursuit of quality despite different kinds of budget constraints. First, a popular idea often expressed among state politicians is that higher education can be an important engine of economic growth. It may help train a skilled workforce for the state if college graduates can be retained, and it may produce economic activity that spurs growth in areas such as biotechnology, medicine, and computers. As long as actions, even costly ones, can be justified on this basis, politicians may support them. Second, it may be that such actions represent a mechanism for institutional self-defense. A university with national prominence and reputation may provide a kind of inoculation against budget incursions from politicians.

Of course, another way to defend an institution is to have effective governance structures that assure the public and the politicians that institutional decision making is efficient, effective, responsive to environmental imperatives, cognizant of the public's interests, and mindful of the institution's long-run interests. Perhaps no amount of reform and adjustment can assure the public that shared governance is an effective and important means of guiding these complex and important institutions. But winning the public's confidence will require institutions to pursue both greater transparency in their decision making and a clearer delineation of responsibilities. Faculty participation in governance needs to be boosted so that governance bodies can confidently assert that they reflect the faculty's interest and best judgments. To do so will require real and perhaps costly measures that make genuine the oft-promised but rarely enacted idea that tasks other than research will be considered in professional promotion and rewarded in practice. Any reform effort will have to overcome the inertia of participants in shared governance whose implicit motto seems to be "upset no one." Most importantly, true progress in reform and in public persuasion can occur only when more research, both thick description and comprehensive data, is available concerning the relationships between practices and institutions of shared governance and organizational performance.

CHAPTER EIGHT

# Collective Bargaining in American Higher Education

RONALD G. EHRENBERG, DANIEL B. KLAFF,
ADAM T. KEZSBOM, AND MATTHEW P. NAGOWSKI

No discussion of governance in higher education would be complete without a consideration of the role of collective bargaining. Historically, most researchers interested in the subject have directed their attention to the unionization of faculty members. Given several recent decisions by the National Labor Relations Board (NLRB) that leave open the possibility that unionization of faculty in private colleges and universities may increase in the future, we discuss collective bargaining for faculty in the first section (Leatherman 2000, A16).

Recently, however, attention has been also directed at the unionization of two other groups in the higher education workforce. Activists on a number of campuses have pressed for academic institutions to pay their low-wage employees a *living wage*, and this has brought attention to the role of staff collective bargaining in academia. In the second section, we present the first empirical estimates of the impact of staff bargaining on staff salaries in higher education.

Finally, the number of public universities in which teaching assistants, and in some cases research assistants, have won the right to bargain collectively began to expand rapidly at the turn of the twenty-first century.

We are grateful to the Andrew W. Mellon Foundation and the Atlantic Philanthropies (Inc.) USA for their support of the Cornell Higher Education Research Institute. Without implicating them for what remains, we are grateful to Ernie Benjamin, Rick Hurd, James Monks, Doug Shapiro, and Anne Machung for their comments on an earlier draft.

A NLRB ruling in 2001 that permitted collective bargaining for teaching assistants at New York University (NYU), led the university in the following year to become the first private one to sign a contract with a union representing teaching assistants. Building on this ruling, graduate assistant organizing campaigns are underway at a number of prestigious private universities. In the third section we address why graduate assistants are increasingly interested in organizing and then present evidence on the effects of graduate student unions on a number of economic variables.

Faculty Unions

Statutes governing bargaining for federal and state government employees, NLRB decisions governing private higher educational institutions, and the Supreme Court decision in the *Yeshiva* case have heavily influenced the growth of collective bargaining for faculty in the United States.[1] President John F. Kennedy's 1962 executive order, which permitted federal government employees limited bargaining rights, led to the signing of the first faculty contract at the U.S. Merchant Marine Academy in 1968.

State governments swiftly followed the executive order and established their own laws governing collective bargaining for public employees in their states. By 1972, thirty-seven states had passed legislation permitting their employees to bargain collectively, although many of them did not cover faculty. The first major faculty contract at a public higher education institution was at the City University of New York in 1969. A 1979 act in California giving collective bargaining rights to faculty and other employees of its four-year colleges led in 1982 to the organization of the eighteen-thousand-faculty-member California State University system.

Collective bargaining for faculty in private higher education took hold in the early 1970s when the NLRB ruled in a case involving Cornell University that nonprofit educational institutions could be required to bargain with their employees. While this case did not apply directly to faculty, the NLRB ruled in another case involving a branch campus of Long Island University that faculty were not necessarily supervisors. This latter ruling was upheld in another NLRB case involving Fordham University. However, the U.S Supreme Court effectively put the brakes on private-sector faculty unionization efforts in 1980, when in the *Yeshiva* case it ruled that faculty were managers and thus were ineligible to bargain collectively with their universities (*NLRB v. Yeshiva University* 944 U.S. 672 [1980]). Indeed, during the decade that followed, a number of institutions, including Boston University and Fairleigh Dickinson University, successfully sought to have previously approved faculty bargaining units decertified.

As a result, faculty unionization in U.S. higher education has become primarily a public-sector phenomenon. In the mid-1990s, about 38 percent of full-time faculty in public higher educational institutions were covered by collective bargaining agreements, while only about 6 percent in private higher educational institutions were covered.[2] Collective bargaining coverage for faculty also varied widely across Carnegie categories of colleges and universities (Carnegie Foundation for the Advancement of Teaching 1994). While over 40 percent of full-time two-year-college faculty were covered by collective bargaining agreements, less than 3 percent of faculty at Liberal Arts I institutions were similarly covered. Lest the reader think that faculty unionization is strictly a two-year-college phenomenon, the proportions of full-time faculty members covered at Carnegie Research, Doctorate, and Comprehensive institutions were over 20 percent at this time.

The number of individuals covered by collective bargaining agreements relating to faculty at public two-year colleges in 1996 exceeded the total number of full-time faculty employed at these institutions that year, at least partially because these bargaining units often include many employees who are not faculty members. While some part-time faculty members are included in these units, nationwide less than 20 percent of part-time faculty are covered by collective bargaining contracts.

There has been a tendency in many academic institutions to increasingly rely on part-time faculty as a way of reducing costs. Between 1987 and 1998, the proportion of adjunct and other faculty employed part-time in the United States rose from 33 to 42 percent, with most of the growth occurring during the first half of the period (Wilson 2001, A17). It is only natural that the low pay and lack of benefits that many of these positions offer would serve as a stimulus for organization of the faculty members that hold them. However, while part-time faculty may have incentives to become unionized, they are difficult to organize for a number of reasons, including that many have other full-time jobs, public-sector part-time faculty are often excluded from full-time units, in some states (e.g., Ohio) part-time employee bargaining units are illegal in the public sector, and part-time faculty have high turnover rates. Having said this, in July 2002, the United Automobile Workers (UAW) won the right to represent over four thousand part-time faculty members at NYU, making it the first adjunct-only faculty union at a major private university and one of the largest adjunct-only faculty unions in the nation (Smallwood 2002c).

Numerous studies have evaluated the impact of collective bargaining coverage on faculty members' salaries relative to faculty salaries at academic institutions where they are not covered by collective bargaining agreements. The result of these studies suggest that at best, faculty unions increase their members' average salaries by a very small percentage, and some found that faculty unions have had no effect.[3] These findings should not be a surprise, for the following reasons: most faculty members covered by union contracts are employed in public higher education institutions, most organized faculty in public higher education lack the legal right to strike, and the two major sources of revenue that finance faculty salaries—tuition and state appropriations—are typically controlled by the legislature and the governor, not by the trustees of the state institutions. With little bargaining power and very few monopoly rents to extract, one should expect unions to have a very small impact on faculty salaries. Indeed, faculty at many of the most prestigious public research universities, who have the most individual bargaining power (in terms of their ability to threaten to leave the institution if their salaries and other conditions of employment are not deemed adequate to them), have systematically chosen not to be represented by unions.

Some observers have feared that faculty unions would press for across-the-board raises in pay rather than merit increases, thus reducing the financial incentives that faculty have to be productive. However, a careful study of faculty contracts in higher education found that more often than not, they contained explicit provisions for merit increases (Rhoades 1998). Often, these contracts required that faculty groups be involved in the determination of which of their colleagues deserved merit increases, but this requirement is not in conflict with what proponents of a strong faculty role in governance should want.

Researchers have also attempted to ascertain the effect of faculty unions on a variety of other outcomes, including research productivity, job satisfaction, turnover behavior, salary differentials across fields, and the probability of obtaining tenure.[4] In the main, these studies have been cross section in nature and have not controlled for the possibility that whether an institution's faculty members are covered by a collective bargaining agreement is not a random event. For example, if collective bargaining is more likely to be established in institutions where faculty are poorly treated by the administration and have low salaries and high turnover rates, it is possible that even if collective bargaining leads to an improvement in faculty salaries, one might still observe a negative relationship between collective bargaining coverage and faculty salaries. However, in this example the direction of causation would run from poor salaries to faculty collective bargaining coverage, not vice versa. The empirical analysis we undertake in the next section attempts to correct for this problem.[5]

One question that has yet to be addressed by researchers is how faculty unions influence the system of shared governance that is in place at many institutions. Shared governance by its nature is cooperative, while collective bargaining may be confrontational.[6] A hypothesis, generated by one of us after participating for many years in faculty senate meetings at an institution without faculty bargaining, is that collective bargaining may actually improve the system of shared governance with respect to economic issues, because it allows faculty participating in shared governance to focus on what is best for the institution as a whole, not solely on what is best for the faculty.

To see this, consider the position of a faculty member participating on a joint faculty-administrative committee during deliberations on the institution's financial plan for the next academic year. If the average faculty salary increase has to be resolved as part of this discussion, the faculty member may focus his attention heavily on increasing this component of the budget, and not worry as much as he should about the other aspects of the budget. On the other hand, if the faculty salary increase pool is determined through collective bargaining and is not part of the budget deliberation, the faculty member can focus all of his attentions on the other aspects of the budget and more carefully consider all of the trade-offs involved. We encourage researchers to investigate the hypothesis that the presence of a faculty union may actually improve the functioning of systems of shared governance, at least with respect to economic issues.[7]

## Staff Unions

In 2001, a twenty-day sit-in at Harvard University brought the living-wage debate to the forefront of American consciousness.[8] After a six-month study, the Harvard Committee on Employment and Contracting Policies, a nineteen-member committee of faculty, staff, administrators, and students that had been appointed by Harvard's president as a result of the discussions to end the sit-in, recommended giving raises to the university's lowest-paid employees and relying more on collective bargaining in the future to ensure that the wages paid by subcontractors did not undercut local union wage scales ("Harvard Panel Recommends Wage Parity: Raises Coming to Cambridge?" *Chronicle of Higher Education*, 11 January 2002, A34). A three-day sit-in at the University of Connecticut that related to the living-wage issue also yielded a substantive victory for campus workers. The protesters there generated an almost two-dollar increase in wages, as well as substantial improvement in benefits for many of the university's workers ("Sit-ins over Staff Wages Have Different Outcomes at Harvard and U. Connecticut," *Chronicle of Higher Education*, 25 March, 2001, A41).

The growth of living-wage movements on almost one hundred campuses reflects the large variation in the wages paid to college and university staff across the country (Van Der Werf 2001). There are many potential explanations for these salary differences, including differences in local cost of living and differences in the resources that the academic institutions have available to pay faculty and staff salaries. One other possible explanation is the influence of staff unions. There have been no studies, however, of the impact of collective bargaining on staff salaries in higher education.

This section of our chapter addresses this issue. After providing some background data on the number of blue-collar and white-collar employees covered by collective bargaining agreements at U.S. higher education institutions, we use data from a 1997–1998 study on the costs of staffing in higher education conducted by the Association of Higher Education Facilities Officers (APPA) and other sources to estimate models that explain the variation across academic institutions in salaries for a number of narrowly defined blue-collar and white-collar occupational groups that are employed by the academic institutions' facilities divisions.[9] Of primary interest to us is the extent to which the salaries of academic staff covered by collective bargaining agreements exceed the salaries of otherwise comparable academic staff that are not covered by such agreements.

Table 8.1 presents data on the employment levels of blue-collar and white-collar staff members employed in U.S. higher education in the mid-1990s, as well as the percentage of each group that was covered by a collective bargaining agreement. The percentage of blue-collar employees represented by staff unions, 42.8 percent, is much larger than the percentage of white-collar employees represented by staff unions, 23.4 percent. Because there are many more white-collar employees, in

Table 8.1. Collective Bargaining Coverage of College and University Staff in 1994

|  | Total Employees | Estimated Employees in Bargaining Units | Percentage Represented |
|---|---|---|---|
| White collar | 1,070,142 | 250,573 | 23.4 |
| Blue collar | 306,335 | 131,232 | 42.8 |
| TOTAL | 1,376,477 | 381,805 | 27.7 |

*Sources*: National Center for Education Statistics 1994, 228–229 (total employees); National Center for the Study of Collective Bargaining in Higher Education and the Professions 1995 (employees in bargaining units).

Table 8.2. Distribution of Academic Institutions by Carnegie Category and Control in the APPA Sample

| Carnegie Category | Funding | | |
|---|---|---|---|
|  | Private | Public | Total |
| Associate | 1 | 13 | 14 |
| Baccalaureate | 23 | 3 | 26 |
| Doctoral | 4 | 16 | 20 |
| Masters | 12 | 42 | 54 |
| Research | 7 | 42 | 49 |
| TOTAL | 47 | 116 | 163 |

the aggregate about 27.7 percent of staff at U.S. colleges and universities were covered by union contracts in the mid-1990s.

The salary and collective bargaining coverage data used in our study come from the APPA's *1997–1998 Comparative Costs and Staffing Report for Educational Faculties* Association of Higher Education Facilities Officers 1999.[10] This data set provided information on salary levels and collective bargaining coverage for forty-seven narrowly defined occupations at 193 U.S. and Canadian colleges, universities, and elementary and secondary schools. We restricted our attention to U.S. higher education institutions that could be classified as Research, Doctoral, Masters, Baccalaureate, or Associate (two-year) institutions (Carnegie Foundation for the Advancement of Teaching 1994).[11] The sample that we used consisted of 163 institutions. Table 8.2 presents the breakdown of the institutions in our sample by Carnegie classification and by form of control. Public institutions constitute the majority of the institutions in each Carnegie category in our sample, except for the Baccalaureate category.

Table 8.3. Mean Occupational Salaries in 1997–1998 for Employees Covered by Collective Bargaining Agreements and Not Covered by Collective Bargaining Agreements in the APPA Sample

| Occupation | Mean Salary without Union | Mean Salary with Union (Ratio) |
|---|---|---|
| Administrative secretary | 21,953 | 26,978 (1.23) |
| Custodian | 16,993 | 22,850 (1.34) |
| Groundskeeper | 18,838 | 26,138 (1.39) |
| Carpenter | 26,206 | 35,962 (1.37) |
| Electrician | 27,701 | 38,629 (1.39) |
| Locksmith | 27,243 | 33,463 (1.23) |
| Heating and cooling | 26,576 | 37,600 (1.41) |
| Painter | 24,468 | 34,645 (1.42) |
| Plumber | 26,852 | 37,575 (1.40) |

*Source*: Authors' computations from the APPA data (Association of Higher Education Facilities Officers 1999). Only institutions that reported union coverage for an occupation and a salary figure for an occupation are included.

We restrict our attention to the nine occupations for which at least 115 institutions in the sample reported both an occupational salary level and whether the employees in the occupation were covered by a collective bargaining agreement. Table 8.3 compares the mean annual salaries of unionized and nonunionized employees for each occupation, and provides the ratio of the mean salary for employees covered by union contracts to that for employees not covered by a union contract. The vast majority of these occupations are blue-collar occupations in the building trades.

In each occupation, employees covered by a union contract earned considerably more than employees not covered by a contract, with the raw differentials in the mean salaries varying across occupations from 23 to 42 percent. The differentials were largest in the skilled trades. Salaries for custodial workers, the group of employees that have been the focus of the living-wage debate on many campuses, were the lowest in the group, and the unionized custodial workers in the sample earned about 35 percent more on average than custodial workers not covered by a collective bargaining agreement.

The estimated differences in the salaries reported in Table 8.3 are raw differences that do not control for characteristics of the institutions or the areas in which the institutions are located, which might be expected to influence staff salaries independent of unionization. For example, if academic institutions whose employees were organized also had greater financial resources, or were located in higher-cost-of-living areas, than institutions whose employees were not organized, one would expect to observe the former paying higher salaries than the latter, even if unionization per se had no effect on the salaries of staff at academic institutions. To estimate whether staff unions do influence salaries, it is necessary to control for the other characteristics of the institutions that might influence salaries.

To accomplish this, we estimated staff salary equations, by occupation, in which the logarithm of the annual salary paid to a staff member in an occupation at the academic institution is specified to a function of a categorical variable indicating whether the particular occupation is unionized at the institution, a vector of categorical variables indicating the Carnegie classification of the institution, a vector of other variables that vary across institutions and are expected to influence staff salaries, and a random error term. Because the dependent variable is the logarithm of salaries, the interpretation of the estimate of the coefficient of the union variable is that it is the estimated percentage by which the salaries of staff in institutions with collective bargaining for the occupation exceed the salaries of staff at institutions without collective bargaining for the occupation, after controlling for the other factors expected to influence salaries.

We included in the set of other variables expected to influence staff salaries a number of variables that influence the resources that the academic institutions have at their command out of which to pay the salaries of staff. These include the logarithm of the institution's endowment per student, the logarithm of its average undergraduate tuition, and for public institutions the logarithm of its state and local government appropriation per student.[12] In our basic specification, we also included the logarithm of the average salary that the institution pays its full professors, under the assumption that this probably represents the best single measure of the financial capacity of the institution. Also included in this vector, to control for differences in cost of living or wage levels across geographic areas, is the logarithm of the mean salary of custodians in the city in which the academic institution is located. When an institution was not located in a city for which we had mean custodian salary data, the mean custodian wage in the state was substituted. Finally, included in this vector is the logarithm of the average math and verbal SAT seventy-fifth-percentile score for entering freshmen at the institution. This variable, as well as the Carnegie category variables, was included to see if the "selectivity" of an academic institution, or its institutional type, influences the salary of its staff, once we have controlled for its financial resources.

Row A of Table 8.4 presents the estimated coefficients of the collective bargaining coverage variable from our basic model. For six of the nine occupations, union coverage is associated, other factors held constant, with higher salaries, with the estimated differentials being in the range of 10 to 17 percent. The differentials are the largest for several of the occupations that historically have been heavily unionized nationwide in the building trades. Relevant to the living-wage debate, we observe that unionized custodians appear to earn about 10 percent more than nonunionized custodians at academic institutions, other factors held constant.

The remaining rows of Table 8.4 summarize the results of the additional econometric modeling we conducted to investigate the sensitivity of the estimated union coefficient to the variables included in the analyses and to the econometric methods we utilized. A key explanatory variable included in the estimating equation that yielded the results in row A was the logarithm of the average salary of full professors at the institution. One can easily argue that this variable should be treated as endogenous and that including it in the model may bias the estimated union coefficient. To see if the inclusion of the full-professor-salary variable mattered, we reestimated our equation excluding this variable from the analyses. The estimated union coefficients from this model specification are found in row B of Table 8.4. The exclusion of the full-professor-salary variable from the right side of the equation leads to slightly higher estimated union–nonunion differentials, with the statistically significant coefficients now ranging from 13 to 21 percent.

The estimates presented in rows A and B of Table 8.4 treat each occupational equation as independent. They ignore the fact that there may be some omitted institutional-level variables that influence the salaries of staff commonly in all occupations. For example, the union–nonunion wage advantage for an occupation at an institution may depend on the fraction of the other staff occupations at an institution that are covered by collective bargaining agreements. Hence the wages for any given staff occupation at an academic institution may depend on the unionization of all staff occupations at the institution.

We attempted to reestimate the models underlying the collective-bargaining-coverage-variablem coefficients reported in row A, adding as an additional explanatory variable the fraction of all nine occupations that were covered by collective bargaining agreements.[13] Unfortunately, when one of the nine occupations was covered by a contract, the vast majority of the other occupations also were covered by a contract. Hence the coverage-by-union-contract variable for an occupation was

Table 8.4. Logarithm of 1997–1998 Occupational Salary Equations: Coefficients of Union Variables Sensitivity Analyses (Absolute Value of *t*-Statistics in Parentheses)

| | Administrative Secretary | Custodian | Groundskeeper | Carpenter | Electrician | Locksmith | Heating and Cooling | Painter | Plumber |
|---|---|---|---|---|---|---|---|---|---|
| A | 0.024 (0.6) | 0.101 (2.7) | 0.007 (0.2) | 0.107 (2.3) | 0.122 (2.6) | 0.071 (1.5) | 0.167 (3.1) | 0.138 (3.0) | 0.135 (2.7) |
| B | 0.044 (0.9) | 0.131 (2.8) | 0.081 (1.1) | 0.155 (2.0) | 0.171 (2.2) | 0.129 (1.9) | 0.187 (2.5) | 0.189 (2.5) | 0.208 (2.7) |
| C | 0.020 (0.5) | 0.072 (2.2) | 0.020 (0.3) | 0.099 (1.6) | 0.130 (2.0) | 0.069 (1.3) | 0.139 (2.3) | 0.135 (2.3) | 0.158 (2.5) |
| D | -0.013 (0.3) | 0.030 (0.7) | -0.067 (1.3) | 0.084 (1.6) | 0.116 (2.2) | 0.032 (0.6) | 0.128 (2.3) | 0.125 (2.4) | 0.113 (2.2) |

*Note:* Row A shows ordinary least squares (OLS) coefficients of the union variable from the basic model; B shows OLS coefficients of the union variable from model that excludes the logarithm of average faculty salary; C, seemingly unrelated regression estimates of the union coefficients from the basic model for the sample of institutions that report data for all 9 occupations; and D, selectivity bias corrected estimates of the basic model.

very highly correlated with the fraction of the nine occupations at the institution that were covered by union contracts. The high degree of collinearity prevented us from estimating such a model.

A second way to get at this issue is simply to treat the nine occupational salary equations as a single system and to allow the error terms to be correlated across equations. Estimating this system using the method of seemingly unrelated regressions will increase the efficiency of our estimates; however, as long as none of the other statistical assumptions is violated, the estimates reported in rows A and B of Table 8.4 will remain unbiased.[14]

The method of seemingly unrelated regressions will increase the efficiency of the estimated coefficients only if the identical explanatory variables do not appear in each equation. In our system, the only explanatory variable that varies across occupations is whether employees in an occupation are covered by a collective bargaining agreement at an institution. We have already indicated that the fraction of occupations organized at an institution is highly correlated with whether any one of the occupations is organized across institutions. Given this fact, it is not surprising that the estimated union coefficients that we obtained when we reestimated the model by seemingly unrelated regressions (the estimates found in row C of Table 8.4) prove to be very similar to the coefficients found in row A of the table. Any differences are probably due to sampling error, since the seemingly unrelated regression model could only be estimated using data on the subset of institutions that reported occupational salary and unionization data for all nine occupations.

Finally, our estimates of the salary advantage that staff who work in unionized academic environments have over staff who work in nonunion academic environments treat staff coverage by a collective bargaining agreement as being exogenous. If, for example, the institutions in which we observe staff covered by a collective bargaining agreement were initially the institutions in which staff compensation was lowest, other factors held constant, our estimates will understate the extent to which academic staff unions have improved their members' compensation relative to the compensation of academic staff at institutions not covered by collective bargaining agreements.

In the absence of having a panel data set that would permit us to estimate how changes in staff salaries at academic institutions are related to changes in collective bargaining coverage, the best way to handle this problem is to use the sample selection bias correction method developed by Heckman (1979) and Lee (1978). To implement this method, we estimate a probit equation for union coverage in an occupation in which union coverage is assumed to be a function of the other right-side variables in our salary equations, as well as the proportion of private-sector employees in the state who are covered by collective bargaining agreements, the proportion of public-sector workers in the state who are covered by collective bargaining, and the interaction of each of these variables with a variable indicating whether the academic institution is public or private.[15] These interaction terms permit the impact of each of the sector coverage variables on the institution's probability of having its staff covered by union contracts to vary with the public or private status of the institution.

The estimated union coefficients that we obtained when the sample selection bias correction method was used are found in row D of Table 8.4. In most cases these estimates prove to be very similar to the ordinary least squares (OLS) estimates reported in row A. The estimated union coefficients for carpenters, electricians, heating and cooling technicians, painters, and plumbers remain statistically significant, and each coefficient is close to its value in the OLS equations. The estimated union coefficients for secretaries, groundskeepers, and locksmiths are statistically insignificantly different from zero, as they were in the OLS estimation. While custodians' salaries appeared to be higher when they were covered by a collective bargaining contract in the OLS specification, the selectivity-corrected estimate of the effects of unions on custodians' salaries is close to zero.

In contemplating what our findings mean, the limitations of our analyses should be kept in mind. The sample of 163 academic institutions used in our study is not necessarily representative of the population of over 3,000 two- and four-year colleges and universities in the United States. The nine occupations whose salaries we analyzed all relate to employees employed in the facilities division, and the effects that we estimated for them are not necessarily representative of the effects for staff unions that one might observe for a wider range of college and university employees working in other areas (e.g., housing and dining, athletics, academic support, student services, external relations).

Nonetheless our findings do suggest that collective bargaining coverage influences staff salaries in higher education, and they imply that a direct way to achieve better salaries for low-paid college and university employees is to encourage them to organize and bargain collectively. Unlike private college and university faculty members, who are effectively precluded from collective bargaining at many

Table 8.5. Universities That Have Recognized Teaching Assistant Unions

| Public Universities before 1999 | Public Universities, 1999 and After | Private Universities |
|---|---|---|
| CUNY | Illinois (Urbana) | New York University (2001) |
| Florida | Massachusetts (Boston) | |
| Florida A&M | Michigan State | |
| Iowa | Oregon State | |
| Kansas | Rhode Island | |
| Massachusetts (Amherst) | Temple University | |
| Massachusetts (Lowell) | UC Berkeley | |
| Michigan | UC Davis | |
| Oregon | UC Irvine | |
| Rutgers (New Brunswick) | UCLA | |
| South Florida | UC Riverside | |
| SUNY Albany | UC San Diego | |
| SUNY Binghamton | UC Santa Barbara | |
| SUNY Buffalo | UC Santa Cruz | |
| SUNY Stony Brook | Washington (Seattle) | |
| Wayne State | | |
| Wisconsin (Madison) | | |
| Wisconsin (Milwaukee) | | |

*Source*: "Unionization Activity of Teaching Assistants," *Chronicle of Higher Education: Almanac*, 2002–2003 and December 6, 2002.

institutions because of the Supreme Court's decision in the *Yeshiva* case, there is no such prohibition to prevent staff at these institutions from organizing.

## Collective Bargaining by Graduate Assistants

The first graduate student union to be recognized as a collective bargaining agent was at the University of Wisconsin in 1969. As noted in an earlier section, collective bargaining at public higher education institutions is governed by state laws, and as state agencies or state courts ruled on the applicability of these laws to graduate assistants, collective bargaining for graduate students gradually spread at public higher education institutions. By 1999, teaching assistants at eighteen public Research and Doctoral universities were covered by collective bargaining agreements (Table 8.5), and in some cases these agreements also covered research assistants at the same campuses. Since the start of 1999, fifteen additional major research and doctoral universities have recognized graduate student bargaining agents, including all the campuses of the University of California.

Teaching assistants at Yale University have been trying to organize and bargain collectively since 1990. The push for collective bargaining for graduate students at private universities got a major boost in February 2001, when the NLRB ruled that graduate assistants at NYU had the legal right to form a union (Smallwood 2001). NYU subsequently agreed to enter into collective bargaining with the union, and a contract settlement was reached in February 2002 (Smallwood 2002a). Organization drives subsequently began at many other private universities, including Brown, Columbia, Cornell, Tufts, and Pennsylvania; a ruling by the NLRB that Brown assistants had the right to form a union has been appealed by the university. In fall 2002, Cornell became the first private university at which teaching assistants voted against forming a union.

The formation of graduate student unions is a bit of an anomaly to economists and collective bargaining scholars. The literature on unions suggests that they are most likely to arise in situations in which workers have long-term attachment to firms. Graduate students do not have permanent employment relationships with the universities at which they study, so why have they increasingly become interested in unionizing?

The University of Wisconsin was a hotbed of student activism in the late 1960s when the first graduate student union was formed, and undoubtedly its formation was heavily influenced by this activism. The late 1960s also represented a booming time in the academic market for new Ph.D.s, with the time needed to earn a doctorate averaging five to six years in many fields and a widespread availability of good academic positions. However, since then things have changed. As Table 8.6 indicates, across all disciplines, the median total number of years enrolled between the granting of baccalaureate and doctoral degrees increased by 1.5 years between 1970 and 2000. Focusing on the increase in the median times across all fields obscures the wide differences in the changes that occurred in many fields. In particular, while median time to earning a degree went up by less than two years in virtually all of the science and engineering fields, it went up by almost three years in the humanities. Humanities, and to some extent social science, graduate students found themselves spending more hours per week as teaching assistants, and service as a teaching assistant slows the time it takes to earn a degree (Ehrenberg and Mavros 1995).

In addition, the fraction of new Ph.D.s finding employment, let alone employment in tenure-track academic jobs, by the time they received their degrees declined substantially. For example, less than 59 percent

Table 8.6. Median Number of Years Enrolled between
Baccalaureate and Doctorate Degrees

| Academic Discipline | 1970 | 2000 |
|---|---|---|
| Engineering | 5.2 | 6.8 |
| Physical sciences | 5.3 | 6.5 |
| Geological sciences | 5.8 | 7.8 |
| Math and computer science | 5.2 | 7.1 |
| Life sciences | 5.3 | 7.0 |
| Psychology | 5.3 | 7.2 |
| Social sciences | 5.8 | 8.1 |
| Humanities | 6.0 | 8.8 |
| Education | 6.3 | 8.3 |
| TOTAL | 6.0 | 7.5 |

*Source*: Authors' calculations from data found at Web-
CASPAR (http://caspar.nsf.gov).

of new Ph.D.s in the humanities reported having definite commitments
of employment or plans for future study at the time they received their
Ph.D., in 1998 (Sanderson et al. 1999). In some fields, such as the life
sciences, at least one and often multiple postdoctoral fellow positions,
frequently at relatively low salaries and without benefits, became the
rule, rather than the exception, before young scholars had a shot at
receiving a tenure-track position (National Research Council 1998). In
sum, an increase in the time it takes to earn a degree and smaller and
more distant payoffs at the end of the graduate school rainbow made
highly educated graduate students a ripe target for unionization efforts.

The time it takes to earn a doctoral degree, the nature of support patterns while in graduate school, the relationships of graduate students to
faculty, and job opportunities after receipt of the Ph.D. vary widely
across fields. Degree times are shortest in the sciences and engineering
fields, where many graduate students work closely with faculty as
research assistants on sponsored research projects, develop research
skills from this work, choose related dissertation topics, and then have
good employment opportunities in the nonacademic as well as academic
sectors. In addition, scientists' external research funding often permits
them to supplement the size of the minimum graduate student stipend
specified by their universities; they have external resources to pay what
is needed to attract first-rate talent. As a result, many graduate students
in the physical sciences and engineering are quite happy with their graduate school experiences.

In contrast, in the humanities there is less involvement of faculty and
graduate students on joint research, a greater proportion of graduate

students are funded via teaching assistantships, writing a dissertation takes considerably longer, and there are only limited nonacademic employment opportunities after receipt of the degree. Faculty members in the humanities only rarely have funds to supplement university teaching or fellowship stipends. Is it any wonder, then, that the push for graduate student unionization is often led by graduate students in the humanities and that often the unionization effort seeks to limit the bargaining unit to assistants (primarily teaching assistants) who are supported by the university rather than include those supported by external funds?[16]

Most universities that have been faced with a graduate student unionization campaign have vigorously opposed it. Public universities that have had collective bargaining relationships with their faculty for many years (e.g., the University of California and State University of New York systems) or collective bargaining relationships with their staff (e.g., the University of Illinois at Urbana), and have not seen these relationships lead to the demise of the university, still vigorously oppose such organizing campaigns. So too do many private universities: a large number of presidents of major private research universities testified before the NLRB, as well as did leaders of higher education organizations such as the Association of American Universities, the American Council on Education, and the Council on Graduate Schools, in opposition to the bid of the NYU graduate student union to be allowed to bargain collectively (Lafer 2001).

Why have these universities opposed graduate student unionization? For some it is clearly the principled belief that a system of shared governance in which the parties (students, faculty, administrators, and trustees) reach decisions through mutual discussions is preferred to a system of conflict. For some it is the worry that graduate student unions will try to get involved in decisions that are more properly left to the faculty and administration, such as the assignment of specific students to different responsibilities and faculty members. For some it is the concern that "one size does not fit all" and that graduate assistant contracts will not allow for the wide diversity of individual arrangements that currently exist across departments within each campus. For some it is the fear that graduate student unions will impose financial costs on universities that they do not want to bear and that these costs will force them to make cutbacks in other areas, or to increase tuition by more than they would prefer to do.

Some of these fears appear to be unfounded, at least for public universities. Public employees in many states, such as New York, are prohibited from striking. Absent the major weapon that a union has to try to impose its desired contract on management, economists predict that the likely impact of the unions on public employees' compensation packages will be small. Certainly the literature discussed in an earlier section suggests that faculty unions' effects on their members' salaries and benefits have been small.

To date there have been no studies of the effects of graduate student unions on economic variables, but a data exchange conducted by a set of major universities provides some suggestive information. Under the condition that we would not divulge the name of any individual institution, or even the name of the data exchange, and would not present the data for any individual institution, we have been granted access to data on the salaries, compensation, and costs of teaching and research assistants at a set of public universities for a number of recent years. We have grouped these universities into four groups. Group A consists of sixteen institutions that have never had a collective bargaining relationship with graduate assistants. The second and third groups consist of four institutions that had collective bargaining arrangements with their graduate assistants before 1995 (group B), and these four institutions plus two more that first began bargaining with graduate assistants in 1995 or 1996 (group B + C). The final group consists of seven institutions that first began bargaining with their graduate assistants during the 1999–2001 period (group D). For simplicity, we restrict our attention to teaching assistants in what follows, but the data for research assistants yields very similar results.

Table 8.7 shows the mean values, across institutions in each group, for a number of economic variables for five academic years, 1996–1997 through 2000–2001. The first panel presents the average stipends that teaching assistants received from the institutions during the academic year. Comparing the institutions where bargaining never occurred (group A) to those whose graduate students were covered by collective bargaining agreements by the first year in our sample (groups B and B + C), we observe that the institutions without collective bargaining had slightly lower average stipends in 1996–1997, but by 2000–2001, their stipends averaged the highest among the three groups. Whether this reflects the inability of graduate student unions to win large salary increases for their members, differences in the tightness of budgets in states where institutions with graduate students who are organized are located and the tightness of budgets in states where institutions with graduate students who are not organized are located, or a concerted effort by nonunion schools to raise stipends to discourage graduate stu-

Table 8.7. Comparison of Teaching Assistant (TA) Salaries, Costs, and Compensation at Public Research Universities with and without TA Unions

| Outcome/Group (number in group) | 1996–1997 | 1997–1998 | 1998–1999 | 1999–2000 | 2000–2001 |
|---|---|---|---|---|---|
| **Average TA academic-year salary** | | | | | |
| A (16) | 10,370 | 10,617 | 10,990 | 11,378 | 11,817 |
| B (4) | 10,401 | 10,670 | 10,537 | 10,724 | 11,223 |
| B + C (6) | 10,561 | 10,891 | 10,950 | 11,352 | 11,686 |
| D (7) | 12,347 | 12,616 | 12,833 | 13,161 | 13,630 |
| **Average TA academic-year compensation** | | | | | |
| A | 9,739 | 9,931 | 10,250 | 10,688 | 11,150 |
| B | 8,953 | 9,107 | 10,009 | 10,141 | 10,649 |
| B + C | 8,999 | 9,269 | 9,892 | 10,271 | 10,653 |
| D | 10,679 | 10,964 | 11,429 | 11,483 | 12,751 |
| **Average TA academic-year cost** | | | | | |
| A | 14,009 | 14,492 | 15,079 | 15,612 | 17,350 |
| B | 14,415 | 14,855 | 16,019 | 17,756 | 17,318 |
| B + C | 13,354 | 14,020 | 14,925 | 16,001 | 16,132 |
| D | 15,345 | 15,676 | 18,375 | 16,256 | 18,627 |
| **Average TA summer salary** | | | | | |
| A | 2,904 | 2,970 | 4,012 | 4,347 | 3,625 |
| B | 2,608 | 2,695 | 4,608 | 5,059 | 4,865 |
| B + C | 2,683 | 2,767 | 4,319 | 4,624 | 4,576 |
| D | 4,182 | 4,752 | 4,607 | 4,788 | 4,785 |
| **Average TA salary/average assistant professor salary** | | | | | |
| A | 0.19 | 0.23 | 0.22 | 0.22 | 0.22 |
| B | 0.20 | 0.22 | 0.21 | 0.21 | 0.20 |
| B + C | 0.20 | 0.23 | 0.23 | 0.22 | 0.22 |
| D | 0.21 | 0.26 | 0.24 | 0.24 | 0.24 |

*Source*: Authors' calculations from confidential data provided to the authors from a set of major research universities that participate in a data exchange program.

*Note*: A, public institutions without TA unions; B, public institutions with TA unions prior to 1995; B + C, group B plus public institutions with TA unions starting in 1995 or 1996; D, public institutions with TA unions starting during the 1999–2001 period; "Compensation" indicates salary less the portion of tuition and fees that TAs must pay; "Cost," salary plus tuition and fees that university forgoes. The value of health insurance benefits provided to TAs is excluded from their salaries. The share of health insurance costs paid for by a fee charged to students that is waived for TAs is included in TA costs.

dents from organizing, cannot be determined from these data. What is of interest, though, is that the highest average stipends in each year occurred at institutions where graduate students organized for bargaining only during the later years of the period (group D). Many of these institutions are located in relatively high-cost-of-living areas, a point that we return to later.

The second panel of data shows the results when we deduct from the stipend paid at each institution the tuition and fees that teaching assistants who were in-state residents had to pay to the university.[17] This is not a perfect measure of the teaching assistants' compensation because the value to the graduate students of any university-provided health insurance benefits would not be included in these numbers, and health insurance coverage has often been an issue that precipitated graduate student organizing efforts. A search of the Web sites of all the institutions in our sample suggested that by 2001–2002 (which is after our sample period) all but two of these institutions (one from group A and one from group B) provided at least partial funding for graduate student health insurance. Nonetheless, focusing on this compensation variable provides some evidence on how graduate student unions influence tuition remission decisions.

In 1996–1997, average teaching assistant compensation was higher at the nonunion institutions (A) than it was at the unionized institutions (B and B + C), which suggests, given the numbers in the previous panel, that required graduate assistant tuition payments were higher at the unionized institutions than they were at the nonunion ones. By 2000–2001, the differential had narrowed somewhat, suggesting that graduate assistants were able to win larger reductions in required tuition and fee payments at schools where graduate students bargained collectively. Again the average compensation of graduate assistants at the group D schools, the ones that organized near the end of the period, was the highest.

The third panel, displays what the costs of graduate assistants are to the institutions. These costs include the stipend and the portion of the students' tuition and fees that are not collected from them. Some of these costs are real costs, for example, the fees that graduate students would otherwise have to pay for mandatory student health insurance coverage. Some are opportunity costs, for example, the forgone tuition revenue that the university does not collect. Omitted from these costs are any university subsidies for benefits, such as health insurance, that the university makes for all graduate students, regardless of whether they are graduate assistants.

Viewed from this perspective, the average teaching assistant costs for the nonunion schools (group A) rose relative to those for the schools where graduate students were organized during the entire period (groups B and B + C), as well as relative to the costs at institutions where graduate students were organized only at the end of the period (group D). These comparisons do not support the view that graduate assistant unions increased universities' academic-year costs for graduate students during the period, although we caution that they may be driven by differential rates of tuition increases at the different sets of institutions during the period.

The next panel in the table provides information on the average stipends paid to graduate students for teaching assistant responsibilities during the summer. The average summer salaries at the nonunion schools started a few hundred dollars above those at the schools where graduate students were unionized throughout the period, but wound up substantially below them by the end of the period. Hence one economic effect of graduate student unions may be to win better stipends for summer work.

Interestingly, the stipends for summer teaching were highest throughout the period at the institutions where graduate students became unionized only at the end of the period. As noted earlier, many of the universities in this category are located in high-cost-of-living areas (see Table 8.5), and it is important to control for cost-of-living differences across areas before drawing any definitive conclusions from the comparisons presented so far.

There are several ways to control for cost-of-living differences. One can use variations in the cost of rental housing across areas to proxy for differences in the cost of living; such data can be obtained from the published *Census of Population* volumes, available from the government every ten years. One can use estimates of the costs of living in different areas prepared by commercial firms that advise corporations about how much to alter their executives' compensation when one relocates them.[18] Or, one can simply say that what is relevant is how much teaching assistants are making relative to young tenure-track faculty, namely, full-time assistant professors.[19] Using all three measures yields similar findings, and we report only the comparisons that adjust for assistant professor salaries here.

The final panel of Table 8.7 presents the latter set of data. We find little support from these comparisons for the proposition that graduate student unions increase the salaries of teaching assistants relative to the salaries of assistant professors. Initially, the ratio of average teaching assistant salary to average assistant professor salary is lowest at the institutions that never had collective bargaining for graduate assistants. However, over the period studied, it rises relative to the ratios at universities where graduate students bargained throughout the period. Similarly, it was highest throughout the period at the institutions that began bargaining with their graduate assistants only during the last sample year. That the ratio of graduate assistant to assistant professor salaries does not vary that much over time at these public institutions should not be too surprising—several of the graduate student contracts specify that the salary increase that their members are to receive will be equal in percentage terms to increases granted to the faculty.[20]

Taken together, the findings suggest that the impact of graduate assistant unions on economic outcomes does not appear to be very large and that concern about the issue of graduate student unions may be overstated.[21] Indeed attracting and retaining top graduate students is an important objective of faculty at all research universities, and so the faculty is often supportive of increased stipends for graduate fellows and assistants. Concern about graduate assistant unions, for the most part, is an administrative, not a faculty concern.

Of course if the cost of graduate students increases too much, it is reasonable to expect that universities will seek alternative ways of meeting their staffing needs for undergraduate courses. If graduate student unions, or the bidding up of teaching assistant stipends in an effort to attract the best and brightest graduate students, lead to substantially increased costs for the students, it is reasonable to expect that ultimately universities will reduce the size of their Ph.D. programs and make more use of lecturers and other non-tenure-track faculty to staff undergraduate courses. Another source of substitute labor is undergraduate teaching assistants. However, as the vote in favor of establishing a union for undergraduate resident hall assistants at the University of Massachusetts in March 2002 should suggest, once the line between financial aid and employment becomes blurred, academic institutions may well be subject to more organizing campaigns of undergraduate students ("Resident Assistants at UMass Vote to Unionize," *Chronicle of Higher Education*, 15 March 2002, A39).[22] Institutions that offer undergraduate teaching assistantships for academic credit, rather than for compensation, might skirt this issue, but many faculty members challenge the legitimacy of giving academic credit for work as a teaching assistant.

Similarly, if graduate student unions bid up the costs of research assistants, and universities require faculty with external sources of funding to pay higher stipend levels and higher levels of tuition for graduate research assistants, faculty members may decide that they are better off employing more postdoctoral fellows and permanent lab staff and fewer graduate research assistants. So one impact of graduate student unions may be smaller Ph.D. programs.

One respected former university president is genuinely concerned that there may be a conflict between collegiality at universities and collective bargaining for graduate students (Duderstadt 2000, 94–95).[23] In addition to worrying about graduate student unions getting involved with issues of class size and the assignment of teaching assistants, he worries that graduate student unions may lead to some breakdowns in the faculty–student mentorship relationship and ultimately a reduction in graduate program quality.

If this were true, one might expect to see things such as the time it takes to earn a degree and completion rates for Ph.D. students increasing at universities that have teaching assistant unions and, as a result, possibly a decline in the quality of students who apply to such programs. In contrast, if graduate student unions are seen as improving the atmosphere for students attending graduate school, such unions might be expected to lead to an improvement in the quality of the applicants and a general increase in program quality. To date, no tests of these hypotheses have been conducted.

## Conclusion

The role of collective bargaining in higher education is likely to increase in the future. Most of the growth of higher education is occurring in the public sector, and it is in the public sector that both faculty and staff unions are the strongest (in terms of shares of individuals who are members) and where there are the fewest legal obstacles to the continued rise of collective bargaining. The decline of faculty salaries in the public sector relative to those in the private sector may also provide further impetus for future faculty organization issues, although the decline in public salaries has often been large in states where faculty unions already exist. Recent NLRB decisions seem to leave open the possibility that the *Yeshiva* decision may not apply to all private-sector faculty members and thus, possibilities may also exist for the growth of unions among faculty in private colleges and universities.

While extensive research has been conducted on the impact of faculty unions on salaries, benefits, and productivity, very little is actually known about how they influence faculty governance. One hypothesis, which has yet to be tested, is that by providing a means by which faculty may advocate for things (such as salaries) that are explicitly important to them, unionization allows faculty members involved in faculty governance to evaluate economic issues facing their institution more broadly from the perspective of the institution as a whole.

The growing living-wage movement on campuses, which has its roots in the notion that academic institutions have an obligation to treat their workers fairly, is also likely to provide a stimulus for efforts to increase union strength among staff at these institutions. Certainly the evidence that staff unions, unlike their faculty counterparts, seem able to improve their economic positions through collective bargaining should stimulate future growth in this area.

Finally, it will likely prove difficult for most major universities to resist the tide of graduate assistant organizing activity that is sweeping the nation. These unions provide a structure under which activist students can develop leadership skills, and the courts appear to be increasingly ruling in unions' favor. Our preliminary evidence suggesting that graduating student unions do not have a large impact on the economic well-being of their members is unlikely to sway die-hard adherents from the notion that graduate student unions will help to alter the imbalance between graduate students and their mentors that is often alleged to exist.

# CHALLENGES FROM NONPROFITS AND NONLEGAL LEGAL INFLUENCES

# CHAPTER NINE

# Nonprofit and For-Profit Governance in Higher Education

## BRIAN PUSSER AND SARAH E. TURNER

T here is a growing consensus in contemporary research on higher education that the next decade will be a period defined by an increasingly competitive political-economic environment for providers of degrees, credentials, and educational services (Green, Eckel, and Barblan 2002; Newman and Couterier 2001). The fundamental drivers of these predictions are often delineated in contemporary accounts of the changing postsecondary landscape: increased competition between nonprofit institutions and the rise of for-profit providers; evolving labor market opportunities and the attendant demand for continuous education; changing student demographics; a retreat from direct public provision of higher education; reductions in state subsidies; competition from for-profit providers; and the emergence of new technologies. Governance structures in any enterprise—higher education included—are fundamental in the determination of what is produced and how it is produced. At issue is how the marketplace, and the emerging competitive political economy, will affect governance structures and processes in higher education.

Among the first institutions incorporated in the United States were colleges and universities, with Harvard College leading the way in the early seventeenth century. A wave of small liberal arts colleges followed in the late eighteenth and early nineteenth centuries, with denominational groups establishing new postsecondary institutions in New

The authors are grateful to David Breneman, Gordon Winston, and Gary Rhoades for their comments on the manuscript, and to David A. Wolcott for his help in the preparation of this work.

England and the midwestern states. The nineteenth century also saw the widespread introduction of colleges and universities chartered by the states, including the opening of the University of Virginia in 1819, followed by the widespread funding of state universities under the Morrill acts of 1862 and 1890. The establishment of these institutions as charitable nonprofits and public institutions with the benefits of tax exemption legitimized the direct production of higher education as an activity recognized in the public interest.[1] Their organizational status also created the strongest measure of differentiation between institutional types at that time: source of funds. Public nonprofits were the recipients of significant direct appropriations from their respective states. Private nonprofits received donations and also benefited from favorable tax treatment, while for-profits relied solely on tuition income and the tax benefits generally accorded business enterprises.

Nonprofit and for-profit institutions of higher education have had distinctly different developmental trajectories over the course of the last century. While public universities were in their ascendancy at the start of the century, proprietary schools were nearly forced out of the market—or at least forced to the shadows of higher education—owing to reports of exploitative practices and financial scandals.[2] Throughout the twentieth century, and particularly after World War II, nonprofit public institutions held the largest share of what had become the largest degree-granting postsecondary system in the world.

Near the end of the twentieth century a new form of for-profit rose to prominence: the corporate university. "For-profit higher education" no longer necessarily implied a storefront sole-proprietorship. The new model brought a blend of the scale economies familiar to public universities, with marketing and organizational practices drawn from the corporate sector. These new for-profits—Strayer, Inc., the University of Phoenix, and so on—saw no conflict between the provision of educational services and profit maximization. What is more, these institutions benefited from many of the same public subsidies as their nonprofit peers, as their students were eligible for extensive financial aid through federal Title IV programs. While federal criteria governing Title IV financial aid programs generally include accredited for-profits, those institutions often compete in an arena free from the regulatory and oversight burdens placed on nonprofits that house significant student populations, operate athletic programs under Title IX, or engage in federally funded research. Where public and private nonprofit and for-profit providers clearly diverge is in their governance processes. Of particular interest is the question of how differences in governance may lead to differences in the response to market forces such as changes in political and economic conditions, student demand, and the introduction of new technologies in the educational process.

The first section of this analysis begins with a comparison of the missions, outputs, and governance structures of colleges and universities with different forms of institutional control. In turn, we consider the variation by institutional control in revenue sources, academic employment, and board governance. Our central conclusion is that while public and private nonprofit universities and for-profit institutions were at one point vastly different in their missions, sources of revenue, and outputs, in certain sectors there has recently been substantial convergence in what these institutions do and how they generate resources. To be sure, there remain meaningful differences in revenue, output, and governance by institutional control; yet, with some significant exceptions among very elite institutions, these differences are narrowing rather than widening (Ehrenberg 2000a). The questions for public policy raised by this convergence of activities are whether governance forms will—or should—follow suit, and whether public and private nonprofit colleges and universities will continue to generate public benefits as governance structures adapt.

## Mission and Constituency: Overlap in Higher Education

Perhaps the easiest way to distinguish between public and private nonprofit institutions, on the one hand, and for-profit institutions, on the other, is to look at their legitimate objective functions. In for-profit colleges, the objective is clear: maximize profits. More formally, this means that we would expect for-profit colleges and universities to choose faculty and other inputs to produce a given level of output or course offerings at the lowest cost. As in the corporate sector more generally, external threats—including the possibility of hostile takeover—are powerful forces that push managers and directors in for-profit higher education to maximize profits.

For nonprofit providers, the legitimate objective functions are far less easily defined (Pusser 2002; Winston 1999). What nonprofit providers maximize depends on institutional mission, with institutions differing in their emphasis on quality versus quantity, the production of public and private goods, and the balance between research and teaching.[3] Glaeser (2002, 3) captured the ambiguity this way: "What nonprofits do maximize is a significant and difficult question." While the compe-

Table 9.1a. Distribution of Institutions by Control (Degree-granting Postsecondary Institutions, 1997–1998)

| Type | N |
| --- | --- |
| 4-year | |
|   For-profit | 216 |
|   Nonprofit, public | 1,880 |
|   Nonprofit, private | 631 |
| 2-year | |
|   For-profit | 529 |
|   Nonprofit, public | 218 |
|   Nonprofit, private | 1,113 |

*Source*: National Center for Education Statistics 1999, Table A1.

tition among colleges and universities in the market for higher education provides one incentive for institutional efficiency, and legislative oversight of public institutions another, public and private nonprofits are free of the residual shareholders and the capacity to distribute profits that provide incentives for administrators to maximize profits in the for-profit sector.

Glaeser (2002) argues that in the face of weak governance structures, colleges and universities have evolved to resemble "worker cooperatives," representing the preferences of faculty, with particular emphasis on the institution of tenure and the rise of the importance of research as a faculty activity. While this model may have characterized the nature of governance in higher education through the late 1970s, when Jencks and Riesman wrote the *Academic Revolution* (1968), the revenue shortfalls of the last three decades brought about yet another transformation in academic organization. To varying degrees across colleges of different types, the locus of control has shifted from faculty to professional administrators to such a degree that Rhoades (1998) has described contemporary faculty members as "managed professionals."

While distinguishing institutional mission is inevitably subject to significant ambiguity, identifying market participation is a relatively straightforward exercise. Tables 9.1a and 9.1b show the distribution of institutions by the broad distinction of baccalaureate and associate degree granting and institutional control.

To be sure, there is considerable specialization, with public nonprofit institutions dominating the two-year sector, private nonprofit institutions dominating four-year degree-granting institutions, and for-profit institutions dominating the category of institutions awarding less than

Table 9.1b. Distribution of Institutions by Enrollment

| | All Postsecondary Institutions | | Degree-granting Institutions | |
|---|---|---|---|---|
| | N | Share (%) | N | Share (%) |
| Public | 11,353,880 | 76.0 | 11,160,838 | 76.8 |
| Private not-for-profit | 3,040,251 | 20.3 | 3,004,925 | 20.7 |
| Private for-profit | 552,777 | 3.7 | 364,273 | 2.5 |
| TOTAL | 14,946,908 | 100.0 | 14,530,036 | 100.0 |

*Source*: National Center for Education Statistics 2001b.

two-year degrees or certification. While there are a number of explanations for the existence of some comparative advantage across institutional types, there is also a considerable degree of plurality, with each
institutional type represented in each sector.

Despite the presence of several very large for-profit institutions like
the University of Phoenix (with enrollment over 75,000), the for-profit
share of total collegiate enrollment is relatively modest, accounting
for less than 4 percent of all enrollment (Table 9.1b). Public nonprofit
colleges and universities, which are generally much larger than their
private nonprofit counterparts, continue to account for the majority of
student enrollment, registering about three-fourths of all students in
1997–1998.

What should be clear at the outset is that while there are many postsecondary institutions that produce quite similar outputs, some institutions are extremely specialized. Whereas path dependence is one
explanation (Goldin and Katz 1999), and the instrumental political
value of public institutions another (Pusser 2003), it is also possible
to suggest several economic arguments. Following Hansmann 1980,
public and nonprofit provision is particularly appropriate when outcomes are difficult to observe or can be revealed only with the passage
of time, where rapid expansion of capacity requires resources not provided for by capital markets, or when there are likely to be externalities associated with the development of particular types of human
capital. It has also been argued that public nonprofit provision is essential where consumer demand is insufficient to ensure the production of
particular socially useful outcomes (Pusser 2002). Given that a number
of activities are efficiently produced through public subsidies to for-
profit firms, the observation that there may be economies of scope in
higher education provides a strong argument for production outside the
for-profit sector.[4]

Despite the traditional distinctions between public nonprofit, private nonprofit, and for-profit postsecondary institutions, we argue that these organizations are undergoing transformation on five dimensions. First, there is an increasing convergence of revenue sources to these institutions. Second, increased political-economic demands for competitive efficiencies in a number of postsecondary sectors are driving a potential convergence in outcomes. Third, new opportunities for postsecondary provision, such as the growing demand for continuing education and services targeted to adults, are transforming the competitive environment for higher education institutions. Fourth, changes in the organization of academic labor, as well as greater distinctions between faculty members and institutional managers, will facilitate convergence in nonprofit and for-profit academic administration. Finally, while the embedded structures and legal constraints on nonprofit governance make adaptation in that realm somewhat slower, given the trends for revenue and outcomes, we suggest that a convergence of nonprofit and for-profit governance structures and processes is likely to follow.

## A Convergence of Revenue Sources

Research on nonprofit organizations has long suggested that a fundamental distinction between nonprofit and for-profit organizations is the source of their revenues (Hansmann 1996; James 1998; Weisbrod 1988; Winston 1998). Yet, while the historical difference in revenue sources is unambiguous, there appears to be a contemporary convergence in revenue sources. Overall, the share of revenue coming from tuition charges as well as revenue coming from fee-for-service activities has risen at all three institutional types. While the share of current revenues accounted for by tuition remains appreciably larger at the private institutions than the public institutions, the tuition share at public institutions rose by approximately 47 percent between 1980 and 1995, relative to an increase of 15.5 percent at private for-profit and 17 percent at private nonprofit institutions (Figure 9.1).

For public institutions, the largest source of revenue—and the factor distinguishing these colleges and universities from private institutions— is state and local appropriations. While private institutions typically receive less than 3 percent of revenues from state and local sources, public institutions historically received over one-half of all revenues from state appropriations. Yet, in the last two decades, the relative importance of state funding has decreased appreciably at public

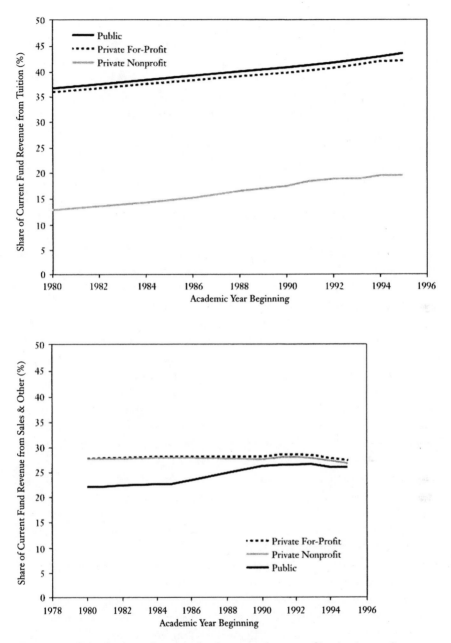

Figure 9.1. Distribution of current fund revenue by type of institution, 1980–1995.

institutions, falling from 49 percent of current fund revenues in 1980 to a bit less than 40 percent of current fund revenues in 1995 (National Center for Education Statistics 2001). While total state appropriations have not fallen appreciably, what is clear is the leveling off in state support, in both total dollars and dollars per student (Figure 9.2). In this regard, as costs have escalated in higher education, state support has not kept pace, leaving public institutions to garner a larger share of their revenues from service activities (Mingle 2000).

In response to uncertainty over state funding, a significant number of public nonprofit institutions have initiated innovative efforts to offer programs and degrees without direct state subsidies, charging tuition quite close to that of for-profit providers (Pusser and Doane 2001). This search for alternative markets for educational services has followed in the private nonprofit sector as well. Some of these programs originate in existing continuing education or extension programs; others have been created anew, as in the case of UCLA's OnLine Learning.net, E-Cornell, and the Universitas 21 consortium. In some instances these entrepreneurial programs are created in partnership with venture capitalists or for-profit corporations. To the extent that these "market rate" programs prosper and generate enrollments, they will expedite the convergence of tuition prices across institutional types.

The burden of increased tuition revenues is borne not only by the consumers or students, but also by the federal government through student aid payments. Individuals often fund tuition payments through federal subsidies, including financial aid programs like the Pell grant program, subsidized student loans, and tax credits. In the three decades since the passage of the Higher Education Act of 1972, federal financial aid, once the sole province of the nonprofit sector, has been increasingly made available to for-profit providers. For-profit providers are also significant beneficiaries of tax subsidies. A significant proportion of the students enrolled in the University of Phoenix have some or all of their tuition paid by their employers, who in turn receive tax deductions for those payments.

While the overall share of Pell grant dollars going to students attending for-profit institutions has declined somewhat since a peak of over 22 percent in 1989–1990, the share of federal financial aid dollars going to students attending for-profit schools is greater than the associated share of total postsecondary enrollment at these schools (Figure 9.3).[5] Without question, both the for-profit and nonprofit sectors of higher education have relied on Pell grants (as well as capital available through student loans) as a source of tuition payments. What is, perhaps, most

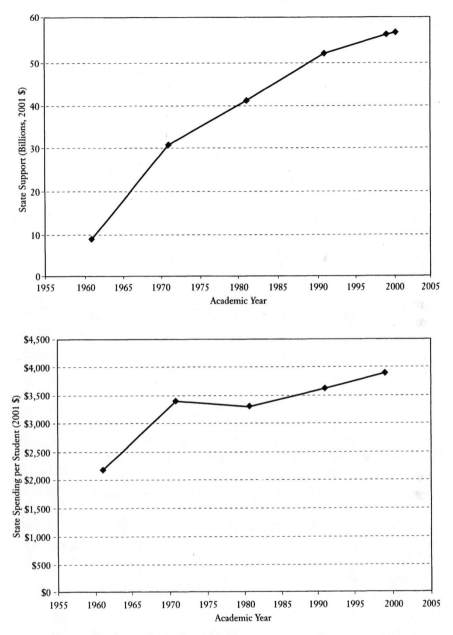

Figure 9.2. State support for higher education.

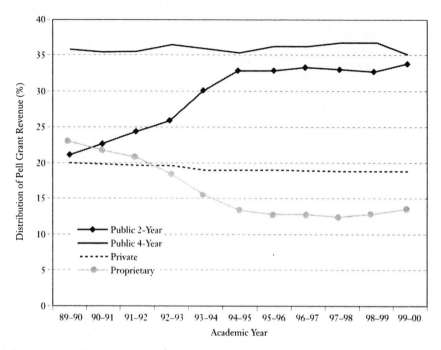

Figure 9.3. Pell Grant revenue by type of institution. Source: College Board 2001, Table 5.

interesting about the distribution of student aid is the large share of Title IV aid distributed to independent students (Figure 9.4). These students are largely beyond the traditional college-going age (over age twenty-four for those without dependents) and must demonstrate the absence of parental support.

In many respects, the provision of postsecondary training in the form of continuing education, certification, or part-time degree programs has been one of the largest growth areas in higher education over the last three decades. Some of this expansion has been fueled by the increased availability of federal financial support for nontraditional students (Seftor and Turner 2002). Income from programs targeted to this group of students represents an increasing share of university revenue in all sectors. More to the point, this is an area in which the traditional distinctions in production technology across sectors are less obvious, as the on-campus activities such as dorms and athletics that are integral to traditional undergraduate education (and largely unique to nonprofit institutions) are peripheral to these activities.

Nonprofits have also increased revenue from entrepreneurial behaviors in a number of arenas. University auxiliary enterprise income from

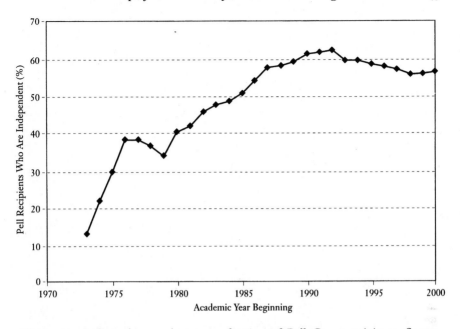

Figure 9.4. Independent students as a fraction of Pell Grant recipients. Source: College Board 2001, Table 7.

the provision of housing, parking, food services, bookstores, and the like have increased rapidly over the past three decades. Figure 9.5 shows the growth in income from university auxiliary enterprises, with this budget line increasing by nearly 60 percent overall between 1975 and 1996. In addition to increasing revenues, it has been argued that these activities increase the size and influence of the administrative cohort of public and private nonprofit universities (Slaughter and Leslie, 1997).

At issue is whether the increase in revenues to nonprofits in activities for which for-profits provide a relatively close substitute, combined with declines in direct appropriations to colleges and universities from government sources, will "squeeze out" the capacity of colleges and universities to produce educational services that are unique to the nonprofit sector and may have a high degree of public benefits. Such programs may include investments in very basic research with few identifiable patent or licensing prospects or providing educational opportunities in a range of abstract topics such as classical languages. Institutions with substantial private endowment income are able to make such activities institutional priorities, while institutions without such support may not have that luxury.

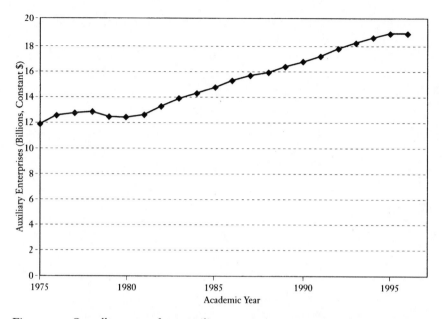

Figure 9.5. Overall revenues from auxiliary enterprises, 1975–1996. Source: National Science Foundation, Web CASPAR database, http://caspar.nsf.gov.

Most plainly, a key expectation is that there will be a growing stratification between the institutions that are able to raise substantial donative revenues or receive direct public appropriations and those lacking access to such resources. In the latter case, there may be little difference in governance or outcomes between those undersourced nonprofit providers of educational services and for-profit providers (Winston 1999).

## Convergence in Outcomes

As might be expected, given a convergence in sources of revenue to nonprofit and for-profit postsecondary providers, there is also considerable evidence of a steady convergence of outcomes. The extent to which this will continue is by no means certain. If nonprofit colleges and universities are true to their missions, convergence in outcomes may be limited. John Whitehead, an experienced nonprofit and for-profit trustee, notes, "A for-profit board has an obligation to *get out* of a bad business while a nonprofit board may have an obligation to *stay in*, if it is true to its mission" (Bowen 1994, 23).

Nonprofit and for-profit providers are increasingly producing degrees using similar forms of delivery, such as evening programs and on-line education. They are also targeting similar populations. Nonprofit continuing education programs offering courses and degrees that attract adult and other nontraditional students are some of the fastest growing enterprises in the nonprofit postsecondary sector. As these programs have competed more directly with for-profits, an isomorphic convergence of price, delivery structure, labor contracts, and curricular content has emerged (Adelman 2000; Marchese 1998). A similar story holds in the market for contract education, where nonprofit community colleges have constructed competitive programs to maintain market dominance against for-profit encroachment (Levin 2001).

In a similar fashion, public and private nonprofits have increasingly promoted the private benefits of their degrees in marketing and outreach (Marginson and Considine 2000), while for-profits have begun to market themselves to accrediting and regulatory agencies as providers of public goods. The University of Phoenix recently revised an application for licensing to practice in New Jersey with the additional claim that the university would build educational capacity in underserved communities around the state (Selingo 2001).

Although there are many indicators that nonprofit and for-profit providers are competing in many of the same markets, full convergence is some ways off. Particularly noteworthy is the absence of for-profit provision in what might be considered the core enterprises of liberal arts colleges (residential undergraduate education) and research universities (doctoral-level training in the arts and sciences). It is in the activities outside the traditional focus of colleges and universities—particularly professional programs—where there are growing similarities across institutional types.


Governance and Organizational Behavior in Higher Education

Understanding the linkage between changes in revenue sources and changes in institutional form is central to understanding contemporary shifts in the structure and process of academic governance. While data support a significant incidence of convergence in revenue sources and outcomes in certain sectors of higher education, whether a convergence in governance structures will take place is less clear. Governance structures and processes in higher education mediate internal and external political-economic demands for what is produced and how it is produced within postsecondary institutions. By tradition, charter, and statutory design, there have been significant differences between for-profit and nonprofit institutions in how governance decisions are made.[6] While all of these institutions have (at least nominally) faculty, administrators, a variety of external and internal stakeholders, and boards of directors, the role of each party in decision making differs markedly between the for-profit sector and the nonprofit sector.

Research on governance in higher education has long addressed the problem of how to characterize the decision-making process of the institutions. Scholars have generally relied on multidimensional models of organizational behavior that portray colleges and universities as at once bureaucratic, collegial, political, and anarchical (Berger and Milem 2000; Pusser 2003). Research on for-profit corporations in general, and those in higher education specifically, has characterized the organizations in a simple, direct fashion, as rational profit maximizers (Ruch 2001).

In a for-profit institution, the nature of the relationship between faculty, administrators, and the board is dictated by corporate control. The structure is straightforward in that the board of directors, representing shareholder interests, sets objectives intended to maximize profits. Management or administrative officers report to the board of directors and are largely responsible for hiring faculty and determining curricular offerings. It is the objective of the board and management to structure employment relationships in a way that provides incentives for high productivity, particularly in areas that are difficult to measure. Indicators of success—and failure—are ultimately quite clear in a for-profit and can be captured by market performance in terms of stock price, dividends, and earnings.

There are few clear metrics for evaluating what constitutes legitimate mission-related activity in nonprofit colleges and universities, how to prioritize those activities, or how to measure their success in pursuing priorities. Governance in this sector involves not only making decisions about what to produce, but also evaluating the extent to which institutional outcomes coincide with institutional mission. Bowen and co-authors (1994) argue that the most important activity of nonprofit boards is the assurance of fidelity to an organization's stated mission. In contrast, for a for-profit board, the overriding concern is the development of strategies to enhance shareholder value, since profit maximization and mission are one and the same.

Analyses of the nature of governance at public and private nonprofit postsecondary institutions have long turned attention to the extent of shared governance in various institutional sectors.[7] Shared governance has generally been understood as a division of authority between faculty, administrators, and governing board (Hines 2000), with the influence of interest groups from the wider political economy largely ignored. More recently attention has been turned to the distinction between internal governance, those processes and procedures made by boards and administrative leaders within institutions, and the external direction of public institutions by system boards, state coordinating agencies, and legislatures (Pusser 2003).

Whether governance was ever limited to or even functionally shared between administrators, faculty, and trustees continues to be a matter of some debate. In recent decades, increased division of labor between administrators and faculty, and the development of professional managers in higher education not drawn from the faculty ranks, make it increasingly more difficult to sustain existing norms of shared governance. Nonetheless, nonprofit boards are distinguished by an explicit charge to protect academic freedom as part of the institutional mission.[8]

If governance is increasingly less collaborative at nonprofit colleges and universities, how are such institutions governed? The strongest similarity in governance between nonprofits and for-profit providers resides in the link between administration and boards of directors. The most significant difference rests in the absence of "ownership" or residual shareholders and the potential ambiguity in mission on the nonprofit side.

In evaluating how well governance works in higher education, it is necessary to distinguish between productive efficiency—getting a given output at the lowest cost—and mission efficiency—choosing the combination of outputs that is true to institutional mission. Increased similarity in the governance of nonprofit and for-profit institutions might have both positive and negative consequences. The positive effects are likely to come in the form of increased productive efficiency, while the adverse consequences may be the decreased attention to providing educational services that fulfill the charitable or public purpose of an institution's charter. What is clear is that convergence will have significant implications for academic work.

## Academic Labor

Division of labor has been a cornerstone of the evolution of the modern university. In the first order, the division of labor was fueled by the evolution of scientific thought and the growth of economies of scale in higher education, producing clear disciplinary specializations (Goldin and Katz 1999). A further wave of specialization has taken hold more recently and concerns the distinction between faculty expertise and management expertise. While it remains common that the "chief executive" of a college or university is someone with faculty experience, colleges and universities now quite frequently employ a cadre of managers not trained as "academics." These include specialists in investment management, athletic coaches, development officers, or deans trained to counsel students.

While this further specialization may enhance the efficient management of the enterprise, it serves to further unravel notions of shared governance (Rhoades 1998). It is certainly possible that an individual trained as an accountant or an investment manager may be more able to make university budgetary decisions than someone trained as a Greek scholar. Yet, if faculty members no longer participate in governance outside their spheres of expertise, it is not clear how long the independent judgment of faculty in their areas of expertise will inform institutional decision making.

Articulated under the heading of academic freedom, the General Declarations of the American Association of University Professors (1915) addressed "freedom of inquiry and research; freedom of teaching within the university or college; and freedom of extramural utterance and action." While no college or university has renounced the general principles of academic freedom articulated by the association, many institutions have substantively changed the nature of faculty employment. The existence of tenure at public and private nonprofit institutions has been a significant mechanism for differentiating governance at public and private nonprofits from governance at for-profit institutions. In for-profit institutions, tenure was never an institutional employment relationship, while nonprofit colleges and universities have only recently begun to substantially alter the composition of the academic labor force (Baldwin and Chronister 2001). The most direct shifts in the nature of the faculty employment relationship have been the reduction in tenure-track appointments and the increased employment of faculty in adjunct and part-time capacities. Between 1987 and 1998, the proportion of faculty at nonprofit colleges and universities with tenure or tenure-track appointments declined from nearly 80 percent to 67 percent (Table 9.2). The reduction in tenure-track employment is a clear manifestation of a differentiation in faculty responsibility for knowledge generation and knowledge dissemination.

Table 9.2. Percentage of Faculty with Tenure or Tenure-Track Appointments, by Type of Institution and Year

|                       | 1987 | 1992 | 1998 |
| --------------------- | ---- | ---- | ---- |
| All institutions      | 79   | 76   | 67   |
| Public research[a]    | 86   | 83   | 70   |
| Private research      | 82   | 73   | 66   |
| Public doctoral[b]    | 85   | 80   | 68   |
| Private doctoral[b]   | 72   | 73   | 76   |
| Public comprehensive  | 87   | 85   | 82   |
| Private comprehensive | 84   | 79   | 66   |
| Private liberal arts  | 74   | 71   | 65   |
| Public 2-year         | 69   | 68   | 55   |
| Other[c]              | 51   | 43   | 57   |

*Source*: National Center for Education Statistics 2002.

[a] All public and private not-for-profit, Title IV–participating, degree-granting institutions in the 50 states and the District of Columbia.

[b] Institutions classified by the Carnegie Foundation as specialized medical schools and medical centers.

[c] Public liberal arts, private 2-year, and religious and other specialized institutions except medical schools and medical centers.

Notably, these changes were not limited to the comprehensive sectors but were spread throughout higher education.

The importance of academic freedom as a tenet of the faculty employment relationship depends to a significant degree on the scope of faculty responsibilities. Where faculty work is narrowly defined to include only teaching from a preselected curriculum, "academic freedom" is of limited importance. For academic freedom to have meaning, faculty must have the latitude to exercise judgment and intellectual creativity. Where faculty responsibilities extend more broadly to include the choice of research questions and the organization of curricula, academic freedom for faculty is a principle with considerable force.

For-profit universities take an entirely different approach to governance, with a very distinct stance on hierarchy, collegiality, and "sharing." In for-profits the faculty are quite clearly employees, few faculty are involved in creating curriculum, and decision making of all sorts is firmly in the hands of managers. As one observer with experience in both nonprofit and for-profit postsecondary institutions put it, "The governance structures and processes of the for-profit university are based on the values of traditional corporate management. Accountability for certain outcomes is fixed with individual managers, who have both the responsibility and the authority to make decisions" (Ruch 2001, 15). In these environments, governance is not "shared" in the way the traditional academy has operationalized the term.

Where nonprofits engage in collective bargaining with faculty unions, governance roles and responsibilities are often negotiated at a system, rather than a campus level. Here too a clear shift from tenure-track to part-time and adjunct faculty is taking place, although the conditions of work for other-than-tenure-track faculty can be improved through collective action.

It is not just the role of faculty that has changed in the evolution of nonprofit governance. The most notable convergence between for-profit and nonprofit governance is in the area of administration and management. Rhoades (1998) suggests that "faculty influence" is now a more appropriate term than "faculty control." With regard to budgets, salaries, reductions in force, elimination of programs, faculty size, class size, student enrollments, intellectual property agreements, and employment policies, Rhoades (p. 5) concludes, "I simply note that these matters are ultimately decided by those who manage faculty, by administrators and boards." In short, it is difficult to avoid the conclusion that decisions about the allocation of institutional resources are increasingly outside the scope of faculty decision making.

Faculty with extensive research portfolios are a modest exception, as the availability of external sources of support such as foundation and government grants provide these individuals with more bargaining power within the institution. In this way, some faculty are able to maintain more control over the allocation of student aid, teaching loads, and equipment purchases. However, these faculty members comprise a relatively small share of those employed at nonprofit institutions, and they tend to be concentrated at a small number of colleges and universities (Slaughter and Leslie 1997).

The control of academic labor in public and private nonprofit institutions is rapidly changing. The power of faculty authority over appointments, promotion, and tenure has been eroded by shifts to part-time and nontenured faculty (Baldwin and Chronister 2001). While the relative shifts have been significant in nonprofit organizations, faculty in nonprofit postsecondary organizations continue to possess a level of influence over academic labor that is unheard of in for-profit institutions. Such key practices in public and private nonprofit institutions as admissions, promotion and tenure, peer review, research and scholarship, and the construction of curriculum are largely under faculty control.

To be sure, there is considerable—and increasing—heterogeneity among institutions in higher education in the extent to which faculty are expected to be "intellectual entrepreneurs" or simply classroom instructors. One indication of this stratification is the widening of the dispersion in teaching loads between faculty at elite research universities and those at liberal arts colleges or comprehensive institutions.

At issue in comparing the responsibilities of faculty in different types of employment situations is what their outside options are. In thinking about how faculty employment relations have changed (or differ across sectors), it is important to also keep in mind the extent to which the terms of employment will affect the composition of the labor pool. To the extent that faculty are increasingly employed to "deliver content" in higher education rather than to "advance knowledge," it is inevitable that the characteristics of the faculty will change as well.

Where for-profit colleges differ most markedly from nonprofits is in the extent to which individual faculty set the curriculum, choosing what to teach and how to teach it. In the for-profit sector, there is a strong division of labor between "content developers" and "content deliverers." This is done in the hope that "unbundling" traditional faculty responsibilities of course design, assessment, and content delivery will generate efficiencies through specialization. Ruch (2001, 118) comments, "In a real sense, faculty in the for-profits are viewed by the business side as being delivery people, as in delivery of the curriculum." The curriculum they deliver is produced, for the most part, at a distance, and adopted through a process that excludes the vast majority of for-profit faculty. As contested as tenure may be in the nonprofit institutions, it is not even an issue in the for-profits.

While the synergistic links between teaching and research are lost, unbundling is essential to maintaining an extremely low-faculty-wage structure in the for-profit sector. It is argued that standardization will reduce the variance in course delivery and facilitate the evaluation of student learning, yet to date there is little evidence that unbundling enhances either teaching or learning. As faculty responsibilities are further divided, the degree of faculty autonomy—and implicitly academic freedom—is eroded within the institution.

Another concern is the shift in control of resource allocation from faculty—defined as those involved in teaching and research—to administrators or managers (Rhoades 1998). In this environment, administrators are increasingly positioned as managers of particular institutional functions (e.g., the library, computer services, or student guidance) and, as such, are assessed based on performance of these functions. While increased accountability of particular service centers may yield some benefits, there is also a potential cost in that the incentives to use the university mission to institutionalize potential benefits are lost.

Governing Boards

Public nonprofit and for-profit postsecondary governing boards are distinctly different in origin, composition, reproduction, compensation, and expertise. This is not surprising, given the traditional distinctions in their missions and constituencies. Private nonprofit boards, while quite distinctive, bear many similarities to for-profit boards.

A key difference in the governance of public and private nonprofit institutions rests in the process of board and administrative appointments and the degree of autonomy the respective boards possess. For private nonprofits, governing boards are essentially self-perpetuating in the sense that current officers choose their successors. For public institutions, such decisions are either directly or indirectly a function of the state or local political process.

The composition of private nonprofit boards often includes student and faculty representation, constituents who are generally absent from for-profit boards. While the faculty senate representative of a large, public nonprofit university generally has voting rights, or a place at the board table, there is rarely direct faculty representation on the boards of for-profit universities. For-profit board members may have significant fiduciary interests in the success of the institutions they preside over, through holdings and stock options. Although board members in both sectors endeavor to avoid conflicts of interest, trustees of public universities receive virtually no compensation for their service. In contrast, individual directors of for-profit universities may receive significant compensation and profit from the sale of stock. As one example, the chair of the board of Apollo Group Inc., the parent company of the University of Phoenix, holds at the time of this writing several hundred million dollars worth of Apollo Group stock.

Perhaps the fundamental distinction at the board level concerns the role of political actors in the composition of public nonprofit boards (Pusser forthcoming). Given their role as democratic institutions, public nonprofits are largely composed of trustees appointed by governors directly, or appointed by governors and subject to legislative approval (Jones and Skolnik 1997). Ex officio members often include governors and other elected officials who serve as voting members of the boards. While politicians may also serve as directors of for-profit postsecondary organizations, they do so as allies of the organization. Political leaders on public nonprofit boards serve quite different roles and often have agendas at odds with the institutional leadership (Pusser 2003).

In for-profits the board governs to maximize shareholder value. In nonprofits the board endeavors to maximize the legitimate functions of the organization. However, the process of relying on political appointments may not allow public postsecondary institutions the diversity, independence, and commitment required to be most effective in a rapidly changing environment. A recent study of public governing board dynamics indicated that governors generally appoint close political allies to trustee positions, without sufficient attention to expertise in either higher education or trusteeship (Pusser 2003).

Over the past decade there has been a significant increase in conflict at the nonprofit public board level. The so-called "activist trustee" movement (Ingram 1996) has been fueled by demands from trustees seeking increased institutional accountability on a range of organizational behaviors. While there has also been increased conflict in for-profit corporate boards of higher education, they have generally been challenges to lack of administrative responsiveness or institutional profitability.

Trustees on nonprofit public postsecondary boards are much less likely to serve on other corporate boards than are trustees of nonprofit private boards or for-profit boards. The prevalence of "board interlocks" has long been a significant concern of researchers on for-profit organizational behavior. In a number of studies, director interlocks have been found to generate substantial effects, including increased organizational control over resources (Pfeffer and Salancik 1978), greater interfirm cooperation (Burt 1983), isomorphic adoption of strategic tactics across firms (Useem 1984), a reduction of information and monitoring costs (Mizruchi 1996), and the maintenance of social elites (Palmer 1983). Board interlocks also offer opportunities for career enhancement for directors and increased legitimacy for the organization (Haunschild and Beckman 1998). While board interlocks are much less prevalent on nonprofit public boards, they have increased rapidly over the past two decades (Thomas, Slaughter, and Pusser 2002). These interlocks are likely to be a key driver of convergence, as they provide a significant source of information for nonprofit trustees about for-profit corporate structures and processes.

Conclusion: Implications of Convergence of Governance Norms

The effect of changes in the sources and distribution of revenue in the nonprofit postsecondary sector is already evident in its emerging structures and procedures. A number of authors have suggested that the increase in entrepreneurial institutional behaviors has led to disproportionate administrative growth (Gumport and Pusser 1997), increased administrative control over internal resource allocation and decision making (Lowen 1997; Slaughter and Leslie 1997), and a convergence in nonprofit and for-profit university activities (Pusser 2002; Slaughter 2001).

One implication of the growing convergence in governance structures is that nonprofit and for-profit institutional outcomes will also converge. In that case, the role of nonprofit colleges and universities in producing positive public benefits may be considerably diminished. Such a convergence would, in a sense, invalidate the strongest argument for public subsidy and nonprofit provision of educational services. That is, public and private nonprofit colleges and universities must— as part of their mission—work to resolve failures in the education market and produce positive externalities that would not evolve from an independent market mechanism. The rationale for the protection and privileges of nonprofit status requires that the governance of public and private nonprofit universities facilitate these outcomes.

A key issue going forward is the degree to which increased convergence in governance will change the objective function and the provision of higher education services with public benefits. Plainly, the issue is not one of changing the underlying behavior of for-profit providers. For these institutions, the target is largely fixed: maximize profits subject to regulatory constraints. While competition may have the virtue of pushing public and private nonprofit providers to more efficient provision of certain types of educational outcomes, it may also push those outcomes aside.

The central question is whether the convergence of governance structures between nonprofit and for-profit providers will lead nonprofits to abandon their charitable missions, shifting toward the emulation of for-profit behavior (essentially, for-profits in nonprofit clothing). Slaughter and Leslie (1997) and Marginson and Considine (2000) suggest that the nonprofit university research enterprise has already moved significantly in the direction of commercial production at the expense of public goods. The costs of a broader institutional shift in behavior are real and require significant future research. Little is currently known about how convergence will shape underprovision to particular educational markets, the tension between long-term strategic planning, and ad hoc decision making, or the role of research and teaching in faculty responsibilities. The emerging question for those who make public policy is whether regulatory and funding incentives can be structured to encourage the positive dimensions of mixed-market provision, while preserving essential public commitments.

# CHAPTER TEN

# The Rise of Nonlegal Legal Influences on Higher Education

MICHAEL A. OLIVAS

The legalization of higher education is an unmistakable trend, one that has drawn commentary, although relatively modest scholarship, given the centrality and importance of the phenomenon. Alexis de Tocqueville's observation of over 150 years ago that persons in the United States eventually take all their disputes to court was once untrue of higher education, which gave rise to relatively little litigation in the nineteenth century. Even in the first half of the twentieth century, only a small number of college cases arose, leaving plaintiffs such as the hapless Miss Anthony without real remedy when she was dismissed on the grounds that she was "not a typical Syracuse girl" (*Anthony v. Syracuse University*, 231 N.Y.S. 435 [1928]).

But the last half of the twentieth century saw a torrent of cases directed at or brought by colleges, so much so that any regular observer of these must rely on a cottage industry of publications to track the thousands of cases each year. There is a law review that focuses solely on college law (*Journal of College and University Law*, a refereed journal–law review hybrid), commercial reporters that report and analyze litigation throughout the circuits and states (*West's Education Law Reporter*, the Education Law Association's monthly *Reporter*, and *Synthesis*, a commercial reporter, among many others), and specialized newsletters (e.g., *Fraternal Law Newsletter* and *Education Daily*) that report cases and developments in great detail. A mature treatise (*The Law of Higher Education*, in its third edition) and casebook (*The Law and Higher Education: Cases and Materials on Colleges in Court*, in its second edition, with supplements) form a set of useful bookends. There are LISTSERVs, CD-ROMs, commercial materials, continuing legal education (CLE) courses, national associations, and all the earmarks of a maturing field of study and area of practice.

Early studies of higher education law trace back to M. M. Chambers, a nonlawyer who, by himself and with E. C. Elliott, actually counted college cases in the courts for the Carnegie Foundation for the Advancement of Teaching. That he could undertake such a Herculean task without computerization probably indicates just how few cases there actually were. His multivolume series started in 1936 with *The Colleges and the Courts: Judicial Decisions regarding Institutions of Higher Education in the United States*, with periodic supplements published from 1941 until 1976 (Elliott and Chambers 1936; Chambers 1941). By then, he turned his full attention to *Grapevine*, another gargantuan task, gathering state appropriation data on a national basis. (Thus, he straddled the harbor with legs on both the law and the finance banks of higher education, a veritable Great Wonder of the College World.) ·

This is first-generation scholarship, largely supplemented today by computerized databases and search engines that bring to your desk almost any case or fact you might require. Very few people do this kind of old-fashioned scholarship today, although some do variants in its smaller subfields such as special education or for treatise or casebook purposes. Another such example is journal articles that carefully examine the annual terms of courts and their college cases.

Second-generation scholarship would include the study of many cases within a social science framework, such as the estimable 1987 book by George LaNoue and Barbara A. Lee, *Academics in Court: The Consequences of Faculty Discrimination Litigation*, where they conducted detailed case studies of important college employment cases, using public policy theory. Other examples include comprehensive studies of college legal issues using implementation theory, communications theory, political theory, and other theoretical approaches to understanding this phenomenon (Olivas 1992). In short, there is a movement afoot to place the legalization of colleges into larger frameworks, all the better to understand how legal change is absorbed by the college body politic and to measure how institutions are changed as a result.

While the number of books and articles is growing, it is still relatively small, slightly larger if you include law books on grades K through 12, as I do in my law school office. This scholarship has examined the increase in the number of court cases, statutes, and regulations governing higher education, both directly and as part of the rise of the modern administrative state. While this topic is large and important, the studies over the last twenty-five years have generally focused on the formal mechanisms of courts, legislatures, and administrative agencies as the major actors in this legalization of the academy. Many forces, which include, among others, insurance carriers, sole-source contract actors, regional and specialized accreditation groups, and regional consortia, exert tremendous private-sector pressures on colleges and universities. Less scholarship has charted these influences, in part because they often come "on cat's feet" and are not formal, broad-scale legal assaults, and in part because their rise is a feature of the widespread globalization of higher education and increased complexity of the modern-day organization. In addition, these influences arise directly from higher education's largely successful self-portrayal of the college sector as salient and essential to the liberal state, and its central role in the economy and polity of modern nation-building.

The second section of this chapter is devoted to the heart of the matter—case studies of nonlegal factors in college governance, ones that even in their nonlegal form give rise to legal or quasi-legal characteristics. That is, they take on the cloak of legal regimes because they dictate a policy response and constitute the complex features of statutory, litigative, or regulatory requirements. University/corporate research parks, the role of donors in determining policy, the marketing of intellectual property and patentable discoveries, and the commercialization of academic science all illustrate my thesis that large-scale development affects campuses in substantial and nonlegal ways that are not strictly statutory, regulatory, or litigative but which mimic legalization. Another topic I considered was the effects of higher education's increased globalization, but I did not follow through in this case study, inasmuch as a formal immigration regime is involved, with its labyrinthine statutory and regulatory components. The restrictions of the USA PATRIOT Act, enacted following 11 September 2001's depredations by air school students enrolled with F-1 or M-1 status, also complicate this case, in ways not yet fully evident (Firestone with Wald 2002). I do not believe I exaggerate when I refer to these factors as a "parallel universe," and I hope that my highlighting them in a systematic way advances the topic. In the final part, I summarize and suggest additional cases for consideration in this vein.

## Insurance Carriers

The first time I heard of insurance carriers wagging the dog was in conjunction with a deanship search in which I was a finalist, easily my most unpleasant professional experience. The board of this private college had reconsidered its admissions policies for both the undergraduate and professional schools, following the recent ruling by the Fifth Circuit Court that public law schools may not use race in admissions (*Hopwood v. State of Texas*, 78 F. 3d 932 [5th Cir. 1996]). But what was memorable to me was that in my interview with the president, he asked me whether I agreed with the campus decision to discontinue the modest use of race in admissions. I said I did not agree that the *Hopwood* decision extended to private colleges in the Fifth Circuit, and that previously, such institutions had never felt themselves bound by Title VI or Texas Attorney General Opinions. He then asked me whether it would make a difference in my view—which I had written about and had been widely quoted as saying—if the campus insurance carrier had required them to do so? Under the mistaken assumption that he wanted my actual opinion on this issue, I said that insurance carriers cannot be allowed to determine college policy. I didn't say this in any mean or harsh way, but his face reddened and he obviously took offense at my response. Indeed, my memory of the exchange is so fresh and clear that I have sought a venue to write about this exact topic.[1]

The more I have investigated the issue of campus carriers determining college policy in significant ways, the more troubled I have become at the insidious and corrosive way the practice has developed.[2] To illustrate this practice, I will give several examples of the role of insurance in higher education, a survey that is not entirely self-evident or intuitive. Finally, I suggest some principles that I believe should drive the relationship, especially for the campus governance implications.

Like other large commercial enterprises, colleges undertake risky business in the normal course of daily activities, whether it is on the employment side (firing an employee for cause), the auxiliary side (a student hurts herself in a college dining room), or the instructional side (a lab fire hurts a student who is mixing chemicals for an experiment). In addition to relying on Section 1983, the Eleventh Amendment, and other federal or state sovereign immunity provisions, colleges enact liability and risk management regimes to limit their exposure. Most major institutions have offices of risk management or have personnel in human resources or legal offices whose responsibilities are predominantly managing risk: risk avoidance, risk control, risk transfer (insurance), and risk retention. While these are each pure "types," they also exist in hybrid or mixed formats in virtually every college.

Risk avoidance is the most drastic type of risk management, as it is the removal of risky behavior or occasion. As an example, some athletic departments have eliminated high-tower formations by cheerleaders, in order to avoid injuries from the collapse of a complex maneuver involving tumbling and climbing on one another. In *Rendine v. St. John's University* (735 N.Y.S. 2d 173 [2001]) exactly such a disaster was at issue, but the plaintiff lost on an assumption-of-risk theory. Closing a science department or program because of inadequate facility safety would be another example. In one recently publicized incident, a college fired a faculty member who refused to move out of his lab and clear it of dangerous chemicals and papers. The college acted to remove the environmental risk in the building.[3]

Risk control is a subset of risk avoidance, or risk avoidance "lite." Rather than completely eliminating the risky program or activity, risk control addresses or ameliorates the risky aspects by modifying or altering the behavior. The institution that barred high-tower maneuvers by cheerleaders could have restricted them to "one-boost" formations, rather than the "four-high" formations that were over twenty feet high. Retrofitting or venting a building might be employed rather than closing a science program that has become dangerous.

The third type of risk management is transferring the risk, predominantly by purchasing insurance, entering into hold-harmless or indemnification arrangements, or employing releases or waivers.

These are the major forms of managing risk, for both foreseeable and unforeseeable harms that might befall an institution. In the summer of 2001, my own institution (University of Houston) suffered terrible storm damage from Tropical Storm Allison, including severe harm to its Law Center and to 95 of the campus's 105 buildings. The Law Center, which has approximately one-third of its square footage underground, had so much water come in from above (the rain) and below (collapsed utility tunnels) that we had to relocate to the basketball arena for nearly four months ("luxury" boxes become less luxurious in such a situation) and to bulldoze nearly 200,000 volumes of ruined library books, journals, and microfiche. Over a year later, our buildings partially rebuilt, we are still negotiating (i.e., fighting) with the Federal Emergency Management Agency (FEMA) for our full share of the insurance funds, which have many restrictions on them. Any car owner or homeowner who has had an accident knows the cycle of claims-adjustments-negotiations-restoration inherent in an insurance policy.

In addition to these complex reimbursement issues, there are issues over who is indemnified under a policy and in what circumstances. For instance, in *Chasin v. Montclair (N.J.) State University* (732 A. 2d 457 [N.J. 1999]), a professor sought reimbursement over court costs and a claim against her that arose in a grading dispute. When she lost in court, she sought such reimbursement, which the carrier refused to pay, insisting that she acted against the advice of college counsel and the provost in the matter. The court disagreed with her, noting that the original issue was governed by statute and that she had violated institutional policy in the matter. In situations like this, the insurance carrier carries great weight.

The hands of colleges are strengthened when they employ insurance carriers to "pool" the risks and purchase group insurance from companies that are organized as mutual risk retention groups or as reciprocal risk retention groups. In this fashion, the policyholders can maintain some control over their risks while smoothing out the costs. Colleges can even purchase very specialized or tailored policies to cover their own unique exposure and risks (McNamee 2002a, 2002b).[4]

Colleges can also attempt to transfer risk by employing releases or waivers to relieve themselves of any liability, but these are both awkward and questionable. Some states will not allow such attempts at risk transferring to the individual parties. For example, in *Emory University v. Porubiansky* (282 S.E. 903 [Ga. 1981]), the Georgia Supreme Court voided a risk transfer practice at Emory University's Dentistry Clinic, where patients were required to waive all liability before dental treatment. Sometimes, courts will void insurance policies or indemnification agreements that cover institutions for gross negligence, on the grounds that covering such behavior serves as no deterrence to the behavior (Kaplin and Lee 2000, 90–101).

The final area of risk management is risk retention, or self-insurance, where colleges set aside their own funds to cover a specific risk that is too expensive to insure against, or where the risk is uninsurable. An example of this is a period of time where a large public university was negotiating with a health maintenance organization and could not get reasonable coverage for catastrophic illnesses, so it set aside a fund to cover that single risk. After a year where several employees died of AIDS, officials decided they could no longer fund the risk internally. Choosing very large deductibles is another form of self-insurance. The FEMA coverage I mentioned earlier is for 75 percent of the loss the University of Houston suffered from Tropical Storm Allison. At the Law Center, this "self-help" portion, which translated into lower rates for the whole institution, meant that we had to come up with $12 to $15 million ourselves.

This Cook's tour of insurance options, while it includes court cases that resolved issues among parties, shows the extent to which policies and risk management as a guiding principle are decidedly nonlegal and are designed to reduce litigation by reducing the occasions of litigation. Being engaged in such audits is almost like being prepared to go to trial. And the time spent on a serious preventive regime is often enormous. Each year, I am obligated to undertake training and formal tested certification on equal employment law, sexual harassment guidelines, and hazardous material disposal, as required by state law of all state employees. Prior to these training programs becoming computerized so that they are Web-based and able to be completed at any time, dozens of people would crowd into classrooms at off-peak hours to listen to trainers provide the information and administer tests. We may be educators, but we do not want to be on the receiving end of instruction.

One cost not often calibrated is the cost to governance, particularly when the carrier tail wags the college dog. I have been involved with a dozen or more lawsuits involving my own institution—ranging from a disgruntled applicant to students denied resident status for paying in-state tuition—as a defendant, participant fact witness, expert witness, or legal consultant to the attorney general's lawyer trying the cases. In one particularly vexing case, I was defended by a former student of mine who had taken my Higher Education Law Seminar, and who was working for the state attorney general's office; she successfully defended the University of Houston in the case. But I have also seen an institution settle cases when the insurance carrier determined it should do so, and have spoken with insurance counsels more than once when they were contemplating a course of action that would force the university's hand or bend it to their will. I have heard discussions that have involved all these options, which were part of the overall trial strategy, where coverage was an issue, but not the driving issue.

I have also heard the opposite, and it is these cases and others like them that scare me: "We'll cover the directors and officers, but we're cutting Dr. X loose," or "We cannot have an admissions policy like that," or (to a private college board) "*Hopwood* says we cannot have a scholarship program/recruiting program that goes into minority high schools," even though *Hopwood* said no such thing and does not control private colleges. Earlier, I mentioned that the carrier of one private college required it to cut back on its admissions and scholarship policies, both of which met the *Bakke* test of giving only slight and targeted assistance to underrepresented minority admittees.

Although this operating procedure surprised and troubled me, it is enough of a practice that a useful insurance primer took note:

In the event that the college or university is presented with a claim and the insurance company is notified, a question that often arises is who controls the defense and settlement of the claim: the insurance company or the college or university? Primary standard form CGL [Comprehensive General Liability] insurance policies generally provide that the insurance company may control the defense of the policyholder, including the selection of defense counsel, and negotiate a settlement.

In theory, the insurance company and the college or university policyholder have similar interests in the quick and efficient resolution of claims, and the policyholder is willing to let the insurance company control the litigation and settlement. The theory continues that the policyholder's interests will be adequately served by such an arrangement, because insurance companies have a fiduciary duty to their policyholders, including a duty of good faith and fair dealing in connection with their obligations. Moreover, counsel hired by the insurance company also has an independent duty to represent the policyholder's interest.

In practice, however, the interests of the policyholder and the insurance company are frequently at odds. Differing visions of what constitutes an adequate defense or a reasonable settlement cause tension to develop between the policyholder and its insurance company. Conflicts first arise when the insurance company and the policyholder disagree about the choice of counsel to handle the defense of claims, and most frequently when they disagree about whether or not to settle a claim. Insurance companies usually refuse to pursue counterclaims or third-party claims even though the policyholder may believe that "the best defense is a good offense" (Ende, Anderson, and Crego 1997, 723–24).

It is one thing for an insurance carrier to litigate aggressively or to play hardball in order to protect its policyholders, but it is another thing entirely to act as the ultimate decision maker on institutional policies and to become the arbiter of bona fide institutional behavior. A good example of this occurred in *Andover Newton Theological School v. Continental Casuality Co* (930 F. 2d 89 [1st Cir. 1991]), a complex case over whether or not the school's insurance carrier was obligated to pay for a jury verdict on a faculty member dismissed in violation of federal age discrimination laws. The merits of this case are complex, and not at issue here, but the carrier refused to pay the jury award on the grounds that to do so would allow policyholders like the school to behave badly and not put into place preventive measures to make certain that discrimination did not occur.[5]

Of course, colleges can lose a given case without rampant institutional malfeasance or misbehavior. Universities are, on the whole, pretty law abiding, so much so that the feedback loop of litigation to campus practice is usually quite good. Newton Theological School never violated mandatory retirement laws again after this case, so the institution will not be a reckless law breaker causing the carrier to pay out for many cases of the same sort. More likely, it is like the University of Texas Law School in *Hopwood*, violating *Bakke* a quarter-century later by getting sloppy and complacent with admissions procedures, rather than flagrant flouting of any law.

Thus, withholding coverage by the carrier to force a college's hand not only is often against a jurisdiction's public policy, but also is not efficacious in its regulating of institutional behavior. Moreover, the carrier was paid to provide coverage and in not doing so may not be fulfilling its contractual obligation to the policyholding institution.[6] Insurance, with all its complexities, is the premier example of nonlegal legal influences on campuses.

Accreditation

As it happens, accreditation is an area where I have a lot of firsthand experience, as I have been on fifteen site inspection teams for law schools, chaired my law school's self-study committee to prepare for an inspection, and serve on the American Bar Association's (ABA) Section on Legal Education and Admission to the Bar Council, which determines accreditation status and policy for the 180 ABA-accredited law schools and other law schools seeking such accreditation. I am, on balance, generally positive about the accreditation process and spend much time on this function.

To be sure, the process of accreditation is not unanimously viewed this way, as critics view this function as either too little (collusion with the accredited units to extort resources from central administrators) or too much (the criteria are elitist and drive historically black institutions away from their traditional functions by requiring excessively high criteria) (Shepherd 2003). But it is the process employed by federal and state governments to ascertain quality and eligibility for student financial aid; it is this certification process at the undergraduate level and licensure at the professional level that drive accreditation. Governments use accreditation standards to fulfill eligibility for governmental student financial assistance or veterans programs, while occupational licensing authorities (such as state bars and state supreme courts) use accreditation as an entrance criterion for admission to professional licensure (e.g., medicine, law, pharmacy).

Many court cases have arisen over accreditation issues, and since the important 1970 *Marjorie Webster Junior College v. Middle States Association of Colleges and Secondary Schools* case (432 F. 2d 650 [D.C. Cir. 1970]), which upheld the authority of a regional accrediting body to determine its own rules, courts have given great leeway to such bodies. There have been actions to rein in accrediting bodies, such as the Department of Justice's decision to limit the authority of the ABA to review faculty salaries, owing to antitrust implications.[7]

However, at the end of the day, accreditation remains a powerful collegial influence on colleges at all levels—implicating governance, curriculum, expenditure decisions, and other facets. Indeed, once the decision was made by one institution to move off campus into a nearby commercial facility that had closed, the law school's neighbors sued to enforce an agreement that had been reached to expand the existing campus facility, located adjacent to their property. They had contested the original agreement for nearly eight years in municipal courts and boards. This was driven by accreditation standards that found the building not adequate for its purposes.

Notwithstanding all the hours billed over legal battles (ABA sources have indicated that the Justice Department's consent decree and related litigation cost well over $2 million), accreditation is an important nonlegal legal dimension. It is the highest form of self-regulation, where institutions agree to submit themselves to highly stylized inspections and thorough self-study.[8] It is consultative, with most self-studies necessitating scores of committees, internal reports, and external constituency meetings. But at heart, accreditation is the process by which we judge ourselves, hold ourselves up for public inspection, and commit resources to implement. Done right, it is a salutary and renewing enterprise.


Consortia

Consortia comprise an interesting facet of higher education in which institutions affiliate with others like themselves in order to facilitate exchanges of personnel, students, facilities, and other resources. As in the instance of accreditation, antitrust activities may be implicated in the complex arrangements. In *NCAA v. University of Oklahoma* (468 U.S. 85 [1984]), for example, a detailed history of the National Collegiate Athletic Association (NCAA) is recounted, including the establishment of a rival consortium (the College Football Association [CFA]), which had negotiated its own college football television contract. The district court had found that the NCAA constituted a "classic cartel," and the U.S. Supreme Court agreed, enabling the rival CFA to pursue its own interests. Since the 1984 decision, there has been a shift in individual athletic conference cooperative arrangements as well, with the most powerful university programs going their own way in choosing or creating new conference arrangements or in negotiating media broadcast contracts.

Examples include the decision by the University of Texas and Texas A&M University to abandon the Southwest Conference and join the Big 12 Conference. With these two schools pulling out, the Southwest Conference collapsed, scattering its members to several other affiliations. And many dollars are at stake. In 1995, CBS paid the NCAA $1.75 billion for an eight-year contract to cover the men's annual basketball championship tourney ("March Madness"). Some schools have such power that they can go it alone, as Notre Dame has done, refusing to abide by the NCAA's football contract. Notre Dame, a truly national football institution, chose to negotiate its own televised football games on network and cable channels so it does not have to share revenue with other conference members or compete for a conference title to be considered for postseason bowl games.[9]

It is interesting to note that in intercollegiate athletics, many of the detailed regulations have been drafted essentially to protect the institutions from their own excessive wrongdoing and from each other's wrongdoing in recruiting high school minors. Perhaps the best example is the highly codified NCAA rules governing the recruiting of athletes, and the invocation of the "death penalty" for institutions (such as SMU) found to have engaged in massive and extraordinary improprieties. Essentially, the institutions agree to police themselves and to submit to private, collective oversight.

That college athletics have legal implications is inarguable. An extraordinary document issued by the Special Committee of Methodist Bishops in 1987, concerning illegal payments to athletes and numerous violations of NCAA regulations by SMU, detailed evidence of substantial wrongdoing. The report included a pattern of rules violations, recruiting abuses, cash payments to athletes, NCAA sanctions, collusion by trustees and administrators to "keep the lid on," decisions by the president of the board (who resigned to become governor of Texas) to continue illegal payments, an agreement to bribe a disgruntled former employee who threatened to go public, public disclosures of the payments, and deceptions toward the faculty. According to the report, a trustee said in 1985:

> NCAA members of the Board would have been naïve not to have known that SMU players were being paid. . . . But the Board of Governors members were

content to win football games, to trust the leadership and look the other way. The institutional attitude and response to the NCAA allegations and investigations were symptomatic of the Board of Governors' attitude toward football in general: "Whatever was happening in the SMU football program was no better but no worse than what was happening in every other major college program." They told themselves that the other schools in the South-west Conference and the NCAA were after SMU. They reasoned that SMU had been down so long, its competitors simply could not stand to see SMU win. "Everybody's doing it, why pick on SMU?"—that was the Board of Governor's stance. That translated into a combative, adversarial relationship with the NCAA and its investigation. The Board of Governors was guilty of more than neglect. Their attitude was one of acquiescence in the actions of a small group of leaders on the Board. As with many of the active participants in this drama, the other members of the Board were able, through their passivity, to deny direct knowledge or direct participation in wrong-doing. The entire Board of Governors, as a Board, was at fault. All members of that Board share some measure of responsibility for the payments to players at SMU and the consequences of that course of action. (Bishops' Committee Report, quoted in Olivas 1997, 941)

On the other end of the spectrum, colleges engage in consortia and interinstitutional arrangements to maximize cooperation and to share resources and reduce overlap. For example, the Cornell Higher Education Research Institute (2001) has undertaken extensive surveys to chart tuition-reciprocity agreements among the 149 public research and doctoral institutions classified as such by the Carnegie Foundation for the Advancement of Teaching (1994); almost half the responding institutions indicated participation in a tuition-reciprocity program—either by a formal consortium arrangement or by a simple student-exchange mechanism. Other examples include the Midwest Student Exchange Program, the New England Regional Student Program, the Western Interstate Commission for Higher Education, and WAMI (a small agreement among the states of Washington, Montana, and Idaho). Many other states have border agreements where students who reside in a border area can attend programs across state lines. Wisconsin and Minnesota, for instance, have such an agreement. There are also more informal arrangements such as various student-exchange programs that allow students to swap institutions for short periods at home tuition rates. The Tuition Exchange, for instance, allows students whose parents teach at one institution to attend another institution in a recip-rocal fashion. If I teach at Rice University and my daughter gets Rice tuition free as a benefit, I can arrange for her to attend Grinnell in exchange. The Tuition Exchange administers this program for over five hundred private colleges that offer family enrollment as an employment benefit.

In addition, there are programs legislatively carved out to "rent" places for students in other, nonregional states. Several states contract each year with the University of Houston, which has one of the fewer than two dozen optometry schools in the United States. Each year, a complex tuition agreement is administered to underwrite nonresident tuition for such sender states; certainly this arrangement is less expensive than starting up a new optometry program in the home state.

The vast array of arrangements requires an infrastructure to administer and oversee the many exchanges and migrations that occur, yet the idea is simplicity itself.[10] For example, even though the University of Houston responded to the Cornell Higher Education Research Institute survey that it had no reciprocity agreements in 2001, the year of the study, the University of Houston's Law Center is home to NACLE, the North American Consortium on Legal Education, which hosts U.S.-Canada-Mexico exchanges and programs among nine member law schools (three in each country). In addition, the University of Houston has a comprehensive exchange with Monterey Tech, in Monterey, Mexico (Chapa-O'Quinn Program), set in motion by philanthropy from a University of Houston law alumnus who established the program with money from a major law case won for his Mexican client. Virtually every U.S. institution has some such similar arrangement with a foreign counterpart college.

Consortium arrangements, from the NCAA to Chapa-O'Quinn, are good examples of how institutions interact, form strategic alliances, and share resources. While they may occasion litigation, they are, at bottom, agreements to share, and thus are indications of nonlegal legal arrangements.

## Sole-Source Goods and Services

The rise of universities as places of commerce can be seen in the recent history of collective bargaining. The National Labor Relations Act (NLRA) governs faculty collective bargaining in private institutions. In 1951, the National Labor Relations Board (NLRB) decided that colleges would not fall under NLRA jurisdiction, as their mission was "noncommercial in nature and intimately connected with the charitable purposes and educational activities" (*Trustees of Columbia University,*

29 LRRM 1098 [1951]). This refusal to assert jurisdiction remained in force until 1970, when the NLRB reversed itself in the *Cornell University* case (which also included Syracuse University). After reviewing the development of labor law trends and higher education finance in the twenty years that had passed, the board noted, "We are convinced that assertion of jurisdiction is required over those private colleges and universities whose operations have a substantial effect on commerce to insure the orderly, effective and uniform application of the national labor policy" (*Cornell University and Syracuse University*, 183 N.L.R.B. 329 [1970]). The board set a $1 million gross revenue test for its standard, a figure that today covers even the very smallest institutions.

Indeed, it appears quaint by today's standards that a mere $1 million would be the threshold for engaging in commerce, for colleges are incontestably commercial institutions; an entire literature now exists on colleges as economic development engines, multiplying many times over the state's investments in higher education. In college towns such as College Station, Ithaca, Iowa City, West Lafayette, and Amherst, institutions of higher education are the predominant employers to the extent that the locales are, in many respects, college-company towns.

On campus, I walk through a student union building and feel overwhelmed by the commercialization around me, particularly in relation to student affairs. The student newspaper today contains sixteen pages, and by my count there are over seventy-five ads, including two full-page ads touting travel and computer specials. (This does not include the want ads or classifieds, which would bring the total to well over one hundred.) There are two vans blocking the driveway, one for a phone carrier company and one for a credit card company. Free, or seemingly free, shirts are widely available. Soft-drink and bottled-water vending machines are arrayed in several places, but they are compliments of the vendors, so they all stock only one brand (and its subsidiaries that make juices and other beverages). There are six fast-food or coffee franchises competing with the college's own cafeteria service, which is subcontracted to a food vending service, which in turn leases counter space to several national chains of donut shops and bagel stores. They cater meals in the various meeting rooms and throughout campus. There is a bank, a branch of a local bank, and two of its ATMs. There are magazine racks with dozens of take-away papers and magazines. The kiosks are peppered with commercial flyers, lost-dog notices, and various announcements. Portable carts offer travel posters, earrings,

CDs, and other student goods and services. There are over a dozen stores or venues, ranging from a pool hall and bowling alley to an herbal wellness center. The bookstore dominates the facility, and it is operated by a national chain that specializes in campus center bookstores. But it is only incidentally a *book*store, as it is filled with more clothes, office supplies, souvenirs, and other goodies than it is with books. You can buy anything it sells with a campus account card or a campus-affinity credit card, which donates a portion of each purchase to the institution. You can even pay tuition, room, and board by use of this card, and many students do so. You can mail, fax, email, and compute with these cards.

These casbahs are the heart of virtually every campus, more so than even the traditional heart, the library, although libraries themselves are morphing into multiservice facilities as well, with coffee bars, printing facilities, and computer services—each of them a cost center auxiliary service. And don't get me started on the retrofitting of college dorms to accommodate today's electronic and audio toys. Speaking of sleeping, my campus has a full-service hotel and conference facility, with students at the professional school of hotel and restaurant management to serve customers.

Now this is not an example of the decline of Western civilization—indeed, I wish I could get a fresh vente decaf with half-and-half in even more places, and most mornings I would kill for a good breakfast taco. But the NLRB would have no hesitation in declaring colleges to be commercial operations.

Neither would the Internal Revenue Service. The IRS has recently issued regulations to govern these developments on campus as unrelated business income ("New IRS Regulations Could Force Colleges To Pay Tax on Some Partnership Deals," *Chronicle of Higher Education*, 26 April 2002, chronicle.com/daily/2002/04/2002042601n.htm). There is no special tax treatment for campus single-source contracts, such as ones agreeing to use Nike or Adidas athletic apparel for all athletic teams in exchange for free gear and payment, or to provide only Coca-Cola or its corporate beverages in campus vending machines. For example, some institutions receive fleets of cars for various functions, including perquisites for high administrative or athletic officials, and then the coach appears in car ads for the dealership, and the college allows car advertisements to be filmed on campus. These transactions would likely be characterized as "unrelated business income." As campuses enter into more of these commercial partnerships, many legal issues arise in the areas of contracting regulations, taxation, conflict-of-interest and procurement regulation, and governance generally, especially as so many commercial activities occur in corporate contexts where trustees or institutional officials may have their own personal or professional ties.

A special note of concern about credit cards and college students. In his excellent book *Credit Card Nation* (2000), Robert Manning includes a very insightful chapter on college student debt issues, where he caustically describes the lending practices of credit card companies and the collusive role that colleges play, both in selling directory information and in providing exclusive and comprehensive access to student data for marketing purposes. He is particularly scornful of the affinity cards, which pose a conflict of interest for colleges, especially when the institutions get a percentage of all sales. In the traditional credit card transaction, the vendor pays a percentage to the card company. That some students pay their tuition, room, and board on credit cards is a very questionable practice. Government student loans are subsidized and payments are deferred while the student is in school; credit card loans accumulate at an interest rate of 20 percent in many cases, and they are not subsidized and payments are not deferred. This is a dreadful choice for students to make, and colleges should not facilitate or prosper from students making the wrong choice. This is a shameful practice, a nonlegal one to be sure, but shameful all the same.

As I sit here among the stacks of books and papers I consulted for this writing project, I realize that this is an unusual take on college governance, a subject I have studied in the twenty-five years since I wrote my Ph.D. dissertation on the same topic. In those days, issues seemed clearer to me, in large patches of black and white; today, I confess it is the grays that intrigue me. And to consider nonlegal influences has taxed my legal analytic skills, where I read cases and statutes carefully and apply legal reasoning. Rather, what impresses me about this particular project is how the nonlegal issues have so cleverly mimicked and aped their legal counterparts. The four examples I discussed—insurance, accreditation, consortia, and sole-source service providers—all have legal implications but arise in contexts other than statutes or cases. Each is a deeply embedded and complex subject that is absorbed into institutional legal regimes, a parallel universe that colleges and universities must inculcate and implement in order to control.

Even though I am a law professor and scholar who tracks these legal issues on campus, I often find myself the least litigious person in the room. Rather, I find litigation a sure sign that all other avenues of resolution have failed, so I try to consider all dispute-resolution alternatives. This is a helpful guide in considering the many nonlegal legal issues that arise on campus, and I offer final thoughts on considering these issues.

• Nonlegal issues such as I have discussed here will ripen into traditional legal issues if special care is not taken. Thus, preventive practices such as risk assessment and institutional audits are useful. Rehearsing for the sure-to-come storm damage might very well have prevented the massive restoration the University of Houston had to undertake after Tropical Storm Allison. More expensive, pressurized "submarine" doors would have held flood waters at bay, had they been installed. Fewer electrical and utility mechanisms would have been constructed underground (not to mention libraries). Pumps and portable buildings would have been more accessible, and a hazardous-material plan would have been in place. Weekend emergency plans would have been developed and implemented.

• Use the experience of other institutions for risk assessment and review. Most higher education professionals are networked or have access to helpful national affinity organizations. Presidents have the American Council on Education; lawyers, the National Association of College and University Attorneys; chief financial officers, the National Association of College and University Business Officers; and professors, the American Association of University Professors, just to cite a few. The LISTSERVs I see suggest to me that virtually no problem arises that your counterpart hasn't encountered. Use the resources available to your office or profession.

• Consider how nonlegal regimes are implemented. Many issues or initiatives founder in the implementation stages, undermining the original policy. There is an extensive literature on this subject, including its importance in higher education (Cerych and Sabatier 1986; Sabatier 1987; Olivas 1992). Institutional leaders can ensure important policies are fully institutionalized by paying attention to how they are planned and implemented.

• Governance scholarship and higher education research should pay attention to the many nonlegal influences that arise on campus.

Even in this very preliminary inquiry, I have learned several things, not all of which I had anticipated. First, it is hard to separate the various strands of complex governance matters. In addition, there are strategic techniques from implementation theory that can be employed to improve the likelihood that policies, once decided upon, will actually be carried out efficaciously. Finally, higher education is embedded in a real world, so larger world events will eventually affect colleges and universities, just as 11 September has led to immigration reform controls, regulation of flight schools, international student requirements, and a comprehensive student data–tracking system.

# Conclusion: Looking to the Future
## Ronald G. Ehrenberg

A number of important themes emerge from the chapters in *Governing Academia*. First, decentralization gives individual units—be they university campuses within a state system, colleges within a university, or departments within a college—an incentive to act in their own best interests, but less of an incentive to work toward the common good. As Heller points out, at the level of a state system, decentralization of control may lead to wasteful overlap between campuses. As Wilson shows, decentralized budgeting in the form of responsibility center management models may cause units not to maximize the quality of the education they are providing students. And, as Lohmann demonstrates, decentralized hiring by departments may lead to ossification, replication of the status quo, and a failure to move quickly into new areas of inquiry that require interdisciplinary approaches.

Each suggests that designs of academic governance structures need to pay serious attention to reducing problems that decentralization may cause. Heller notes that states establish governance structures and funding mechanisms that will promote state goals, but that institutions work within these constraints to maximize their own goals.[1] He also notes that there does not appear to be any single form of state governance that unambiguously works best in each situation. Indeed, it appears that states tend to oscillate between more and less state control and oversight of their systems. Wilson suggests that responsibility management center budgeting systems require strong academic leadership at the center of the university to ensure academic quality in each of the university's colleges. In my book *Tuition Rising* (2000a), I similarly stress the importance of either the university having strong central academic leadership or the central administration having sufficient resources (from its own endowments or from revenue that it receives from "taxing" each of its colleges) to induce cooperative behavior and get colleges to buy-in to university-wide priorities. Lohmann suggests that one way for colleges and universities to overcome the resistance of departments to hire new faculty members with interest in emerging interdisciplinary areas is to assign positions jointly to the departments and the interdisciplinary programs.

A second theme is that there may not be any single optimal design for a governance structure either for a system of state academic institutions (Heller), for boards of trustees (Hermalin), or for the organization of the university (Lohmann). Rather, what arises reflects the local history of each organization and the very different constraints it faces. Put another way, the variety of governance structures and organizational forms that we observe in place at a point in time may be present for very good reasons. It is natural for institutional arrangements to evolve as conditions change; hence the movement first away from, and then back toward, central control of the public university system in some states may reflect adaptation to changing circumstances and needs rather than irrational behavior.

A related inference that can be drawn from Hammond's chapter is that as the issues facing universities and the importance of different areas of inquiry change, it may be important for universities to consider reorganizing their hierarchy so as to facilitate the things they consider most important. For example, Cornell University recently established a "virtual" college of information sciences, with the dean having control over a number of faculty positions, as a way of stimulating the infusion of information sciences into the teaching and research programs at all of Cornell's colleges; the prior department of information science, which was located within the College of Engineering, was unlikely to be able to do this. Establishment of this virtual college is very consistent with Lohmann's suggestions about how to create new interdisciplinary programs.

The third and final theme is that the changing environment that higher education faces is likely to continue to influence the forms of governance we see in academia and the way academic institutions behave. Recent decades have seen the growing use of part-time and non-tenure-track faculty as academic institutions try to cope with financial pressures. It is not surprising, therefore, that Kaplan finds that faculty authority in governance tends to be concentrated in academic matters and that more and more financial matters are the purview of the administration. The growing threat from for-profit providers leads Pusser and Turner to worry about whether the traditional nonprofit higher education sector will maintain its concern for the public good and continue to act in the public welfare. The rush to commercialize faculty research findings is but one example.

Most of the growth of enrollments in higher education is in the public sector, where there are fewer impediments to increased faculty unionization than there are in the private sector. The growth in graduate student unionization that my chapter coauthors and I pointed out suggests that there will be a cadre of new entrants to the academic profession who are much more sympathetic to the notion of faculty unions than the generations of academics that preceded them. It is thus reasonable to predict that in the years ahead we will see increased collective bargaining coverage of tenure-track faculty in public higher education. The financial stresses that have caused academic institutions to substitute part-time and non-tenure-track faculty for tenure-track faculty will probably continue, and it is likely that these faculty members will increasingly become a fertile ground for unionization activities. The *Yeshiva* decision applied only to tenure-track faculty, so this pressure for unionization of adjunct and non-tenure-track faculty will be felt in private as well as public higher education.

Projections undertaken even before the financial crisis and recession of 2001 and 2002 suggest that most states will not have the resources to meet the increased demand for college enrollments that is occurring now and that is projected to occur during the first decade or so of the twenty-first century (Ehrenberg 2000c). This imbalance of resources and enrollment pressure will likely lead to increased demands for accountability in public higher education and to pressures for increased centralization and control of state university systems.

One way states try to achieve increased accountability is by adopting performance incentives in their budgetary processes or, more directly, by adopting performance budgeting systems in which institutional budgets are directly tied to one or more measures of institutional achievement. While there is evidence that states are increasingly adopting such systems, there is little evidence that this adoption has had any measurable effects on how public institutions behave.[2]

Demands for accountability will also lead to increased demands, at least in the public sector, for more constituent representation—in particular, faculty and students—on boards of trustees. Freedman suggests that it would be wise for institutions to resist such pressures, because he fears that "constituent trustees" often perceive themselves as acting as representatives of their constituents, rather than as acting in a fiduciary capacity.

The growing need to raise revenues from sources other than tuition or state appropriations will lead to increased pressure on both private and public academic institutions to increase their annual appeals and their endowment. This will in turn likely also create pressure on private institutions to expand the size of their boards of trustees, to enable the institutions to "reward" more large donors with seats on their boards and to keep the donors involved with the institution so that the likelihood of their making future gifts increases. In both private institutions and public institutions, where board size is often established by state law, we are also likely to see more constituent units (colleges, departments, and programs) establishing advisory boards to facilitate the units' own search for revenues. The growth of these unit boards will increase the difficulties that the central administration of each academic institution faces in trying to maintain academic and economic control over all of the institution's activities. As units increasingly search for contributions on their own, the potential for the types of financial abuses that have often been associated with fund-raising for big-time athletic programs increases (Zimbalist 1999).

The growing importance of donors to academic institutions is also likely to place more pressure on the institutions to respond to the preferences of donors, in terms of both setting the university's priorities and its operation. An extreme example of such pressures recently occurred when one major donor to Case Western Reserve University (CWRU) in Cleveland announced that until the institution's board of trustees was reorganized in a manner that he considered satisfactory, he would withhold all of his contributions from CWRU *and* from all of the other Cleveland area organizations to which he was a major donor. Given the overlapping board structure of these organizations, with important CWRU board members also serving on the boards of the other organizations, the donor believed that withholding his contributions from other Cleveland area organizations would lead those organizations to put pressure on CWRU to reform its board structure (Pulley 2002).[3] Such a form of secondary boycott, while legal because the donor was, after all, withholding his own voluntary contributions, raises serious ethical issues.

The growth of nonlegal legal influences that affect academia—statutory, consortia, and regulatory requirements—which Olivas discusses are also likely to continue. Increasingly accreditation agencies are playing a more interventionist role and requiring institutions to develop strategic plans. Or to take another example, the NCAA certification reviews of Division I varsity athletic programs include gender and racial/ethnic equity as criteria, which puts added pressures on universities to carefully monitor their recruitment of athletes and coaches and their expenditures on various sports.

Equity was evaluated, for example, in the 1999 NCAA certification review of Cornell's varsity athletic programs in terms of the salaries paid to coaches of men's and women's teams, the gender and racial/ethnic representation of coaches, the gender and racial/ethnic makeup of varsity athletics, and the distribution of athletic funding between male and female teams. Although gender equity requirements are written into federal law, there is no such federal law for race/ethnic requirements (Ehrenberg 2000a, ch. 17).

At one point in the Cornell certification review process, in my role as chair of the internal review committee, I explained to a representative of the Ivy League, who was aiding us in preparing for our external certification review, that if the review criticized the university for having a smaller share of underrepresented minority groups among its varsity athletes than among its undergraduate student population, the university had a right to be upset. Cornell was proud that the proportion of its varsity athletes from underrepresented groups was *smaller* than the proportion of its undergraduate students from underrepresented groups, even if this made it seem like we weren't putting enough effort into attracting underrepresented minority athletes. Put simply, Cornell recruits underrepresented minority students primarily for academic, not athletic reasons, and the notion that an accrediting agency might penalize a university for doing so seemed quite silly.

Fortunately, Cornell was never penalized by the review committee for putting more effort into recruiting minority students for academic purposes than for intercollegiate sports. This example highlights the importance of the governance structure of an institution—the trustees, the central and college administrations, and the faculty—being fully aware of what the institution's core academic values are and being able to explicitly articulate them to external constituents. As the external pressures on academic institutions from all of the forces described here rise, and the difficulty of governing these institutions increases, the ability to do so is likely to become more and more important to the institutions' futures.

# Appendix: Statewide Postsecondary Governance Structures

| State | Governance Structure | Members (appointment process) | Number of University Systems/Governing Boards |
|---|---|---|---|
| Alabama | Coordinating | 12 (10 gubernatorial and 2 legislative) | 2 (U. of Alabama and Troy State) |
| Alaska | Coordinating | 14[a] | 1 (U. of Alaska) |
| Arizona | Planning | 13 (gubernatorial) | 2 (university and community colleges) |
| Arkansas | Coordinating | 12 (gubernatorial) | 3 (U. of Arkansas, Arkansas State U., Southern Arkansas U.)[b] |
| California | Planning | 16[a] | 3 (U. of California, California State U., and California Community Colleges) |
| Colorado | Coordinating | 9 (gubernatorial) | 4 (U. of Colorado, Board of Agriculture, state colleges, community colleges)[b] |
| Connecticut | Coordinating | 11 (7 gubernatorial and 4 legislative) | 3 (U. of Connecticut, Connecticut State U., community-technical colleges)[b] |
| Delaware | Planning | 13 (gubernatorial) | 3 (U. of Delaware, Delaware State U., technical and community colleges) |
| District of Columbia | Governing | 16 (11 mayoral, 3 alumni, 1 student, U. of District of Columbia president) | 1 (U. of the District of Columbia) |
| Florida | Governing | 7 (elected officials serve ex officio) | 39 single-institution boards |
| Georgia | Governing | 16 (gubernatorial) | 1 (U. System of Georgia) |
| Hawaii | Governing | 12 (gubernatorial) | 1 (U. of Hawaii) |

| State | Governance Structure | Members (appointment process) | Number of University Systems/ Governing Boards |
|---|---|---|---|
| Idaho | Coordinating | 8 (7 gubernatorial, 1 elected official) | 1 (U. of Idaho)[c] |
| Illinois | Coordinating | 15[a] | Each institution has its own board |
| Indiana | Coordinating | 14 (12 gubernatorial, 1 student, 1 faculty) | 8 (Ball State U., Indiana State U., Ivy Tech State C., Indiana U., Indiana U.-Purdue U. Fort Wayne, Purdue U., Vincennes U., U. of Southern Indiana) |
| Iowa | Governing | 9 (gubernatorial) | None |
| Kansas | Governing | 9 (gubernatorial) | None for 4-year institutions; individual governing boards for community colleges |
| Kentucky | Coordinating | 16 (15 gubernatorial, 1 elected official ex officio) | 1 (Kentucky Community and Technical College System)[b] |
| Louisiana | Coordinating | 16 (15 gubernatorial, 1 student) | 3 (Louisiana State U., Southern U., U. of Louisiana) |
| Maine | Governing | 16 (gubernatorial) | 1 (U. of Maine System) |
| Maryland | Coordinating | 12 (gubernatorial) | 4 (U. System of Maryland, Morgan State U., St. Mary's C., Baltimore City Community C.)[d] |
| Massachusetts | Coordinating | 12 (11 gubernatorial and 1 appointed official ex officio) | 2 (U. of Massachusetts, Board of Higher Education)[e] |
| Michigan | None | | 42 single-institution boards[f] |
| Minnesota | Planning | 8 (gubernatorial) | 2 (U. of Minnesota, Minnesota State Colleges and Universities) |
| Mississippi | Governing[g] | 12 (gubernatorial) | None |
| Missouri | Coordinating | 9 (gubernatorial) | 4 (U. of Missouri, Lincoln U., Truman State U., Linn State Technical C.)[h] |
| Montana | Governing | 10 (7 gubernatorial and 3 elected officials ex officio) | None |
| Nebraska | Planning | 11 (gubernatorial) | 2 (U. of Nebraska, Nebraska State Colleges)[b] |
| Nevada | Governing | 13 (elected) | None |
| New Hampshire | Planning | 22 (12 gubernatorial and 10 appointed officials) | 2 (U. System of New Hampshire, Community Technical College System) |
| New Jersey | Planning | 8 (gubernatorial) | 31 single-institution boards |
| New Mexico | Coordinating | 15 (gubernatorial) | 15 single-institution boards |
| New York | Coordinating | 16 (legislative) | 2 (State U. of New York, City U. of New York) |

| State | Governance Structure | Members (appointment process) | Number of University Systems/ Governing Boards |
|---|---|---|---|
| North Carolina | Governing[i] | 32 (legislative) | 75 single-institution boards (including community colleges) |
| North Dakota | Governing | 7 (gubernatorial) | None |
| Ohio | Coordinating | 11 (9 gubernatorial and 2 elected officials ex officio) | 19 (Bowling Green State U., U. of Akron, Wright State U., Central State U., Cleveland State U., Shawnee State U., U. of Toledo, Youngstown State U., Ohio U., Ohio State U., Kent State U., U. of Cincinnati, Miami U., 6 community colleges) |
| Oklahoma | Coordinating | 9 (gubernatorial) | 16 (U. of Oklahoma, Oklahoma Colleges, Oklahoma Agricultural and Mechanical Colleges, and 13 single-institution boards) |
| Oregon | Coordinating | 11 (gubernatorial) | 1 (Oregon University System)[j] |
| Pennsylvania | Planning | 22 (gubernatorial) | 19 (State System of Higher Education, Pennsylvania State U., Temple U., Lincoln U., U. of Pittsburgh, and 14 single-institution community college boards) |
| Rhode Island | Governing | 15 (13 gubernatorial and 2 legislative) | None |
| South Carolina | Coordinating | 14 (gubernatorial) | 13 (U. of South Carolina, 2-year colleges, and 11 single-institution boards) |
| South Dakota | Governing | 9 (gubernatorial) | None |
| Tennessee | Coordinating | 15 (11 gubernatorial and 4 elected officials ex officio) | 2 (U. of Tennessee, State University and Community College System) |
| Texas | Coordinating | 18 (gubernatorial) | 60 (U. of Texas, Texas A&M U., Texas State U., U. of Houston, U. of North Texas, Texas Tech U., and 54 single-institution boards, including 50 community college districts) |
| Utah | Governing | 18 (16 gubernatorial and 2 appointed officials ex officio) | 10 single-institution boards |
| Vermont | None | | 2 (U. of Vermont and Vermont State Colleges) |
| Virginia | Coordinating | 11 (gubernatorial) | 15 (Virginia Community College System and 14 single-institution 4-year boards) |

| State | Governance Structure | Members (appointment process) | Number of University Systems/ Governing Boards |
|---|---|---|---|
| Washington | Coordinating | 9 (gubernatorial) | 7 (community college and 6 single-institution 4-year boards) |
| West Virginia | Coordinating | 9 (7 gubernatorial and 2 appointed officials ex officio) | 13 single-institution boards |
| Wisconsin | None | 17 (15 gubernatorial, 2 appointed officials ex officio) | 2 (U. of Wisconsin and Wisconsin Technical College System) |
| Wyoming | Coordinating | 18[a] | 8 (U. of Wyoming and single-institution boards for 7 community colleges) |

*Source*: Adapted from Education Commission of the States 2002.

[a] The appointment process is so complex that it cannot be summarized easily here; the reader is referred to the Education Commission of the States report for more details.

[b] The remaining institutions in the state have single-institution boards.

[c] Each community college has a locally elected board.

[d] The remaining community colleges have individual governing boards.

[e] The Board of Higher Education has authority over the 9 state colleges and 15 community colleges.

[f] Three of the university boards are popularly elected, 10 are gubernatorially appointed, and 29 community colleges have locally elected boards.

[g] Mississippi also has a statewide coordinating agency for community colleges with 10 gubernatorially appointed members.

[h] In addition, there are seven single-institution boards for 4-year institutions and 12 for community colleges.

[i] The state also has a statewide governing board for community colleges with 20 members, 10 appointed by the governor, 8 by the legislature, and 2 elected officials *ex officio*.

[j] The Oregon State Board of Education has governing authority over the state's 17 community colleges.

# Notes

Introduction

1. The reasons for these high rates of increase are numerous and are discussed in Ehrenberg 2000a.

2. A November 2002 statewide referendum victory, backed by opponents of the new plan, reinstated a statewide system governing board, and the new campus boards of trustees will have only those powers that the state system governing board delegates to them.

3. *NLRB v. Yeshiva University* (944 U.S. 672 [1980]). The decision held that Yeshiva's full-time faculty members were managerial employees because they determined curriculum, grading systems, admissions and matriculation standards, academic calendars, and course schedules and also played influential roles in faculty hiring, tenure, and promotion decisions. As such, they were precluded from collective bargaining under the National Labor Relations Act.

Chapter 1. Presidents and Trustees

1. It is a canard, I must add, that public trustees are preoccupied with securing preferential football seating, and that private trustees are principally concerned with influencing the admissions applications of their friends' children!

Chapter 2. Higher Education Boards of Trustees

1. As a shorthand, I use "board of trustees" to refer to governing bodies of college and universities and "board of directors" to refer to the governing bodies of for-profit corporations. Similarly, a "trustee" is an overseer of a college or university, while a "director" is an overseer of a for-profit corporation.

2. Adam Smith (1776, 700), commenting on director-overseen companies, complained that "negligence and profusion . . . must always prevail, more or less, in the management of the affairs of such a company."

3. For modern-day faculty who complain of the tyranny students exercise through course evaluations, school rankings, etc., it may be worth noting that in Bologna the tyranny was quite real: Professors could not leave the campus without the permission of the students and had to make a monetary deposit against their return if permission was granted. Professors were also subject to fines for "poor" lectures (Kerr and Gade 1989, 11).

4. A short list of critics, of varying degrees of vehemence, includes Chait and Taylor (1989), Kerr and Gade (1989), Bowen (1994), and Taylor, Chait, and Holland (1996). Many of their criticisms of nonprofits' boards echo complaints leveled at for-profits' boards by Smith (1776), Berle and Means (1932), and more modern critics (some of whom are discussed in the text—see, too, Hermalin and Weisbach 2003, for a more complete survey of boards and their critics).

5. Most corporate directors can be classified as inside directors or outside directors. Inside directors are employees or former employees of the firm. They generally are not thought to be independent of the CEO, because the success of their careers is often tied to the CEO's. Outside directors are not employees of the firm and usually do not have any business ties to the firm aside from their directorship. Outside directors are typically CEOs from other firms or prominent individuals in other fields. Finally, a small minority of directors fall into neither category; often these are attorneys or businesspeople who have a long-standing relationship with the firm. These directors are usually referred to as "affiliated" or "gray" directors.

6. In the literature, "firm performance" is a convenient phrase meant to capture various possible measures of a firm's success (e.g., return to investors, profitability, and successful execution of the firm's strategy). In many of the empirical studies, firm performance is operationalized in a precise way (e.g., stock return or performance on some accounting measure). In the more limited theoretical literature, firm performance has typically meant economic profits in static models or firm value (the present discounted value of economic profits) in dynamic models.

7. In the corporate setting, Jensen (1993) and Lipton and Lorsch (1992) were among the first to suggest a negative relation should hold between board size and corporate performance. Yermack (1996) was the first to provide compelling statistical evidence in support of this view. Eisenberg, Sundgren, and Wells (1998) provide additional statistical support.

8. As is, to some extent, done in the corporate context—see note 6.

9. One can think of question 1 as the regression, $p_{t+s} = \phi c_t + \varepsilon_t$, where $p$ is a performance measure (e.g., profits in the corporate context), $c$ is a measure(s) of board characteristics (e.g., insider-outsider ratio), $\phi$ is the coefficient(s) to be estimated, $\varepsilon$ is an error term (including, possibly, other controls), $t$ is a time index, and $s > 0$ to reduce joint endogeneity problems.

10. The one study of which I'm aware in the nonprofit—but *not* higher education—context (Herman and Renz 1998) suggests some relation between the prestige of board members and organizational effectiveness. Given, however, that this study lacks controls for joint endogeneity—do, for instance, effective organizations attract high-prestige board members or do high-prestige board members make organizations effective?—it is impossible to view the results as indicative of any causal relationship *from* board characteristics *to* institutional performance. Furthermore, the subjective manner in which the variables are measured also raises questions about how one might interpret the results.

11. Although, interestingly, a survey of presidents and board chairs finds that they generally feel their board structure, at least in terms of size, is good (see Table 3 of Kerr and Gade [1989, 89]).

12. Among them, Coughlan and Schmidt (1985), Warner, Watts, and Wruck (1988), Weisbach (1988), Barro and Barro (1990), Jensen and Murphy (1990), Blackwell, Brickley, and Weisbach (1994), Kaplan (1994), and Huson, Parrino, and Starks (2000).

13. "Busy" could also be a proxy for professional directors. Such people may have motives to develop reputations for *not* rocking the boat and for being supportive of the CEO in order to increase the number of directorships they're offered.

14. Ehrenberg, Cheslock, and Epifantseva (2001) consider some of the determinants of college and university presidents' pay, but composition of the board of trustees or other characteristics of the trustees are not among the determinants considered. It would appear from Ehrenberg and colleagues that there are not many other studies of presidential pay.

15. The norm was one-year terms in the Hermalin and Weisbach 1988 data, but these days, in response to the takeover wave of the late 1980s, the norm is three-year staggered terms.

16. Whether turnover rates on university and college boards are in fact lower than those for corporate boards is ultimately an empirical question. One possible study would, therefore, be to compare these rates.

17. That elected officials believe fee increases influence state elections is evidenced by the current governor of California, Gray Davis, who has steadily resisted fee increases at the University of California as part of his attempt to establish his "bona fides" as an "education governor."

18. Chait and Taylor (1989) offer a list of possible decisions, including the decision to begin offering graduate education, discontinue church affiliation, establish new academic departments, and set investment policies. An interesting historical decision would be the decision to go coeducational. A topical set of decisions to analyze would be those connected with affirmative action and minority outreach.

19. In state schools, this view could be questioned on the grounds that the legislature and governor, through their control of the purse strings, might be the ultimate authorities. In California, for example, the immense power the governor has over the state budget makes him essentially a "super-regent" with respect to many University of California decisions, particularly when it comes to fees. This view could also be questioned for a school that is owned by a religious organization, in which case important authority may reside with church officials who are not directly connected to the school.

20. This isn't to say that boards of trustees do not, from time to time, involve themselves in decisions that are inappropriate uses of their time. See Chait and Taylor 1989 or Bowen 1994 for anecdotes. Kerr and Gade (1989) offer some survey data on the prevalence of "inappropriate" decision making (see, e.g., their Tables B-9, B-10, and B-17).

21. Free-riding is an externality problem long recognized by economists. For a formal analysis of it in the context of a team, see Holmstrom 1982.

22. Recently, economists have begun to model such shifting of power (see, e.g., Aghion and Tirole 1997 or Levitt and Snyder 1997), but such analyses are quite abstract and do not deal with board-management issues per se.

23. Alternatively, if there is a cost to replacing a president (e.g., search costs, costs of disruption, etc.), then the rational decision is to fire only if the incumbent is worse than the expected ability of a randomly drawn replacement minus the replacement costs.

24. The only possible problem would be with interpreting the single dimensional performance variable in the Hermalin and Weisbach model in the higher education context. This is not a critical problem because the model can be readily extended to have *the* performance variable be some statistic over multidimensional performance measures.

25. See Chait and Taylor 1989, Bowen 1994, and Taylor, Chait, and Holland 1996 for discussions of the problem of trustees who see their positions as largely honorific.

26. The reason for this is as follows. The incumbent board has an ideal level of monitoring given the preferences of the existing members. The president/CEO always prefers as little monitoring as possible. So by agreeing to less monitoring than their ideal (e.g., by adding even less vigilant members to the board), the incumbent members suffer only a

second-order loss—they're moving from their optimum—while the president/CEO enjoys a first-order gain; hence the bargaining must always lead to less monitoring than that which the incumbent board would otherwise have done. (This prediction of a steady decline or "entropy" in board effectiveness could be seen as a weakness of the Hermalin and Weisbach model. There are, however, radical breaks in corporate governance, such as from takeovers, that could periodically "reset" board effectiveness—see Hermalin and Weisbach 1998, p. 106, for a discussion. Interestingly, many of these "reset" mechanisms don't operate in higher education, which further bolsters the view that boards of trustees may be less effective monitors than corporate boards.)

27. Bowen (1994), among others, warns of this danger in nonprofit boards.

28. It is worth noting that this powerful trustee "solution" is not always desirable, at least from some perspectives. Bowen (1994) warns against institutional capture by a large donor, urging nonprofits to diversify their donor base. Governor Gray Davis's refusal to increase fees despite funding problems at the University of California is almost surely not the best course of action from the university's perspective.

29. This view is echoed by a significant number of faculty, who, among other criticisms, believe the board cedes too much authority to the president (40 percent hold this view according to survey results reported in Kerr and Gade 1989, Table B-11).

30. To the item, "understands and observes the line between policy and administration," 86 percent of public institution chairs rated the board's performance as good or excellent, while only 69 percent of the presidents of these institutions did (the numbers are 94 percent and 88 percent, respectively, for private institutions)—see Table B-9 of Kerr and Gade 1989. To the item, "effectively reviews the performance of the president," 80 percent of chairs rated the board's performance as good or excellent, while only 68 percent of presidents did (see Table B-8).

31. As discussed earlier, one possible exception would be between board size and performance. Measuring performance in the higher education context is, however, difficult, and moreover, it is not clear that any relation uncovered is causal.

32. A point also made by Kerr and Gade (1989).


Chapter 3. State Oversight of Academia

1. For recent books on aspects of public higher education governance, see Heller 2001; MacTaggart 1996, 1998; and Richardson et al. 1999.

2. Parts of this section have been adapted from Heller 2002.

3. Brubacher and Rudy (1976) and Rudolph (1990) provide good summaries of the early history of state support for private institutions.

4. McLendon (2003) provides an excellent overview of the history of state coordination and governance of higher education.

5. The small literature base was noted in one study: "The empirical literature on state regulation and its impact on campuses is sparse" (Volkwein, Malik, and Napierski-Pranci 1998, 58).

6. To put it more colloquially, "A happy administrator is a productive administrator."

7. Toma (1990) does not present a theoretical or empirical basis in the literature for this presumption regarding the responsiveness of tenure versus nontenured faculty. The differences in tenure rates between public and private institutions are actually small. In the 1980–1981 academic year, 65.7 percent of all faculty at public four-year institutions were tenured, while 56.0 percent of their private college counterparts were tenured (National Center for Education Statistics 2001a, Table 244).

8. While Toma (1990) addresses the potential endogeneity problem of the board structure, she does not mention in the article the possibility of collinearity between her predicted measure of board centralization and the other covariates in her models, some of which were used to predict the board structure.

9. This relationship was only marginally statistically significant, however ($p \leq 0.10$).

## Chapter 5. Herding Cats in University Hierarchies: Formal Structure and Policy Choice in American Research Universities

1. For a sustained critique of the "organized anarchies" metaphor of Cohen and March (1974), as well as its intellectual predecessor, the "garbage can" model of Cohen, March, and Olsen (1972), see Bendor, Moe, and Shotts 2001.

2. For a brief review of the history of governing boards in higher education in America, see Duryea 1973.

3. From Article 4 of the *Bylaws of the Michigan State University Board of Trustees*. See http://www.msu.edu/dig/DOCUMENTS/bylaws.html.

4. Reformatted and lightly edited from Article 4 of the *Bylaws of the Michigan State University Board of Trustees*.

5. From Section 2.1.2.2 of the *Michigan State University Bylaws for Academic Governance*. See http://www.msu.edu/dig/acadgov/agbylaw/agbylaws.pdf.

6. From Section 2.1.2.1 of the *Michigan State University Bylaws for Academic Governance*.

7. For the organization chart at Michigan State University, see http://opbweb.opb.msu.edu under the heading of "Long Range Planning."

8. Gulick's essay (along with the larger "principles of administration" literature) was subjected to a scornful attack by Herbert Simon in his well-known essay "The Proverbs of Administration" (1946). For a defense of Gulick's essay against Simon's criticisms, see Hammond 1990.

9. See Hammond 1994 for a reanalysis of *Strategy and Structure* and the extensive literature on corporate structures that it stimulated.

10. Personal communications to the author from three eminent experts on research on higher education institutions—Robert Birnbaum at the University of Maryland (28 March 2001), Marvin Peterson at the University of Michigan (19 March 2001), and M. Christopher Brown at the University of Illinois (23 March 2001)—all emphasized the almost complete lack of a research literature on the impact of alternative organizational forms on university decision making.

11. For just one example, Brown's *Organization and Governance in Higher Education* (2000), an edited volume that contains forty separate selections, makes *no* reference to the impact of the universities' formal structures.

12. For relevant histories, see Furner 1975 and Haskell 1976.

13. At the least, searching for "political economy department" with the Google search engine on the World Wide Web turned up no such examples in the top forty or fifty listings.

14. For an interesting discussion of divisions within several other social sciences as well, see Dogan and Pahre 1989.

15. Trow (forthcoming) provides an interesting historical analysis of the origins of the numerous biology-related departments at the University of California at Berkeley.

16. For an analysis of the role of professional schools in American universities, see Halpern 1987.

17. For a history of the creation of the U.S. Department of Agriculture, its Agricultural Experiment Stations, and the Stations' linkages with universities, see Carpenter 2001.

18. For a recent review of contingency theory, see Donaldson 2001.

19. I focus more on the provost, as the chief academic officer, rather than on the university president because I am primarily interested in the academic parts of the university. A focus on the university president would require broadening my focus to include such activities as development (fund-raising), public relations, governmental relations (i.e., lobbying the legislature), physical plant, student services, intercollegiate athletics, as well as academic activities. The comparative organization of these activities would be a worthy subject of research. Indeed, even the organization of residence halls for students presents some challenging organizational issues inasmuch as the activities of physical plant, food service, student services (e.g., advisors and counselors), campus safety (policing), and computer services all converge on each residence hall.

20. For simplicity I assume that the chair of each department is sending a sincere—a nonstrategic—message upward about research opportunities and prospects. While it is unlikely that a chair will explicitly downgrade his or her department's research opportunities and prospects, as do the latter two chairs in the illustration, the differential evidence they could use to support their claims would alert the relevant dean that there are fewer such opportunities than in other departments. Moreover, a department chair would not want to overpromise what could be achieved with the help of the new development officer: failure to live up to the promise is likely to have negative long-range consequences for the department.

21. It is possible that a chair interested only in what is good for the university might nonetheless distort information because he thinks this will lead the provost to make a better decision for the university. This might happen especially if the chair believes that other chairs are sending distorted information for their own self-interested reasons. Our chair might then believe that he has to distort his own information in order to counteract the ("illegitimate") actions of the others. Since the other chairs might fear the same thing about our first chair, there may be a stable equilibrium in which everyone lies (or at least shades the truth), even though everyone may prefer to tell the truth and may prefer that everyone else tell the truth too.

22. For simplicity, we shall also assume that the subordinates do not know what their superiors' choices would be. This inhibits their ability to engage in strategic behavior, which will be taken to mean that they simply recommend the candidate who is, in their judgment, the best by whatever criteria they happen to use.

23. The preferences of the chairs, deans, and provost are to be treated here as "latent," in the sense that when presented with a pair of options, each official will spend time and energy deciding which is the better option; the choices that each would make, if required to, are summarized in Figure 5.3. What is listed for the administrators and top-level administrator here should not be treated as clear-cut preferences that they have at the outset. If they had such clear-cut preferences at the outset, they might feel they have little reason to consult their respective subordinates.

24. For an extensive examination of this general point, using concepts from axiomatic social choice theory, see Hammond and Miller 1985 and Miller 1992, ch. 4.

25. My remarks in this paragraph and the next were stimulated by the astute observations of an anonymous reviewer, and I rely heavily on the reviewer's own words for my discussion.

26. The strategizing required in two-level hierarchies is described in Hammond and Horn 1985, while the far greater complexities of strategizing in three-level hierarchies are analyzed in Hammond and Horn 1984.

27. The inclination to press for one solution over another might happen for purely cognitive reasons, but the different political interests of the departments and programs may

lead their chairs to deliberately interpret ambiguous instructions in ways that are beneficial to their own departments and programs.

28. As with an earlier section, this paragraph and the next rely heavily on the insightful remarks of an anonymous reviewer.

## Chapter 6. Tiebout Competition versus Political Competition on a University Campus

1. See Whalen 1991 for a detailed description of responsibility center management (RCM), and also Cross's (1996) brief but informative description and history of the system, highlighting some of its fundamental problems. While emphasizing the relevance of economic theory for RCM, Cross notes the dearth of academic literature on RCM per se. Krause and Wilson (2000) provide one formal model, which is discussed briefly in the chapter. For the related issue of competition among different universities, see Epple, Romano, and Sieg 2000 and Debande and Demeulemeester 2000.

2. Actual RCM systems do allow some variation in compensation rates, such as between undergraduate and graduate students, across different professional schools, and between in-state and out-of-state students. As an extension of my basic model, I briefly discuss differences in compensation rates for in-state and out-of-state students at a public university.

3. Wilson (2002) provides a more extensive discussion of some of these points but does not provide a formal model that can be used to compare RCM with centralized provision of education.

4. One interpretation of these profits is that they are used in ways that make the members of the unit better off than what is needed to induce them to provide their labor services to the unit. Under this interpretation, profits could be distributed to these members either as direct compensation or in the form of wasteful expenditure activities.

5. In practice, units can to some extent vary the attributes of their educational programs across students, thereby mitigating, but not eliminating, this second component. However, such variations give rise to other problems, which I discuss later.

6. This argument does not distinguish between the private marginal benefit of education, which students use to make decisions, and the social marginal benefit of education. It is sometimes argued that education confers external benefits on the economy. This argument reinforces the idea that educational services are underprovided, and provides a rationale for state universities. The importance of such external benefits is not clear, however.

7. See Masten 2000 for an extended discussion of political processes within universities.

8. I assume here that the equilibrium budgets are sufficient to finance any fixed costs that might exist. Note also that $\alpha$ is fixed under my constant cost assumption. More general technologies are discussed at the end of the section titled "The Formal Analysis."

9. See Bernheim and Whinston 1986a, 1986b for the theory of common agency, and see Grossman and Helpman 2001 for applications to special-interest politics.

10. The quality variables may be interpreted as measuring the impact of education expenditures on the future earnings of students, along with other nonmonetary benefits. By treating these quality levels as independent of student behavior, I am not explicitly modeling the production process by which students also contribute inputs to the production of their own education, an idea that Rothschild and White (1995) have emphasized.

11. Actually, the results extend to a wide class of symmetric distribution functions.

12. Recall also that the total compensation level is assumed not to exceed the university's total budget; that is, the center does not collect fixed fees from the unit that are then

used to finance a value of $r(N_A + N_B)$ that exceeds the revenue the center receives from tuition and other sources.

13. Generalizations of this cost structure are discussed later. Following the previous discussion of costs, $\alpha e_i N_i$ may be measured by valuing labor costs at the minimum payments needed to induce members of the unit to provide their labor services to the unit.

14. This expression does not include fixed costs or fixed subsidies and fees, which are independent of $N_i$, but these extra terms do not affect the choice of $e_i$.

15. See Grossman and Helpman 2001, ch. 8, especially pp. 268–270. They refer to schedules satisfying the global truthfulness property as "compensating schedules."

16. Unless the appropriate symmetry assumption is imposed on the joint distribution of $s$ and $v$, units would not choose the same quality levels in equilibrium. Asymmetric units are considered in the section titled "Extensions."

17. In other words, there is a difference between the social and private marginal benefit of education, and this difference varies across different groups of students. The previous analysis has assumed away such differences.

18. Groen and White (2000) investigated the relative preferences of state governments and universities for in-state and out-of-state students.

19. See, for example, Ehrenberg's (2000b) revealing discussion of Cornell University's experience in this regard.

20. Of course, counterexamples to this conjecture can be found by comparing units offering fields of study that differ in their tendency to garner support from central administrators.

21. Similarly, Garvin (1980) models the "prestige" of a university as depending on the prestige of each of the individual departments within the university.

22. See Courant and Knepp 2001.

23. Rey (2001) develops a formal model that captures this possibility.

## Chapter 7. How Academic Ships Actually Navigate

1. For examples, see Jencks and Riesman 1968; Trow 1977; Blau 1973; Baldridge 1971; Pfeffer and Salancik 1974.

2. The Tailored Design Method (TDM) breaks down the steps of survey work into pieces and considers how each step in the process can be approached to maximize survey response. The survey instrument itself should look attractive and have a colorful cover. It should have official sanction that communicates the importance of the project and the breadth and gravity of support from the project within the respondent's population. Before the survey is sent out, the respondents should receive a personalized letter introducing the survey, notifying them of its pending arrival, and asking for their participation in completing the form. The survey can then be sent a short while later. Before the deadline, an attempt should be made to contact the population once or twice to remind respondents about the deadline and again ask for the forms to be completed and returned. Such protocols have been associated with marked improvements in survey response rates. While the average response rate has been found to be 28 percent, utilizing this method has garnered, depending on the survey and the difficulty of the survey task, response rates between 40 and 80 percent.

3. Available at http://caspar.nsf.gov.

4. References to the number of higher education institutions in the United States often mention a figure larger than three thousand. This number includes all community colleges and the specialty institutions such as colleges of business, nursing, and teaching. This study focused only on institutions accredited to grant bachelor's degrees in the liberal arts.

5. Since the contemporary survey was to incorporate questions from the AAUP's governance survey of 1970, permission to use the prior survey was sought from AAUP's Committee T (The Committee on Governance), which eagerly provided immediate support for the project. The American Council of Academic Deans (ACAD) also agreed to support the project and add its name to the sponsor list. The cooperation of these two groups was essential in communicating to respondents both the serious nature of the research and the national scope of the project.

6. Ideally, faculty representatives would have been sent the survey directly, but no mailing list of such individuals involved in campus governance existed, and so the survey depended on the goodwill and cooperation of administrators.

7. If this seems confusing or contradictory, consider the following example. If one group is excluded from a national census, the population of mentally ill homeless people, for instance, the census can still provide a representative sample of the remaining groups of the population since their increased likelihood of being sampled is distributed across all of the other groups. See the survey report for a fuller statement of the response ratios from all Carnegie classes.

8. In fact, if the institutions that were experiencing the greatest conflict over governance were also those least likely to respond to the survey, then the nonrespondent population could significantly bias the survey results and conclusions drawn from the study. The degree to which this may be the case would require further follow-up among the nonresponding institutions, and such an effort exceeded the capacities of the current survey administration.

9. The survey also allowed respondents the opportunity to provide written commentary on the issues raised in the questionnaire, and about half of the respondents chose to provide additional written comments about the state of governance on their campus. These answers have yet to be recorded and analyzed, however, so a more nuanced picture of on-campus relations remains to be drawn.

10. To maintain the survey's amenability for respondents, the questions from the 1970 effort were trimmed from thirty-one to fifteen by measuring the correlations among answers and discarding those questions whose answers were highly correlated and unlikely to produce information that could not be gained by asking only one question.

The five categories for faculty participation are as follows:

*Determination*: The faculty of an academic unit or its duly authorized representatives have final legislative or operational authority with respect to the policy or action, and any other technically required approvals or concurrences are only pro forma.

*Joint Action*: Formal agreement by both the faculty and other components of the institution is required for confirmatory action or policy determination. Negative action can be accomplished by a veto by either faculty or administration and the board. The separate components need not act simultaneously but should act within a reasonable time interval. In no case should the interval be longer than an academic year.

*Consultation*: There is a formal procedure or established practice which provides a means for the faculty (as a whole or through authorized representatives) to present its judgment in the form of a recommendation, vote, or other expression sufficiently explicit to record the position or positions taken by the faculty. This explicit expression of faculty judgment must take place prior to the actual making of the decision in question. Initiative for the expression of faculty judgment may come from the faculty, the administration, or the board.

*Discussion*: There is only an informal expression of opinion from the faculty or from individual faculty members, or there is formally expressed opinion only from administratively selected committees.

*None*: There is no faculty participation. In cases where the specific item is lacking (e.g., there is no long-range budgetary planning) or where the item is mandated, say, by the state legislature (e.g., admission requirements for some state schools), then the form of faculty participation is none.

11. "Redbook" refers to an AAUP publication encompassing all documents and statements about academic policies and practices issued by that organization. It is republished periodically. It was recently re-released, but this discussion refers to statements in the 1995 edition (American Association of University Professors 1995).

12. Two different readers read these responses independently and then compared their categories, discussing any disagreements until they arrived at an agreed-on category. This led to a list of thirty-five different categories of free response from institutions.

13. Table 7.19 does not show this percentage since it does not count the incidence of objectives, which may have been reported twice by an institution but were then grouped under the same thematic heading. Table 7.19 counts only the number of institutions that gave at least one response classified according to that thematic category.

14. This finding supports the conclusion of Adler, who in 1977 ran a replication of the 1970 AAUP survey and concluded that faculty participation in governance had increased over those seven years. He attributed this change to the rise in faculty collective bargaining at many institutions.


## Chapter 8. Collective Bargaining in American Higher Education

1. Our discussion on the early history of faculty collective bargaining is drawn from Education Commission of the States 1974; Means and Semas 1976; Ladd and Lipset 1973; and National Center for the Study of Collective Bargaining in Higher Education and the Professions 1997.

2. We computed these percentages from knowledge of whether full-time faculty in each institution were covered by a collective bargaining agreement (National Center for the Study of Collective Bargaining in Higher Education and the Professions 1997) and used full-time faculty employment data from WebCASPAR. (http://caspar.nsf.gov).

3. See, for example, Ashraf 1997; Barbezat 1989; Kesselring 1991; Rees 1993. Monks (2000) estimated faculty union impacts of 7 to 14 percent on their members' salaries relative to comparable nonunion faculty members' salaries, which are larger than the estimates found in other studies, but his study included faculty at two-year public institutions, which most other studies excluded.

4. See, for example, Meador and Walters 1994; Lillydahl and Singell, 1993; Rees 1994. Rees's study, which addresses turnover, used longitudinal data and was not subject to the criticism that follows.

5. One study that did use longitudinal data for a set of Canadian universities (Hosios and Siow 2001) found that the adoption of collective bargaining was associated with an increase in the senior faculty–junior faculty wage premium and a reduction in salary dispersion across fields of study. Neither result is surprising, because the researchers also found that the leaders of campus unions tended to be senior faculty who were employed in lower-paying disciplines.

6. This statement ignores the recent movement toward mutual gains bargaining, which is discussed in Corry 2000.

7. Somewhat ironically, a bill recently passed by both houses of the Washington State legislature would have given faculty members at Washington's public four-year colleges the right to bargain collectively, but only if the faculty senates at these institutions were eliminated. See Fogg 2002. At the urging of university presidents and faculty senates at the

state's institutions, the governor vetoed the provision that would have prevented bargaining and faculty governance from coexisting.

8. This section summarizes and extends materials first presented in Klaff and Ehrenberg 2002.

9. The acronym APPA is derived from the earlier name of the organization, the Association of Physical Plant Administrators of Universities and Colleges.

10. We are grateful to Joseph Lally, director of business operations for Cornell's Facilities Services Division, for granting us access to these data, under the condition that we not identify the specific institutions that participated in the survey.

11. In addition to excluding Canadian and elementary and secondary institutions, we also excluded specialized U.S. institutions such as seminaries and conservatories.

12. For public institutions this is a weighted average of its in-state and out-of-state tuitions, with the weights depending on the fraction of its students that come from each category.

13. Ehrenberg and Goldstein (1975) followed a similar procedure in their study of the impact of public-sector unions on the wages of different occupational categories of public employees.

14. The seemingly unrelated regression model was developed by Zellner (1962).

15. A table with the estimated coefficients of the union coverage equation for each occupation is available from the authors on request.

16. In both the NYU and Brown campaigns the union successfully sought to limit the scope of the bargaining unit in this way.

17. The rules governing whether graduate assistants who were residents of other states prior to entering graduate school qualify for in-state student tuition, both while they are assistants and during other points in their graduate career, vary widely across institutions. We leave consideration of union effects on these rules for another time.

18. See, for example, the cost-of-living comparisons for 309 U.S job markets provided by Maze Recruiters and Associates at http://mazerecruiters.com/job.htm.

19. These data are available from the American Association of University Professors and from WebCASPAR.

20. For example, the 1999–2002 contract between the Regents of the University of Michigan and the Michigan Graduate Employees Organization (Article X) specifies the minimum percentage salary increases that graduate assistants will receive each year under the contract, and then adds that if the faculty (who are not covered by a collective bargaining agreement) were to receive a greater average percentage increase in any year, then the graduate students would receive the same percentage increase (available at http://www.umich.edu~urel/gsi-sa/contract/99-02-toc.html). The recently signed 2002–2005 contract similarly ties graduate assistant salary increases to faculty salary increases, but the assistants are to receive a 0.5 percent smaller increase in the first year of the contract (Smallwood 2002b).

21. An important concern of graduate students in many organizing efforts has been workload issues. Our analyses of the survey data found no evidence that graduate student unions had decreased their members' workloads relative to those of graduate assistants at institutions without unions.

22. The Massachusetts Labor Relations Board had ruled earlier in the year that resident assistants had the right to join a union. This ruling applies only to public higher education institutions in the state.

23. Iseminger (1999) reported, however, that a survey of nearly 300 faculty at five universities with graduate student unions for at least four years found that over 90 percent of the respondents felt that the unions had not inhibited faculty members' ability to advise and instruct graduate students.

Chapter 9. Nonprofit and For-Profit Governance in Higher Education

1. Nonprofit organizations recognized under Section 501(c)3 of the Internal Revenue Code are known as the "charitable" nonprofits and include a range of organizations providing public benefits as educational, religious, literary, scientific, social welfare, or other charitable functions.

2. The release of the Flexner report in 1910, which documented unscientific practices in many for-profit medical schools, was one of the events that led to the decline of for-profit medical schools and the rise of the training of physicians in the university environment. In addition, what might be thought of as technological change in higher education—the development of complementarities between teaching, research, and economic development—also contributed to the decline of the for-profit institutional form in higher education during the early twentieth century.

3. It is obvious that MIT and Amherst have different institutional missions. MIT places a greater emphasis on engineering and the sciences, while Amherst emphasizes the humanities and the liberal arts and places a greater weight on small class sizes. While such differences in mission may be known at a descriptive level, it is hard to find an explicit codification of either institutional mission. Each institution does have a mission statement, but translating the mission to well-defined objectives is difficult. For example, MIT's Web site (http://web.mit.edu/mission.html) states, "The mission of MIT is to advance knowledge and educate students in science, technology, and other areas of scholarship that will best serve the nation and the world in the twenty-first century. The Institute is committed to generating, disseminating, and preserving knowledge, and to working with others to bring this knowledge to bear on the world's great challenges. MIT is dedicated to providing its students with an education that combines rigorous academic study and the excitement of discovery with the support and intellectual stimulation of a diverse campus community. We seek to develop in each member of the MIT community the ability and passion to work wisely, creatively, and effectively for the betterment of humankind."

4. One example is that if producing research and producing graduate students are both activities that generate externalities, and these activities are complements, it is efficient to produce them jointly in a nonprofit setting rather than separately in a commercial setting. Presumably, these arguments are most persuasive in the context of large, complex research universities with a range of "outputs" including research, undergraduate education, graduate training, and local economic development (Goldin and Katz 1999).

5. The marked decline in Pell revenues to for-profits in the period 1988–1994 coincided with state and federal investigations and increased regulation of for-profit providers. With the emergence of corporate for-profits as a significant lobbying force, the constraints on for-profit access to a variety of forms of federal subsidy are likely to be reduced, and those subsidies increased. The University of Phoenix recently placed on its board of directors a former head of the House Committee on Education and the Workforce. The present assistant secretary for postsecondary education in the U.S. Education Department was previously Phoenix's chief Washington lobbyist (Lobbyist Watch 2001; Ways and Means Committee 2002). This process is not unique to Phoenix, as many other for-profit institutions and associations have become significant political contributors (Selingo 1999).

6. In this chapter, we focus on the comparison between corporate for-profit providers and nonprofit providers. Corporate for-profit colleges, like Strayer and the University of Phoenix, are part of publicly traded corporations, as distinct from sole-proprietorships or other small operations owned by individuals or partnerships. Notably, small proprietary institutions are the numerical majority of for-profit institutions in higher education,

although they enroll a small share of students. These institutions receive public subsidy through tax exemption and tax deductibility of contributions.

7. Although the courts have not ruled definitively on the issue of shared governance in public and private nonprofit universities, they have addressed some aspects of internal governance and have generally favored trustee or board authority. Courts have suggested that there is no compelling reason for trustees to refrain from intervening in university affairs, for example, in teaching, research, or publication, if to fail to interfere would constitute an irresponsible neglect of their oversight duties as commonly understood (Van Alstyne 1990). The Supreme Court, in *Minnesota State Board for Community Colleges v. Knight*, refused to recognize a "constitutional right of faculty to participate in policymaking in academic institutions," and concluded, "Faculty involvement in academic governance has much to recommend it as a matter of academic policy, but it finds no basis in the Constitution" (Rabban 1990, 296).

8. Former University of Chicago President Hanna Gray describes the link between faculty responsibility and trustee responsibility: "[Faculty] are individual talents and intellectual entrepreneurs, demanding developers of their disciplines . . . who have in fact certain constitutional rights in the process of governance and hold the most important authority that exists in the university, that of making ultimate academic judgments. And boards exist to ensure this freedom and creativity and to protect the processes and health of the environment that make them possible" (Bowen 1994, 22).

Chapter 10. The Rise of Nonlegal Legal Influences on Higher Education

1. I have also written about this search in a different context, that of a faculty colleague speaking ill of me in this process (Olivas 2000).

2. For this review, I am indebted to Kaplin and Lee 1995, 137–43; 2000, 98–103; Ende, Anderson, and Crego 1997.

3. See Flores 2002 for information on this unusual case.

4. For example, see www.ue.org (United Educators' Web site), www.eiia.org (religious schools' insurance Web site), and www.nrra-usa.org (National Risk Retention Association's Web site).

5. Interestingly, another arena in which this conflict is occurring is in the issue of who controls legal tactics between the dioceses of the Catholic Church and their various insurers over settlements regarding sexually abusive priests (Liptak 2002).

6. A recent news story pointed out that some insurance premiums at colleges had increased by over 300 percent (Williams 2002).

7. The ABA was recently involved in two legal actions concerning its authorization of accreditation. It won one and had to enter a consent decree in the second matter. See *Massachusetts School of Law v. A.B.A.*, 107 F. 3d 1026 (3d Cir. 1997) (failure to grant accreditation was not a state action and did not injure the law school); see also *U.S. v. ABA 1995* (consent decree limiting ABA accreditation authority).

8. For thoughtful pieces on the accreditation process, see Finkin 1994; Martin 1994. For an article that is very critical of the process, see Shepherd 2003.

9. For a review of the Notre Dame television contract matter, see Blum 1995.

10. See www.wiche.edu/sep/wue/htm or www.tuitionexchange.org for examples.

Conclusion: Looking to the Future

1. Groen and White (2002) address the conflicting objectives of state universities and government over the fraction of their student bodies that come from out of state.

2. See, for example, Burke and Minassians 2001 and Burke and Associates 2002 for evidence on the adoption of performance budgeting and the establishment of performance incentives, and Zumeta 2001 for a discussion of whether they have led institutions to modify their behavior.

3. Interestingly one of the individual's concerns was that the Case Western Reserve University board had become so large, because of its expansion to include many potential major donors, that it could no longer function effectively.

# References

Adelman, C. 2000. *A Parallel Postsecondary Universe: The Certification System in Information Technology*. Washington, D.C.: U.S. Government Printing Office.

Adler, D. 1977. *Governance and Collective Bargaining*. Washington, D.C.: American Association of University Professors.

Aghion, P., and J. Tirole. 1997. "Formal and Real Authority in Organizations." *Journal of Political Economy* 105:1–29.

American Association of University Professors. 1915. *Report of the Committee on Academic Freedom and Tenure*. Washington, D.C.: American Association of University Professors.

——. 1971. "Report of the Subcommittee of Committee T." *AAUP Bulletin* 57 (Spring): 68–124.

——. 1995. *Policy Documents and Reports*. Washington, D.C.: American Association of University Professors.

Ashraf, J. 1997. "The Effect of Unions on Professors' Salaries: The Evidence over Twenty Years." *Journal of Labor Research* 18 (Summer): 439–50.

Association of Higher Education Facilities Officers. 1999. *1997–98 Comparative Costs and Staffing Report for Educational Facilities*. Alexandria, Va.: Association of Higher Education Facilities Officers.

Baldridge, J. V. 1971. *Power and Conflict in the University*. New York: Wiley.

Baldwin, R. G., and J. L. Chronister. 2001. *Teaching without Tenure: Policies and Practices for a New Era*. Baltimore: Johns Hopkins University Press.

Barbezat, D. 1989. "The Effect of Collective Bargaining on Salaries in Higher Education." *Industrial and Labor Relations Review* 42 (April): 443–55.

Barro, J., and R. Barro. 1990. "Pay, Performance, and Turnover of Bank CEOs." *Journal of Labor Economics* 8:448–81.

Bendor, J., T. M. Moe, and K. W. Shotts. 2001. "Recycling the Garbage Can: An Assessment of the Research Program." *American Political Science Review* 95:169–90.

Benjamin, R. 1993. *The Redesign of Governance in Higher Education*. Santa Monica: Rand.

Berger, J. B., and J. F. Milem. 2000. "Organizational Behavior in Higher Education and Student Outcomes." In *Higher Education: Handbook of Theory and Research*, edited by J. C. Smart. Vol. 15, 268–338. New York: Agathon Press.

Berger, M. C., and T. Kostal. 2002. "Financial Resources, Regulation, and Enrollment in U.S. Public Higher Education." *Economics of Education Review* 21:101–10.

Berle, A., and G. Means. 1932. *The Modern Corporation and Private Property*. New York: Macmillan.

Bernheim, B. D., and M. D. Whinston. 1986a. "Common Agency." *Econometrica* 54:923–42.

———. 1986b. "Menu Auctions, Resource Allocation, and Economic Influence." *Quarterly Journal of Economics* 101:1–31.

Biemer, P. P., and R. S. Fesco. 1995. "Evaluating and Controlling Measurement Error in Business Surveys." In *Business Survey Methods*, edited by B. G. Cox, D. A. Binder, and B. Nanjamma Chinnappa. New York: Wiley.

Birnbaum, R. 1988. *How Colleges Work: The Cybernetics of Academic Organization and Leadership*. San Francisco: Jossey-Bass.

Blackwell, D., J. Brickley, and M. Weisbach. 1994. "Accounting Information and Internal Performance Evaluation: Evidence from Texas Banks." *Journal of Accounting and Economics* 17:331–58.

Blau, P. 1973. *The Organization of Academic Work*. New York: Wiley.

Blum, D. 1995. "All Part of the Game." *Chronicle of Higher Education* (24 February): A39–40.

Borokhovich, K., R. Parrino, and T. Trapani. 1996. "Outside Directors and CEO Selection." *Journal of Financial and Quantitative Analysis* 31:337–55.

Boulding, K. 1964. "A Pure Theory of Conflict Applied to Organizations." In *The Frontiers of Management Psychology*, edited by George Fisk, 41–49. New York: Harper and Row.

Bowen, H. 1977. *Investment in Learning: The Individual and Social Value of American Higher Education*. San Francisco: Jossey-Bass.

Bowen, W. G. 1994. *Inside the Boardroom: Governance by Directors and Trustees*. New York: Wiley.

Bowen, W. G., T. I. Nygren, S. E. Turner, and E. A. Duffy. 1994. *The Charitable Nonprofits*. San Francisco: Jossey-Bass.

Brenneman, D. 1994. *Liberal Arts Colleges: Thriving, Surviving, or Endangered?* Washington, D.C.: Brookings Institution.

Brown, M. C. 2000. *Organization and Governance in Higher Education*. 5th ed. Boston: Pearson Custom Publishing.

Brubacher, J. S., and W. Rudy. 1976. *Higher Education in Transition: A History of American Colleges and Universities, 1636–1976*. 3d ed. New York: Harper and Row.

Bucovetsky, S. 1991. "Asymmetric Tax Competition." *Journal of Urban Economics* 30:67–181.

Burke, J. C., and Associates. 2002. *Funding Higher Public Higher Education for Performance: Popularity, Problems and Prospects*. Albany: Rockefeller Institute Press.

Burke, J. C., and H. Minassians. 2001. *Linking State Resources to Campus Results: From Fad to Trend—The Fifth Annual Report*. Albany: Rockefeller Institute Press.

Burke, J. C., and S. Modarresi. 1999. *Performance Funding and Budgeting: Popularity and Volatility—The Third Annual Survey*. Albany: Nelson A. Rockefeller Institute of Government, State University of New York.

Burt, R. S. 1983. *Corporate Profits and Cooptation: Networks of Market Constraints and Directorate Ties in the American Economy*. New York: Academic Press.

Burton, R. M., and B. Obel. 1984. *Designing Efficient Organizations: Modelling and Experimentation*. Amsterdam: North-Holland.

Carnegie Foundation for the Advancement of Teaching. 1994. *A Classification of Institutions of Higher Education*. Princeton, N.J.: Carnegie Foundation for the Advancement of Teaching.

Carpenter, D. P. 2001. *The Forging of Bureaucratic Autonomy: Reputations, Networks, and Policy Innovation in Executive Agencies, 1862–1928*. Princeton, N.J.: Princeton University Press.

Cerych, L., and P. Sabatier. 1986. *Great Expectations and Mixed Performance: The Implementation of European Higher Education Reforms*. Stoke-on-Trent, U.K.: Trenton Books.

Chaffee, E. E. 1984. *After Decline, What? Survival Strategies at Eight Private Colleges*. Boulder, Colo.: National Center for Higher Education Management Systems.

——. 1985. "Three Models of Strategy." *Academy of Management Review* 10:89–98.

Chait, R., and B. Taylor. 1989. "Charting the Territory of Nonprofit Boards." *Harvard Business Review* 67:44–54.

Chambers, M. M. 1941–1976. *The Colleges and the Courts: Recent Judicial Decisions regarding Higher Education in the United States*. New York: Carnegie Foundation.

Chandler, A. D., Jr. 1962. *Strategy and Structure: Chapters in the History of Industrial Enterprise*. Cambridge: MIT Press.

Clark, B. R., and T. I. K. Youn. 1976. *Academic Power in the United States: Comparative Historic and Structural Perspectives*. Washington, D.C.: American Association for Higher Education.

Cohen, M. D., and J. G. March. 1974. *Leadership and Ambiguity: The American College President*. New York: McGraw-Hill.

——. 1986. *Leadership and Ambiguity: The American College Presidency*. 2d ed. Boston: Harvard Business School Press.

Cohen, M. D., J. G. March, and J. P. Olsen. 1972. "A Garbage Can Model of Organizational Choice." *Administrative Science Quarterly* 17:1–25.

College Board. 2001. *Trends in Student Aid*. Washington, D.C.: College Board. Available at http://www.collegeboard.com/press/cost01/html/TrendsSA01.pdf.

Conway, J. K. 2001. *A Woman's Education*. New York: Knopf.

Core, J., R. Holthausen, and D. Larcker. 1999. "Corporate Governance, Chief Executive Officer Compensation, and Firm Performance." *Journal of Financial Economics* 51:371–406.

Cornell Higher Education Research Institute. 2001 (Spring). "Survey of Tuition Reciprocity Agreements." Available at www.ilr.cornell.edu/cheri/survey2001/summary.

Corry, D. J. 2000. *Negotiations: The Art of Mutual Gains Bargaining*. Aurora, Ont.: Canada Law Book.

Coughlan, A., and R. Schmidt. 1985. "Executive Compensation, Managerial Turnover, and Firm Performance: An Empirical Investigation." *Journal of Accounting and Economics* 7:43–66.

Courant, P. N., and M. Knepp. 2001. "Budgeting with the UB Model at the University of Michigan." Unpublished manuscript, University of Michigan.

Crawford, V. P., and J. Sobel. 1982. "Strategic Information Transmission. *Econometrica* 50:1431–51.

Cross, J. G. 1996. "A Brief Review of 'Responsibility Center Management.'" Unpublished manuscript, University of Michigan.

Dahl, R. A. 1957. "The Concept of Power." *Behavioral Science* 2:201–15.

Debande, O., and J. L. Demeulemeester. 2000. "Quality and Variety Competition Between Higher Education Institutions." Unpublished manuscript, European Investment Bank, Luxembourg.

Denis, D., and A. Sarin. 1999. "Ownership and Board Structures in Publicly Traded Corporations." *Journal of Financial Economics* 52:187–224.

Dillman, D. A. 2000. *Mail and Internet Surveys: The Tailored Design Method.* 2d ed. New York: Wiley.

DiMaggio, P., and W. Powell. 1983. "The Iron Cage Revisited: Institutional Isomorphism and Collective Rationality in Organizational Fields." *American Sociological Review* 48 (April): 147–60.

Dogan, M., and R. Pahre. 1989. "Fragmentation and Recombination of the Social Sciences." *Studies in Comparative International Development* 24:1–18.

Donaldson, L. 2001. *The Contingency Theory of Organizations.* Thousand Oaks, Calif.: Sage Publications.

Duderstadt, J. 2000. *A University for the 21st Century.* Ann Arbor: University of Michigan Press.

Duryea, E. D. 1973. "Evolution of University Organization." In *The University as an Organization,* edited by J. A. Perkins, 15–37. New York: McGraw-Hill.

Education Commission of the States. 1974. *Collective Bargaining in Postsecondary Educational Institutions.* Denver: Education Commission of the States.

———. 2002. *Postsecondary Governance Structures Database.* Denver: Education Commission of the States.

Ehrenberg, R. G. 2000a. *Tuition Rising: Why College Costs So Much.* Cambridge: Harvard University Press.

———. 2000b. "Internal Transfer Prices." In *Tuition Rising: Why College Costs So Much,* edited by R. G. Ehrenberg, 157–70. Cambridge: Harvard University Press.

———. 2000c. "Financial Forecasts for the Next Decade." *Presidency* 3 (April): 30–35.

Ehrenberg, R. G., and G. S. Goldstein. 1975. "A Model of Public Sector Wage Determination." *Journal of Urban Economics* 1 (June): 223–45.

Ehrenberg, R. G., and P. G. Mavros. 1995. "Do Doctoral Student Financial Support Patterns Affect Their Times to Degree and Completion Rates?" *Journal of Human Resources* 30 (July): 581–609.

Ehrenberg, R., J. Cheslock, and J. Epifantseva. 2001. "Paying Our Presidents: What Do Trustees Value?" *Review of Higher Education* 25:15–37.

Eisenberg, T., S. Sundgren, and M. Wells. 1998. "Larger Board Size and Decreasing Firm Value in Small Firms." *Journal of Financial Economics* 48:35–54.

Elliott, E. C., and M. M. Chambers. 1936. *The Colleges and the Courts: Judicial Decisions regarding Institutions of Higher Education in the United States.* New York: Carnegie Foundation.

Emerson, R. M. 1962. "Power-Dependence Relations." *American Sociological Review* 27 (April): 31–41.

Ende, H., E. Anderson, and S. Crego. 1997. "Liability Insurance: A Primer for College and University Counsel." *Journal of College and University Law* 23:609–753.

Epple, D., R. Romano, and H. Sieg. 2000. "Peer Effects, Financial Aid, and Selection of Students into Colleges and Universities: An Empirical Analysis." Unpublished manuscript, Carnegie Mellon University.

Fama, E., and M. C. Jensen. 1983a. "Separation of Ownership and Control" *Journal of Law and Economics* 26 (June): 301–26.

———. 1983b. "Agency Problems and Residual Claims." *Journal of Law and Economics* 26 (June): 327–48.

Finkin, M. W. 1994. "The Unfolding Tendency in the Federal Relationship to Private Accreditation in Higher Education." *Law and Contemporary Problems* 57:89–120.

Firestone, D., with M. L. Wald. 2002. "Flight Schools See Downside to Crackdown." *New York Times*, 27 May, 1A.

Flawn, P. T. 1990. *A Primer for University Presidents.* Austin: University of Texas Press.

Flexner, A. 1910. *Medical Education in the United States and Canada: A Report to the Carnegie Foundation for the Advancement of Teaching.* Carnegie Foundation for the Advancement of Teaching Bulletin No. 4. New York: Carnegie Foundation for the Advancement of Teaching.

Flores, M. 2002. "Regents Sack Veteran UTSA Prof." *San Antonio Express-News*, 15 February, 1B.

Fogg, P. 2002. "Bill in Washington State Would Allow Professors to Bargain Collectively, If. . . ." *Chronicle of Higher Education* (29 March): A12.

Freedman, J. O. 1987. "A Common Wealth of Liberal Learning: Inaugural Address of James O. Freedman Delivered at His Installation as Fifteenth President of Dartmouth College." Hanover, N.H.: Dartmouth College.

———. 1996. *Idealism and Liberal Education.* Ann Arbor: University of Michigan Press.

French, J. R. P., Jr., and B. Raven. 1968. "The Bases of Social Power." In *Group Dynamics.* 3d ed. Edited by D. Cartwright and A. Zander, 259–69. New York: Harper and Row.

Furner, M. O. 1975. *Advocacy and Objectivity: A Crisis in the Professionalization of American Social Science.* Lexington: University of Kentucky Press.

Garvin, D. 1980. *The Economics of University Behavior.* New York: Academic Press.

Gibbard, A. 1973. "Manipulation of Voting Schemes: A General Result." *Econometrica* 41:587–601.

Glaeser, E. 2002. "The Governance of Not-for-Profit Firms." NBER Working Paper No. w8921. Cambridge, Mass.: National Bureau of Economic Research.

Goldin, C., and L. Katz. 1999. "The Shaping of Higher Education: The Formative Years in the United States, 1890 to 1940." *Journal of Economic Perspectives* 13 (Winter): 37–62.

Graham, H. D., and N. Diamond. 1997. *The Rise of American Research Universities: Elites and Challengers in the Postwar Era.* Baltimore: Johns Hopkins University Press.

Green, M., P. Eckel, and A. Barblan. 2002. *The Brave New (and Smaller) World of Higher Education: A Transatlantic View.* Changing Enterprise Series. Washington, D.C.: American Council on Education.

Groen, J., and M. J. White. 2000 (June). "In-State versus Out-of-State Students: The Divergence of Interests between Public Universities and State Governments." CHERI Working Paper No. 25. Ithaca, N.Y.: Cornell Higher Education Research Institute. Available at http://www.ilr.cornell.edu/cheri.

Grossman, G. M., and E. Helpman. 2001. *Special Interest Politics*. Cambridge: MIT Press.

Gulick, L. 1937. "Notes on the Theory of Organization." In *Papers on the Science of Administration*, edited by L. Gulick and L. Urwick, 1–45. New York: Institute of Public Administration, Columbia University.

Gumport, P., and B. Pusser. 1997. "Restructuring the Academic Environment." In *Planning and Management for a Changing Environment*, edited by M. D. Peterson, D. D. Dill, and L. Mets, 453–78. San Francisco: Jossey-Bass.

Hall, P. D. 1997. *A History of Nonprofit Boards in the United States*. Washington, D.C.: National Center for Nonprofit Boards.

Hallock, K. 1997. "Reciprocally Interlocking Boards of Directors and Executive Compensation." *Journal of Financial and Quantitative Analysis* 32:331–34.

Halpern, S. A. 1987. "Professional Schools in the American University." In *The Academic Profession: National, Disciplinary, and Institutional Settings*, edited by Burton R. Clark, 304–30. Berkeley: University of California Press.

Hammond, T. H. 1986. "Agenda Control, Organizational Structure, and Bureaucratic Politics." *American Journal of Political Science* 30:379–420.

———. 1990. "In Defense of Luther Gulick's 'Notes on the Theory of Organization.'" *Public Administration* 68:143–73.

———. 1993. "Toward a General Theory of Hierarchy: Books, Bureaucrats, Basketball Tournaments, and the Administrative Structure of the Nation-State." *Journal of Public Administration Research and Theory* 3:120–45.

———. 1994. "Structure, Strategy, and the Agenda of the Firm." In *Fundamental Issues in Strategy: A Research Agenda*, edited by R. P. Rumelt, D. E. Schendel, and D. J. Teece, 97–154. Boston: Harvard Business School Press.

Hammond, T. H., and J. H. Horn. 1984. "Clones, Coalitions, and Sophisticated Choice in Hierarchies." Paper presented at the annual meeting of the Public Choice Society, Phoenix, Ariz.

———. 1985. "'Putting One over on the Boss': The Political Economy of Strategic Behavior in Organizations." *Public Choice* 45:49–71.

Hammond, T. H., and G. J. Miller. 1985. "A Social Choice Perspective on Authority and Expertise in Bureaucracy." *American Journal of Political Science* 29:611–38.

Hammond, T. H., and P. A. Thomas. 1989. "The Impossibility of a Neutral Hierarchy." *Journal of Law, Economics, and Organization* 5:155–84.

———. 1990. "Invisible Decisive Coalitions in Large Hierarchies." *Public Choice* 66:101–16.

Hansmann, H. 1980. "The Role of the Nonprofit Enterprise." *Yale Law Journal* 89:835–901.

———. 1996. *The Ownership of Enterprise*. Cambridge: Harvard University Press.

Haskell, T. 1976. *The Emergence of Professional Social Science: The American Social Science Association and the Nineteenth Century Crisis in Authority*. Urbana: University of Illinois Press.

Haunschild, P. R., and C. M. Beckman. 1998. "When Do Interlocks Matter? Alternate Sources of Information and Interlock Influence." *Administrative Science Quarterly* 43(4): 815–44.

Hearn, J. C., and C. P. Griswold. 1994. "State-Level Centralization and Policy Innovation in U.S. Postsecondary Education." *Educational Evaluation and Policy Analysis* 16(2): 161–90.

Heckman, J. J. 1979. "Sample Selection Bias as a Specification Error." *Econometrica* 47 (January): 153–61.

Heller, D. E., ed. 2001. *The States and Public Higher Education Policy: Affordability, Access, and Accountability*. Baltimore: Johns Hopkins University Press.

———. 2002. "The Policy Shift in State Financial Aid Programs." In *Higher Education: Handbook of Theory and Research*, edited by J. C. Smart. Vol. 17, 221–61. New York: Agathon Press.

Hermalin, B., and M. Weisbach. 1988. "The Determinants of Board Composition." *RAND Journal of Economics* 19:589–606.

———. 1998. "Endogenously Chosen Boards of Directors and Their Monitoring of the CEO." *American Economic Review* 88:96–118.

———. 2003. "Boards of Directors as an Endogenously Determined Institution: A Survey of the Economic Literature." *Economic Policy Review* 9:7–26.

Herman, R., and D. Renz. 1998. "Nonprofit Organizational Effectiveness: Contrasts between Especially Effective and Less Effective Organizations." *Nonprofit Management and Leadership* 9:23–38.

Hines, E. R. 2000. "The Governance of Higher Education." In *Higher Education: Handbook of Theory and Research*, edited by J. C. Smart. Vol. 15, 105–56. New York: Agathon Press.

Hirsch, W. Z., and L. Weber, eds. 2001. *Governance in Higher Education: The University in a State of Flux*. London: Economica; distributed by Brookings Institution.

Hirschman, A. O. 1970. *Exit, Voice and Loyalty: Responses to Decline in Firms, Organizations, and States*. Cambridge: Harvard University Press.

Holmstrom, B. 1982. "Moral Hazard in Teams." *Bell Journal of Economics* 13:324–40.

Hosios, A., and A. Siow. 2001 (November). "Unions without Rents: The Curious Economics of Faculty Unions." Mimeograph, University of Toronto.

Huson, M., R. Parrino, and L. Starks. 2000. "Internal Monitoring and CEO Turnover: A Long-Term Perspective." Working paper, University of Texas, Austin.

Ingram, R. T. 1996. "New Tensions in the Academic Boardroom." *Educational Record* 77 (Spring–Summer): 49–55.

Institute for Higher Education Policy. 1998. *Reaping the Benefits: Defining the Public and Private Value of Going to College*. Washington, D.C.: Institute for Higher Education Policy.

Iseminger, J. 1999. "Study: Bargaining Doesn't Inhibit Grad Education." *Wisconsin Week*, 20 October. Available at http://www.news.wisc.edu/wisweek/

James, E. 1998. "Commercialism among Nonprofits: Objectives, Opportunities, and Constraints." In *To Profit or Not to Profit: The Commercial Transformation of the Nonprofit Sector*, edited by B. A. Weisbrod, 271–86. Cambridge: Cambridge University Press.

Jencks, C., and D. Riesman. 1968. *The Academic Revolution*. 1st ed. Garden City, N.Y.: Doubleday.

———. 1977. *The Academic Revolution*. With a new foreword by Martin Trow. Chicago: University of Chicago Press.

Jensen, M. 1993. "The Modern Industrial Revolution, Exit, and the Failure of Internal Control Systems." *Journal of Finance* 48:831–80.

Jensen, M., and K. Murphy. 1990. "Performance Pay and Top-Management Incentives." *Journal of Political Economy* 98:225–64.

Jones, G. A., and M. L. Skolnik. 1997. "Governing Boards in Canadian Universities." *Review of Higher Education* 20(3): 277–95.

Kaplan, S. 1994. "Top Executive Rewards and Firm Performance: A Comparison of Japan and the U.S." *Journal of Political Economy* 102:510–46.

Kaplin, W. A., and B. A. Lee. 1995. *The Law of Higher Education*. 3d ed. San Francisco: Jossey-Bass.

———. 2000. *The Law of Higher Education*. Supplement to 3d ed. Washington, D.C.: National Association of Colleges and University Attorneys.

Keller, M., and P. Keller. 2001. *Making Harvard Modern: The Rise of America's University*. New York: Oxford University Press.

Kerr, C., and M. Gade. 1989. *The Guardians: Boards of Trustees of American Colleges and Universities*. Washington, D.C.: Association of Governing Boards of Universities and Colleges.

Kesselring, R. 1991. "The Economic Effects of Faculty Unions." *Journal of Labor Research* 12 (Winter): 61–72.

Klaff, D. B., and R. G. Ehrenberg. 2002. "Collective Bargaining and Staff Salaries in American Colleges and Universities." CHERI Working Paper No. 21. Ithaca, N.Y.: Cornell Higher Education Research Institute. Available at http://www.ilr.cornell.edu/cheri.

Knoke, D., P. V. Marsden, and A. L. Kalleberg. 2002. "Survey Research Methods." In *The Blackwell Companion to Organizations*, edited by Joel A. C. Baum, 781–804. Malden, Mass.: Blackwell.

Krause, G., and J. D. Wilson. 2000. "Responsibility Center Budgeting within a University." Unpublished manuscript, Michigan State University.

Ladd, E. C., and S. M. Lipset. 1973. *Professors, Unions, and American Higher Education*. Washington, D.C.: American Enterprise Institute for Public Policy Research.

———. 1975. *The Divided Academy: Professors and Politics*. New York: McGraw-Hill.

Lafer, G. 2001. "Graduate Students Fight the Corporate University." *Dissent* 48 (Fall): 63–71.

LaNoue, G., and B. A. Lee. 1987. *Academics in Court: The Consequences of Faculty Discrimination Litigation*. Ann Arbor: University of Michigan Press.

Leatherman, C. 2000. "Union Movement at Private Colleges Awakens after a 20-Year Slumber." *Chronicle of Higher Education* (21 January): A16.

Lee, L. 1978. "Unionism and Wage Rates: A Simultaneous Equations Model with Qualitative and Limited Dependent Variables." *International Economic Review* 19 (June): 415–33.

Levin, J. S. 2001. *Globalizing the Community College: Strategies for Change in the Twenty-First Century*. New York: Palgrave Press.

Levitt, S., and C. Snyder. 1997. "Is No News Bad News? Information Transmission and the Role of 'Early Warning' in the Principal-Agent Model." *RAND Journal of Economics* 28:641–61.

Light, R. J., J. D. Singer, and J. B. Willett. 1990. *By Design: Planning Research in Higher Education*. Cambridge: Harvard University Press.

Lillydahl, J. H., and L. D. Singell. 1993. "Job Satisfaction, Salaries and Unions: The Determination of Faculty Compensation." *Economics of Education Review* 12 (September): 233–45.

Liptak, A. 2002. "Religion and the Law, Insurance Companies Often Dictate Legal Strategies Used by Dioceses." *New York Times*, 14 April.

Lipton, M., and J. Lorsch. 1992. "A Modest Proposal for Improved Corporate Governance." *Business Lawyer* 48:59–77.

Lobbyist Watch. 2001. "University of Phoenix Parent Company Names Former GOP Congressman to Board." *Chronicle of Higher Education* (2 February): A21.

Lodge, D. 1984. *Small World: An Academic Romance*. London: Secker and Warburg.

Lohmann, S. 2003. "How Universities Think." Manuscript. University of California, Los Angeles.

Lorsch, J. 1989. *Pawns or Potentates: The Reality of America's Corporate Boards*. Boston: Harvard Business School Press.

Lowen, R. S. 1997. *Creating the Cold War University*. Berkeley: University of California Press.

Lowry, R. C. 2001a. "The Effects of State Political Interests and Campus Outputs on Public University Revenues." *Economics of Education Review* 20:105–19.

——. 2001b. "Governmental Structure, Trustee Selection, and Public University Prices and Spending: Multiple Means to Similar Ends." *American Journal of Political Science* 45(4): 845–61.

Mace, M. 1986. *Directors: Myth and Reality*. Boston: Harvard Business School Press.

MacTaggart, T. J. 1996. *Restructuring Higher Education: What Works and What Doesn't in Reorganizing Governing Systems*. San Francisco: Jossey-Bass.

——. 1998. *Seeking Excellence through Independence: Liberating Colleges and Universities from Excessive Regulation*. San Francisco: Jossey-Bass.

Main, B., C. O'Reilly III, and J. Wade. 1995. "The CEO, the Board of Directors, and Executive Compensation: Economic and Psychological Perspectives." *Industrial and Corporate Change* 4:293–332.

Manning, R. 2000. *Credit Card Nation*. New York: Basic Books.

March, J. G., and H. A. Simon. 1958. *Organizations*. New York: Wiley.

Marchese, T. 1998. "Not-so Distant-Competitors: How New Providers Are Remaking the Post-secondary Marketplace." *AAHE Bulletin* 50 (May–June): 3–11.

Marginson, S., and M. Considine. 2000. *The Enterprise University*. Cambridge: Cambridge University Press.

Martin, J. C. 1994. "Recent Developments concerning Accrediting Agencies in Postsecondary Education" *Law and Contemporary Problems* 57:121–49.

Masten, S. E. 2000. "Commitment and Political Governance: Why Universities, Like Legislatures, Are Not Organized as Firms." Unpublished manuscript, University of Michigan Business School.

McLendon, M. K. 2003. "State Governance Reform of Higher Education: Patterns, Trends, and Theories of the Public Policy Process." In *Higher Education: Handbook of Theory and Research*, edited by J. C. Smart. Vol. 18. Dordrecht, Netherlands: Kluwer.

McLendon, M. K., D. E. Heller, and S. P. Young. 2001 (April). "State Post-secondary Policy Innovation: Politics, Competition, and the Interstate Migration of Policy Ideas." Paper presented at the annual meeting of the Midwest Political Science Association, Chicago.

McNamee, M. 2002a. "Insuring Ourselves." *NACUBO Business Officer* 35 (March): 35–37.

——. 2002b. "Coping with Today's Hard Insurance Market." *NACUBO Business Officer* 35 (May): 24–25.

Meador, M., and S. J. K. Walters. 1994. "Unions and Productivity: Evidence from Academe." *Journal of Labor Research* 15 (Fall): 373–86.

Means, H. B., and P. W. Semas, eds. 1976. *Faculty Collective Bargaining.* Washington, D.C.: Educational Project for Educators.

Miller, G. J. 1992. *Managerial Dilemmas: The Political Economy of Hierarchy.* New York: Cambridge University Press.

Mingle, J. R. 2000. "Higher Education's Future in a 'Corporatized' Economy." Occasional Paper No. 44. Washington, D.C.: Association of Governing Boards of Universities and Colleges.

Mizruchi, M. S. 1996. "What Do Interlocks Do: An Analysis, Critique, and Assessment of Research on Interlocking Directorates." *Annual Review of Sociology* 22:271–98.

Monks, J. 2000. "Unionization and Faculty Salaries: New Evidence from the 1990s." *Journal of Labor Research* 21 (Spring): 305–14.

National Center for Education Statistics. 1994. *Digest of Education Statistics, 1994.* NCES publication no. 94–115. Washington, D.C.: National Center for Education Statistics.

———. 1999. *Postsecondary Institutions in the United States: 1997–98.* Washington, D.C.: U.S. Department of Education. Available at http://nces.ed.gov/pubs99/1999174 .pdf.

———. 2001a. *Digest of Education Statistics, 2000.* NCES publication no. 2001-034. Washington, D.C.: U.S. Department of Education.

———. 2001b. *Fall Enrollment in Title IV Degree-Granting Postsecondary Institutions: 1998,* by Frank B. Morgan. NCES publication no. 2002-162. Washington, D.C.: U.S. Department of Education.

———. 2002. *Tenure Status of Postsecondary Instructional Faculty and Staff: 1992–98,* by Basmat Parsad and Denise Glover. NCES publication no. 2002-210. Washington, D.C.: U.S. Department of Education.

National Center for the Study of Collective Bargaining in Higher Education and the Professions. 1995. *Directory of Staff Bargaining Agents in Institutions of Higher Education.* New York: National Center for the Study of Collective Bargaining in Higher Education and the Professions.

———. 1997. *Directory of Faculty Contracts and Bargaining Agents in Institutions of Higher Education.* New York: National Center for the Study of Collective Bargaining in Higher Education and the Professions.

National Research Council. 1995. *Research-Doctorate Programs in the United States: Continuity and Change.* Washington, D.C.: National Academy Press.

———. 1998. *Trends in the Early Careers of Life Scientists.* Washington, D.C.: National Academy Press.

Nelson, C. 1999. "The War against the Faculty." *Chronicle of Higher Education* (16 April): B4.

Nesse, R. M., and G. C. Williams. 1994. *Why We Get Sick: The New Science of Darwinian Medicine.* New York: Vintage Books.

Newman, F., and L. Couterier. 2001. "The New Competitive Arena: Market Forces Invade the Academy." *Change* 33 (September–October): 10–17.

Olivas, M. A. 1992. "The Political Economy of Immigration, Intellectual Property, and Racial Harassment." *Journal of Higher Education* 63 (September–October): 570–98.

———. 1997. *The Law and Higher Education: Cases and Materials on Colleges in Court*. 2d ed. Durham: Carolina Academic Press.

———. 2000. "Ideological Balance in Immigration Law Teaching and Scholarship." *University of Illinois Law Review* 101–26.

O'Reilly, C., III, B. Main, and G. Crystal. 1988. "CEO Salaries as Tournaments and Social Comparisons: A Tale of Two Theories." *Administrative Science Quarterly* 33:257–74.

Pahre, R. 1995. "Positivist Discourse and Social Scientific Communities: Towards an Epistemological Sociology of Science." *Social Epistemology* 9:233–55.

Palmer, D. 1983. "Broken Ties: Interlocking Directorates and Inter-corporate Coordination." *Administrative Science Quarterly* 28:40–55.

Parsons, T., and G. Platt. 1973. *The American University*. Cambridge: Harvard University Press.

Paxson, M. C., D. A. Dillman, and J. Tarnai. 1995. "Improving Response to Business Mail Surveys." In *Business Survey Methods*, edited by B. G. Cox, D. A. Binder, and B. Nanjamma Chinnappa, 303–15. New York: Wiley.

Pfeffer, J., and G. R. Salancik. 1974. "Organizational Decision-Making as a Political Process: The Case of the University Budget." *Administrative Science Quarterly* 19(1): 135–51.

———. 1978. *The External Control of Organizations: A Resource Dependence Perspective*. New York: Harper and Row.

Pulley, J. L. 2002. "Money Talks; More So When It Walks." *Chronicle of Higher Education* (25 October): A29.

Pusser, B. 2002. "Higher Education, the Emerging Market, and the Public Good." In *The Knowledge Economy and Post-secondary Education*, edited by P. A. Graham and N. Stacey, 105–26. Washington, D.C.: National Academy Press.

———. 2003. "Beyond Baldridge: Extending the Political Model of Higher Education Governance." *Educational Policy* 17 (January): 121–40.

———. Forthcoming. *Burning Down the House: Politics, Governance, and Affirmative Action at the University of California*. Albany: SUNY Press.

Pusser, B., and D. J. Doane. 2001. "Public Purpose and Private Enterprise: The Contemporary Organization of Post-secondary Education." *Change* 33 (September–October): 18–22.

Rabban, D. M. 1990. "A Functional Analysis of 'Individual' and 'Institutional' Academic Freedom under the First Amendment." *Law and Contemporary Problems* 53:227–302.

Rees, D. I. 1993. "The Effects of Unionization on Faculty Salaries and Compensation: Estimates from the 1980s." *Journal of Labor Research* 14 (Fall): 399–422.

———. 1994. "Does Unionization Increase Faculty Retention?" *Industrial Relations* 33 (July): 297–321.

Rey, E. D. 2001. "Teaching versus Research: A Model of State University Competition." *Journal of Urban Economics* 49:356–73.

Rhoades, G. 1998. *Managed Professionals: Unionized Faculty and Restructuring Academic Labor*. Albany: SUNY Press.

———. 2001. "Whose Property Is It? Negotiating with the University." *Academe* 87 (October–November): 38–43.

Rhodes, F. H. T. 2001. *The Creation of the Future: The Role of the American University*. Ithaca, N.Y.: Cornell University Press.

Richardson , R. C., Jr., K. Reeves Bracco, P. M. Callan, and J. E. Finney. 1999. *Designing State Higher Education Systems for a New Century.* Phoenix: Oryx Press.

Rosenzweig, R. M. 1998. *The Political University.* Baltimore: Johns Hopkins University Press.

Rosovsky, H. 1990. *The University: An Owner's Manual.* New York: Norton.

Rothschild, M., and L. J. White. 1995. "The Analytics of the Pricing of Higher Education and Other Services in Which the Customers Are Inputs." *Journal of Political Economy* 103:573–86.

Ruch, R. S. 2001. *Higher Education, Inc.: The Rise of the For-Profit University.* Baltimore: Johns Hopkins University Press.

Rudolph, F. 1990. *The American College and University: A History.* Athens: University of Georgia Press.

Sabatier, P. 1987. "Knowledge, Policy-Oriented Learning, and Policy Change: An Advocacy Coalition Framework." *Knowledge Creation, Diffusion, Utilization* 8:649–692.

Sanderson, A., et al. 1999. *Doctorates Received from U.S. Universities: Summary Report 1998.* Chicago: National Opinion Research Council.

Satterthwaite, M. A. 1975. "Strategy-Proofness and Arrow's Conditions: Existence and Correspondence Theorems for Voting Procedures and Social Welfare Functions." *Journal of Economic Theory* 10:187–217.

Schmidt, P. 1996. "More States Tie Spending on Colleges to Meeting Specific Goals." *Chronicle of Higher Education* (24 May): A26.

——. 1997. "Rancor and Confusion Greet Change in South Carolina Budgeting." *Chronicle of Higher Education* (4 April): A26.

Schuster, J. H., D. G. Smith, K. C. Sund, and M. M. Yamada. 1994. *Strategic Governance: How to Make Big Decisions Better.* Phoenix: Oryx Press.

Seftor, N., and S. Turner. 2002. "Financial Aid and the College Enrollment of Non-traditional Students: Evidence from the Pell Program." *Journal of Human Resources* 37(2): 336–52.

Selingo, J. 1999. "For-Profit Colleges Aim to Take a Share of State Financial Aid Funds." *Chronicle of Higher Education* (24 September): A41.

——. 2001. "Aiming for a New Audience, University of Phoenix Tries Again in New Jersey." *Chronicle of Higher Education* (21 September): A23–24.

Shepherd, G. B. 2003. "No African-American Lawyers Allowed: The Inefficient Racism of the ABA's Accreditation of Law Schools." *Journal of Legal Education* 53(1): 103–156.

Simon, H. A. 1946. "The Proverbs of Administration." *Public Administration Review* 6:53–67.

Slaughter, S. 2001. "Professional Values and the Allure of the Market." *Academe* 87 (October–November): 22–26.

Slaughter, S., and L. L. Leslie. 1997. *Academic Capitalism.* Baltimore: Johns Hopkins University Press.

Smallwood, S. 2001. "A Big Breakthrough for T.A. Unions." *Chronicle of Higher Education* (16 March): A10.

——. 2002a. "NYU and Its TA Union Reach a Pact on a Contract." *Chronicle of Higher Education* (15 February): A18.

———. 2002b. "U. of Michigan Strikes Deal with TA Unions." *Chronicle of Higher Education* (19 March). Available http://chronicle.com.

———. 2002c. "UAW Wins Union Election to Represent Part-Time Faculty Members at New York U." *Chronicle of Higher Education* (10 July). Available at http://chronicle.com.

Smith, A. 1776. *An Inquiry into the Nature and Cases of the Wealth of Nations.* New York: Modern Library.

South Carolina Legislative Audit Council. 2001. *A Review of the Higher Education Performance Funding Process.* Columbia: South Caroline Legislative Audit Council.

Taylor, B., R. Chait, and T. Holland. 1996. "The New Work of the Nonprofit Board." *Harvard Business Review* 74:36–46.

Thomas, S. L., S. Slaughter, and B. Pusser. 2002. "Playing the Board Game: An Empirical Analysis of University Trustee and Corporate Board Interlocks." Working paper, Institute of Higher Education, University of Georgia, Athens.

Tiebout, C. M. 1956. "A Pure Theory of Local Public Goods." *Journal of Political Economy* 64:416–24.

Toma, E. F. 1986. "State University Boards of Trustees: A Principal-Agent Perspective." *Public Choice* 49:155–63.

———. 1990. "Boards of Trustees, Agency Problems, and University Output." *Public Choice* 67:1–9.

Trow, M. A. 1977. *Aspects of American Higher Education, 1969–1975.* Berkeley: Carnegie Council on Policy Studies in Higher Education.

———. Forthcoming. "Biology at Berkeley." In *Fostering Scientific Discovery: Organizations, Institutions, and Major Breakthroughs in Biomedical Science,* edited by J. R. Hollingsworth, J. Hage, and E. J. Hollingsworth. New York: Cambridge University Press.

Useem, M. 1984. *The Inner Circle.* Cambridge: Oxford University Press.

Van Alstyne, W. W. 1990. "Academic Freedom and the First Amendment in the Supreme Court of the United States: An Unhurried Historical Review." *Law and Contemporary Problems* 53(3): 79–154.

Vancil, R. 1987. *Passing the Baton: Managing the Process of CEO Succession.* Boston: Harvard Business School Press.

Van Der Werf, M. 2001. "How Much Should Colleges Pay Their Janitors? Student Protests Force Administrators to Consider Issues of Social Justice and Practicality." *Chronicle of Higher Education* (3 August): A27.

Volkwein, J. F., and S. M. Malik. 1997. "State Regulation and Administrative Flexibility at Public Universities." *Research in Higher Education* 38(1): 17–42.

Volkwein, J. F., S. M. Malik, and M. Napierski-Pranci. 1998. "Administrative Satisfaction and the Regulatory Climate at Public Universities." *Research in Higher Education* 39(1): 43–63.

Warner, J., R. Watts, and K. Wruck. 1988. "Stock Prices and Top-Management Changes." *Journal of Financial Economics* 20:461–92.

Ways and Means Committee. 2002. "Senate Confirms Former Congressional Aide as Top Higher Education Policy Maker." *Chronicle of Higher Education* (29 March): A23.

Webster, D. 1819. "The Dartmouth College Case: Peroration of Daniel Webster." Available at http://www.constitution.org/dwebster/peroration.htm.

Weeks, K. M., and D. Davis, eds. 1982. *Legal Deskbook for Administrators of Independent Colleges and Universities*. 2d ed. Washington, D.C.: National Association of College and University Attorneys and Center for Constitutional Study, Baylor University.

Weisbach, M. 1988. "Outside Directors and CEO Turnover." *Journal of Financial Economics* 20:431–60.

Weisbrod, B. A. 1988. *The Nonprofit Economy*. Cambridge: Harvard University Press.

Whalen, E. L. 1991. *Responsibility Center Budgeting: An Approach to Decentralized Management for Institutions of Higher Education*. Indianapolis: Indiana University Press.

Williams, A. Y. 2002. "Colleges Scramble for Insurance as Premiums Rise to New Levels." *Chronicle of Higher Education* (3 May): A27–28.

Williamson, O. E. 1985. *The Economic Institutions of Capitalism*. New York: Free Press.

Wilson, J. D. 1991. "Tax Competition with Interregional Differences in Factor Endowment." *Regional Science and Urban Economics* 21:423–52.

———. 2002. "The Efficiency Implications of Responsibility Center Management within State Universities." In *Incentive-Based Budgeting Systems in Public Universities*, edited by D. M. Priest, W. E. Becker, D. Hossler, and E. P. St. John, 25–54. Northampton, Mass.: Edward Elgar.

Wilson, R. 2001. "Proportion of Part-Time Faculty Members Leveled off from 1992 to 1998, Data Shows." *Chronicle of Higher Education* (4 May): A17.

Winston, G. 1998. "Why Can't a College Be More Like a Firm?" In *New Thinking on Higher Education: Creating a Context for Change*, edited by J. Meyerson, 1–14. Bolton, Mass.: Anker.

———. 1999. "Subsidies, Hierarchy, and Peers: The Awkward Economics of Higher Education." *Journal of Economic Perspectives* 13 (Winter): 13–36.

Wu, Y. 2000. "Honey, I Shrunk the Board." Working paper, University of Chicago.

Yermack, D. 1996. "Higher Valuation of Companies with a Small Board of Directors." *Journal of Financial Economics* 40:185–212.

Zellner, A. 1962. "An Efficient Method of Estimating Seemingly Unrelated Regressions and Testing for Aggregation Bias." *Journal of the American Statistical Association* 67 (June): 348–65.

Zimbalist, A. 1999. *Unpaid Professionals: Commercialism and Conflict in Big-Time College Sports*. Princeton, N.J.: Princeton University Press.

Zumeta, W. 1996. "Meeting the Demand for Higher Education without Breaking the Bank: A Framework for the Design of State Higher Education Policies for an Era of Increasing Demand." *Journal of Higher Education* 67(4): 367–425.

———. 2001. "Public Policy and Accountability in Higher Education: Lessons from the Past and Present for the New Millennium." In *The States and Public Higher Education Policy: Affordability, Access, and Accountability*, edited by Donald E. Heller, 155–97. Baltimore: Johns Hopkins University Press.

# Contributors

*Ronald G. Ehrenberg* is the Irving M. Ives Professor of Industrial and Labor Relations and Economics at Cornell University, director of the Cornell Higher Education Research Institute (CHERI), and a research associate at the National Bureau of Economic Research. From 1995 to 1998, he served as Cornell's vice president for Academic Programs, Planning, and Budgeting.

*James O. Freedman* is president emeritus of Dartmouth College and the University of Iowa. Most recently he served as president of the American Academy of Arts and Sciences. He is the author of *Crisis and Legitimacy: The Administrative Process and American Government, Idealism and Liberal Education,* and *Liberal Education and the Public Interest.* He serves on the boards of trustees of Brandeis University and Hebrew Union College–Jewish Institute of Religion.

*Thomas H. Hammond* is professor of political science at Michigan State University. His research interests focus on the impact of political institutions on public policymaking.

*Donald E. Heller* is associate professor and senior research associate in the Center for the Study of Higher Education at Pennsylvania State University. He is the editor of *The States and Public Higher Education Policy: Affordability, Access, and Accountability* and *Condition of Access: Higher Education for Lower Income Students.* Heller earned Ed.M. and Ed.D. degrees in higher education at the Harvard Graduate School of Education.

*Benjamin E. Hermalin* is the Willis H. Booth Professor of Banking and Finance and a professor of economics at the University of California, Berkeley. He recently served as interim dean of the Walter

313

A. Haas School of Business. He has done extensive research on governance issues, particularly boards of directors, and is frequently invited to comment on such issues in the press and in other forums.

*Gabriel E. Kaplan* is currently an assistant professor of public affairs at the University of Colorado's Graduate School of Public Affairs. His research explores the links between institutional performance and higher education management and governance. He has worked as a consultant on higher education issues internationally and served as a policy aide in Congress.

*Adam T. Kezsbom* received his B.S. from the School of Industrial and Labor Relations at Cornell University in 2002.

*Daniel B. Klaff* is a senior at the School of Industrial and Labor Relations at Cornell University and is the Co-author of a forthcoming paper in the *Industrial and Labor Relations Review*.

*Susanne Lohmann* received a Ph.D. in economics and political economy from Carnegie Mellon University in 1991. She is professor of political science and director of the Center for Governance at UCLA. She has published on central banking and collective action. Lohmann has received numerous fellowships, honors, and awards, including being appointed a fellow of the Center for Advanced Study in the Behavioral Sciences in 1998/99, and a fellow of the John Simon Guggenheim Memorial Foundation in 2000/01. She is completing a book titled *How Universities Think*.

*Matthew P. Nagowski* is a junior at the School of Industrial and Labor Relations at Cornell University, concentrating in economics, history, and mathematics/statistics. He enjoys backpacking, swimming, and playing Ultimate Frisbee. When not pursuing his studies in Ithaca, Matthew resides with his parents, Peter and Barbara Nagowski, in Buffalo, New York.

*Michael A. Olivas* is the William B. Bates Distinguished Chair at the University of Houston Law Center (UHLC), where he serves as director of the Institute for Higher Education Law and Governance, and as the UHLC associate dean for Student Life. He is the former general counsel to the American Association of University Professors and is the author of nine books, including *Dollars, Scholars, and Public Policy* (Johns Hopkins University Press). He has been elected to the National Academy of Education and the American Law Institute, the only member elected to both bodies.

*Brian Pusser* is an assistant professor in the Center for the Study of Higher Education at the University of Virginia. His research addresses the political economy of higher education organization and governance.

He is the author of *Burning Down the House: Politics, Governance, and Affirmative Action at the University of California* (SUNY Press, forthcoming).

*Sarah E. Turner* is associate professor of education and economics at the University of Virginia. She has published on the effect of financial aid on collegiate attainment and the link betwen higher education and local labor markets. In 2002, she received the Milken Institute Award for Distinguished Economic Research for her work on the paper "Trade in University Training."

*John Douglas Wilson* is professor of economics at Michigan State University. He received his Ph.D. in economics from MIT and has taught at Columbia University, the University of Wisconsin, and Indiana University. He was also chair of the Department of Economics at Indiana University. He is now editor-in-chief of the journal *International Tax and Public Finance*.

# Index

Page numbers followed by *t* refer to tables; those followed by *f* refer to figures

317

Wilson, J. D., 154, 155, 157, 276, 291 n 1
Wu, Y., 36

Yale University, 223
Yermack, D., 36, 37, 286 n 7
Yeshiva University (*NLRB v. Yeshiva*

*University*), 3, 210–11, 222–23, 278, 285 n 3
Young, S. P., 64–65

Zumeta, W., 52, 56, 62